Economic Crisis, Elite Conflict and Institutional Change in Empires

Tolga Demiryol

Economic Crisis, Elite Conflict and Institutional Change in Empires

PETER LANG

Bibliographic Information published by the Deutsche Nationalbibliothek
The Deutsche Nationalbibliothek lists this publication in the Deutsche Nationalbibliografie; detailed bibliographic data is available online at http://dnb.d-nb.de.

Library of Congress Cataloging-in-Publication Data
A CIP catalog record for this book has been applied for at the Library of Congress.

ISBN 978-3-631-89618-1 (Print)
E-ISBN 978-3-631-89656-3 (E-PDF)
E-ISBN 978-3-631-89657-0 (E-PUB)
10.3726/b20538

Peter Lang – Berlin · Bruxelles · Lausanne · New York · Oxford

This publication has been peer reviewed.

www.peterlang.com

To my father

Acknowledgment

This book is based on my doctoral research in the Department of Politics at the University of Virginia. I would like to thank my advisors, Professor David Waldner and Professor Herman Mark Schwartz, for their support.

Table of Contents

Chapter 1 Introduction

This book offers an innovative theory of institutional change, drawing on historical evidence from the Ottoman and Habsburg Empires. Even though these two empires shaped the economic and political structures of contemporary states across a vast geopolitical space,[1] they have received limited *comparative* attention from economists, sociologists, and political scientists.[2] Historical, in-depth studies on the Ottomans and the Habsburgs are certainly rich yet they are rarely comparative. The lack of a comparative methodological approach has limited our ability to explicate the causal dynamics of macro-structural change in imperial contexts. This book seeks to fill this gap by offering a comparative-historical study of the fiscal institutions of the Habsburgs and Ottomans from the seventeenth to the nineteenth century.

---

1 John Komlos, *Economic Development in the Habsburg Monarchy and in the Successor States: Essays*, East European Monographs (Boulder; New York: East European Monographs; Distributed by Columbia University Press, 1990); David F. Good, *Economic Transformations in East-Central Europe: Legacies from the Past and Prospects for the Future* (Routledge, 1994); Carl Brown, *Imperial Legacy: The Ottoman Imprint on the Balkans and the Middle East* (New York: Columbia University Press, 1996); Michael E. Meeker, *A Nation of Empire: The Ottoman Legacy of Turkish Modernity* (Berkeley: University of California Press, 2002).

2 Among the exceptions to this critique, I would like to single out Karen Barkey's research on the Ottoman and Habsburg Empires. Barkey and Von Hagen, After Empire: Multiethnic Societies and Nation-Building: The Soviet Union and the Russian, Ottoman, and Habsburg Empires, Karen Barkey, Hasan Kayali, Joseph W. Escherik, and Eric Van Young, "Changing Modalities of Empire: A Comparative Study of Ottoman and Habsburg Decline," in *Empire to Nation: Historical Perspectives on the Making of the Modern World* (Rowman & Littlefield Publishers, In, 2006); Karen Barkey, *Empire of Difference: The Ottomans in Comparative Perspective* (New York: Cambridge University Press, 2008); Karen Barkey and Rudi Batzell, "Comparisons Across Empires: The Critical Social Structures of the Ottomans, Russians and Habsburgs during the Seventeenth Century," in *Tributary Empires in Global History*, ed. Peter Fibiger Bang and C. A. Bayly, 227–61. Cambridge Imperial and Post-Colonial Studies Series (London: Palgrave Macmillan UK, 2011); Also see, Mehmet Sinan Birdal, *The Holy Roman Empire and The Ottomans: From Global Imperial Power to Absolutist States* (I.B.Tauris, 2011); Sanjay Subrahmanyam, "A Tale of Three Empires: Mughals, Ottomans and Habsburgs in Comparative Contexts." *Common Knowledge* 12, no. 1 (2006): 66-92.

1. The Puzzle: The Reversal of Fortunes

The Habsburg and Ottoman Empires shared several common traits. They were large, agrarian, and multi-ethnic dynastic monarchies with remarkably parallel life cycles. Both states were established in the late thirteenth century (the Habsburg Empire in 1284 and the Ottoman Empire in 1299), reached their imperial boundaries in the early sixteenth century, and survived until after the First World War. Yet, the developmental paths of the Habsburg and Ottoman states diverged during the seventeenth-century economic crisis, an external shock that initiated institutional transformations in Europe and beyond. Even though the ruling elites of both states were facing a common challenge, they responded to it in opposite ways: the Habsburg rulers gradually centralized resource extraction, whereas the Ottoman elites' post-crisis strategy involved decentralization of taxation.

My argument explains why the ruling elites in these two states acted differently in the face of strikingly similar economic problems. In addition to accounting for the variation in post-crisis strategies, my theory also sets out to explicate how these initial differences put these two states on divergent developmental paths that proved remarkably resilient in the long run.[3] These two path-dependent trajectories would eventually take the Habsburg and Ottomans to outcomes that contrasted sharply with their initial sets of institutions. I call this puzzle the *reversal of fortunes*.[4]

---

3 On path dependence, see S. J. Gould, Albert Somit, and Steven Peterson, "Punctuated Equilibrium in Fact and Theory," in *The Dynamics of Evolution* (1992); James Mahoney, "Path Dependence in Historical Sociology," *Theory and Society* 29, no. 4 (2000); Paul Pierson, "Increasing Returns, Path Dependence, and the Study of Politics," *American Political Science Review* (2000).

4 Acemoglu, Johnson, and Robinson use the term "reversal of fortunes" in an article where they analyze the sources of variation in the levels of economic development among some countries that are former colonies of European powers. The reversal, they argue, suggests that it is economic institutions not geography that shaped the fortunes of these countries. Daron Acemoglu, Smith Johnson, and James A. Robinson, "Reversal of Fortune: Geography and Institutions in the Making of the Modern World Income Distribution," in *NBER Working Paper no. 8460* (National Bureau of Economic Research, 2001). For further analysis of colonial rule on economic prospects, see Acemoglu, Johnson, and Robinson, "The Colonial Origins of Comparative Development: An Empirical Investigation "; James Mahoney, "Long-Run Development and the Legacy of Colonialism in Spanish America." *American Journal of Sociology* 109, no. 1 (2003): 50-106.

Here is the reversal: before the seventeenth century, the Habsburg state had a decentralized administration and low infrastructural capacity. The state depended on the cooperation of local intermediaries, a well-entrenched class of nobility, to collect taxes, administer distant localities, and provide for the military. Yet, by the mid-nineteenth century, the Habsburgs had managed to centralize the fiscal apparatus with much higher infrastructural capacity. The Habsburg elites then deployed this capacity to reform agricultural relations, remove barriers to trade, and facilitate industrial development thereby promoting steady economic growth throughout the empire in the nineteenth century.[5]

Even though the Ottoman state started with a centralized fiscal and administrative apparatus, better economic resources, and higher infrastructural capacity, it ended up with a decentralized fiscal state and lower infrastructural power. Furthermore, the Ottoman ruling elites, unable to overcome the fiscal troubles, adopted a predatory economic policy to extract resources from society. These predatory economic policies delayed industrialization and facilitated the peripheralization of the Ottoman economy.[6] Consequently, even though both

5 The earlier generation of economic historians considered the Habsburg Empire in the nineteenth century as an economic failure, epitomized in Gerschenkron's description of the Habsburg experience as an "economic spurt that failed." Recent students of Austrian economic history, however, showed that throughout the nineteenth century, all regions of the Habsburg Empire, including Hungary, grew at a steady rate. Alexander Gerschenkron, *An Economic Spurt That Failed: Four Lectures in Austrian History* (Princeton, NJ: Princeton University Press, 1977); David F. Good, *The Economic Rise of the Hapsburg Empire, 1750-1914* (Berkeley: University of California Press, 1984); David Good, "Issues in the Study of Habsburg Economic Development," *East Central Europe* 6, no. 1, Komlos, *Economic Development in the Habsburg Monarchy and in the Successor States: Essays*; Richard Rudolph, "The Pattern of Austrian Industrial Growth from the Eighteenth to the Early Twentieth Century," *Austrian History Yearbook* XI (1975); Richard Rudolph and John Komlos, "Social Structure and the Beginning of Austrian Economic Growth," in *Economic Development in the Habsburg Monarchy and in the Successor States* (New York: Columbia University Press).

6 Kemal Karpat, "The Transformation of the Ottoman Empire, 1789-1908," *International Journal of Middle East Studies* 3, no. 2 (1972); Donald Quataert, *Manufacturing in the Ottoman Empire and Turkey, 1500-1950*, Suny Series in the Social and Economic History of the Middle East (Schoharie, NY: State University of New York Press, 1994); Ilkay Sunar and Huri İslamoğlu-İnan, "State and Economy in the Ottoman Empire," in *The Ottoman Empire and the World Economy* (Cambridge University Press, 1987); Immanuel Wallerstein et al., "The Incorporation of the Ottoman Empire into the World-Economy," in *The Ottoman Empire and the World Economy* (CUP, 1987); Çağlar Keyder, *State and Class in Turkey: A Study in Capitalist Development* (London: Verso, 1987).

empires ultimately collapsed under nationalist pressures and military decay, they left contrasting institutional and economic legacies to their successors.[7]

2. Theory, Data, and Methodology

In explaining the reversal of fortunes in the Habsburg and Ottoman cases, I draw on and seek to contribute to the literature on European state formation. Scholars of empires typically contend that the deeper socio-structural conditions of institutional change in empires are so dissimilar to those of the Western European states that it would be misleading to look at imperial transformations through the European lens. While there are indeed differences between the two contexts, I contend that they do not necessarily rule out the relevance of the causal dynamics and processes of European state formation for empires.

My goal in bridging the study of Western European state formation and imperial institutional transformations is *not* to construct a one-size-fits-all explanation but rather to identify the key causal mechanisms that are neutral with respect to the antecedent conditions. If we can identify such causal mechanisms, we can combine them with a textured analysis of the antecedent conditions of each case and thereby construct highly tailored explanations of individual instances while still achieving a certain degree of generalization.[8]

I identify the key causal dynamic of the emergence of modern states in Western Europe and imperial transformations as the *intra-elite conflict* over the distribution of economic resources. Elite fractions (e.g., ruling families, big landowners, lesser nobility, church, etc.) engaged in constant conflict and bargaining with each other and the institutional configurations across Europe reflected the outcomes of these conflicts.

---

7 Carl Brown, *Imperial Legacy: The Ottoman Imprint on the Balkans and the Middle East* (New York: Columbia University Press, 1996); Valerie Bunce, "The National Idea: Imperial Legacies and Post-Communist Pathways in Eastern Europe." *East European Politics and Societies* 9, no. 3 (2005): 406-42; Craig J. Calhoun, Frederick Cooper, Kevin W. Moore, and Social Science Research Council (U.S.), *Lessons of Empire: Imperial Histories and American Power* (New York: New Press: Distributed by W.W. Norton, 2006); Valentina P. Dimitrova-Grajzl, "The Great Divide Revisited: Ottoman and Habsburg Legacies on Transition." *Kvlos* 60, no. 4 (2007): 539-58.

8 The argument regarding the identification of causal mechanisms that are neutral concerning antecedent conditions is based on David Waldner, "From Intra-Type Variations to the Origins of Types: Recovering the Macroanalytics of Statebuilding" (University of Virginia: Unpublished manuscript, 2004).

Placing intra-elite conflict at the core of the explanatory framework,[9] I show that the coalitional choices made by the Habsburg and Ottoman elites in the aftermath of the crisis put these two states onto two different path-dependent courses. I construct a causal model linking the differences in the structure of intra-elite conflict to institutional outcomes by way of political coalitions among elites with shared institutional interests.

I offer two abstract causal mechanisms to explain how such distributional conflicts produce the variation in institutional outcomes: *balancing against threat* and *redistributive institution building*. The first mechanism suggests that in their effort to fortify their relative position vis-à-vis their rivals, ruling elites engage in balancing behavior and form coalitions with those social sectors whom they consider the least threatening to their capacity to extract resources. The second mechanism posits that the same strategic rationale drives the elites to forge institutions that would (a) provide side payments or payoffs to their new coalition partners and (b) undermine their rivals by rechanneling access to economic resources. In other words, while the first mechanism links distributional conflict to coalitions, the second mechanism causally connects coalitions to institutional outcomes.

The primary finding of my research is that the incorporation of urban capital holders by the elites into the ruling political coalition was essential for the formation of centralized fiscal structures (Habsburg case), while the exclusion of the capital holders from the coalition due to strategic reasons resulted in fiscal decentralization (Ottoman case).

9 My understanding of the centrality of intra-elite conflict in institutional change is closely informed by Waldner's comparative study of political economic development in Turkey, Syria, Korea, and Taiwan; Lachmann's work on the emergence of capitalist structures in Europe before the sixteenth century; and Spruyt's coalitional theory of state formation and regime change. David Waldner, *State Building and Late Development* (Ithaca, NY: Cornell University Press, 1999); Richard Lachmann, *Capitalists in Spite of Themselves: Elite Conflict and Economic Transitions in Early Modern Europe* (New York: Oxford University Press, 2000); Hendrik Spruyt, "Institutional Selection in International Relations: State Anarchy as Order," *International Organization* 48 (1994).

I use comparative-historical analysis[10] and process tracing[11] to demonstrate how differences in the structure of the intra-elite conflict, particularly the distribution of power and perceptions of threat among competing elite fractions, shaped elite preferences regarding capital incorporation. Rather than imputing preferences from outcomes, I focus on the formation of interests and provide direct evidence, whenever possible, regarding the revealed preferences of actors.[12] I systematically analyze the formation of the preferences of the main actors in each case (ruler, capital, and nobility), the political coalitions these actors formed, and how each coalitional configuration produced the variation in fiscal structures.

Using comparative-historical analysis to produce causal explanations raises two methodological challenges: achieving external validity and managing potential selection bias. I consider the internal validity of arguments as a requisite of explanatory adequacy[13] and aim to explain the phenomena at a high level of specificity, paying particular attention to the context of the Habsburg and Ottoman cases. However, internal validity is of limited value in the complete absence of external validity.[14] To maximize internal validity without sacrificing the generalizability of my findings, I follow an approach that combines detailed

---

10 Paul Pierson, "Big, Slow-Moving and...Invisible: Macrosocial Processes in the Study of Comparative Politics," James Mahoney and Dietrich Rueschemeyer, *Comparative Historical Analysis in the Social Sciences*, Cambridge Studies in Comparative Politics (Cambridge, UK; New York: Cambridge University Press, 2003).

11 Alexander L. George and Andrew Bennett, *Case Studies and Theory Development in the Social Sciences*, Bcsia Studies in International Security (Cambridge, MA: MIT Press, 2005); Andrew Bennett and Colin Elman, "Qualitative Research: Recent Developments in Case Study Methods," *Annual Review of Political Science* (2006).

12 Admittedly, relying on "agent self-avowal," i.e. the historical agents' accounts of their actions also involves the potential for "lies, biases, and self-delusion." Clayton Roberts, *The Logic of Historical Explanation* (University Park, PA: Pennsylvania State University Press, 1996).

13 Waldner, "From Intra-Type Variations to the Origins of Types: Recovering the Macroanalytics of Statebuilding."

14 When a researcher is interested in the pathway from the independent variable X to the dependent variable Y in a particular context, that relationship cannot be justifiably sequestered from the more general question of the role of Xs on the generation of Ys. If the internal validity of a particular causal story is well established, then one might reasonably posit that that finding could travel across cases. If it does not, this *might* in turn cast doubt on the internal validity of that case study. Thus, the relationship between internal and external validity is essentially complementary.

comparative-historical analysis of individual cases with an emphasis on abstract and portable causal mechanisms.

By causal mechanisms, I mean the essentially unobservable units with a capacity to change entities and generate outcomes. They allow us to transcend the empiricist equation of covariation with causality by providing a systematic set of statements that provide a plausible account of how and why two phenomena are associated. This of course contrasts sharply with the "black box explanations" common but not limited to deductive models where the link between explanans and explanandum is assumed to be devoid of structure, and reduced to a regression coefficient.[15] Causal mechanisms are the "cogs and wheels," linking independent and dependent variables.[16] In principle, such mechanisms are abstract; they can travel across time and space, while outcomes remain sensitive to historically contingent conditions.

Causal mechanisms allow us to account for the similarity in processes and divergence in outcomes across cases. As Elster argues, the "distinctive feature of a mechanism is not that it can be universally applied to predict and control social events but that it embodies a causal chain that is sufficiently general and precise to enable us to locate it in widely different settings."[17] Thus, identifying the causal mechanisms involved in intra-elite conflicts and combining them with detailed analyses of specific conditions of each case allow me to construct an explanation that is internally valid and generalizable given the scope conditions of my theory.

This methodology differs from the traditional comparative case studies: instead of comparing cases that are similar in all but one aspect, I engage in a

---

15 Hempel Carl, "The Function of General Laws in History," in *Readings in the Philosophy of Science*, ed. M. Martin and L. C. McIntyre (Cambridge, MA: MIT Press, 1997).

16 It must also be noted that despite the widely shared conviction among qualitative methodologists about the *necessity* of causal mechanisms for explanatory adequacy, their conceptualizations of causal mechanisms differ. For Hedstrom and Swedberg, causal mechanisms essentially denote the microfoundations of behavior that causally link macrostructures. Daniel Little, on the other hand, reserves the term primarily for casual relations that are apparent across a family of cases. "Causal relations attach to types," in his words, "not tokens." Peter Hedström and Richard Swedberg, *Social Mechanisms: An Analytical Approach to Social Theory*, Studies in Rationality and Social Change (Cambridge, UK; New York: Cambridge University Press, 1998); Daniel Little, *Microfoundations, Method and Causation: On the Philosophy of the Social Sciences*, Science and Technology Studies (New Brunswick, NJ: Transaction Publishers, 1998).

17 Jon Elster, *Political Psychology* (Cambridge; New York: Cambridge University Press, 1993), 5.

paired comparison of uncommon cases. The goal is to identify the fundamental causal mechanisms and explore how they combine differently with antecedent conditions to generate diverse outcomes.[18]

The second limitation of comparative-historical research is selection bias in choosing from multiple historical accounts of the same event or phenomenon.[19] Discussions on selection bias in comparative research typically focus on the implications of selecting cases on the dependent variable and other forms of selectivity.[20] Comparative-historical analyses, however, might also commit a second type of bias if they draw selectively on a few historical accounts ignoring competing historical theories and interpretations.

I follow several strategies to deal with this problem. First, in explaining various aspects of the Habsburg and Ottoman cases, I "triangulate" using the different interpretations and claims from multiple historiographical schools. I seek to provide a balanced interpretation of historical facts by covering a broad spectrum of research published in German, Turkish[21], and English. Second, whenever available, I use primary sources (memoirs, government reports, and imperial decrees) to adjudicate among competing historical explanations and theories. Third, I use what Lustick called "explicit triage."[22] If I favor an explanation or interpretation over others, I explicitly note alternative interpretations and address why I consider them inferior.

3. Contributions

This book offers two main contributions. First, it adds to coalitional theories in state formation literature by bridging the gap between the demand- and

---

18 Victoria Tin-bor Hui, *War and State Formation in Ancient China and Early Modern Europe* (New York, NY: Cambridge University Press, 2005).

19 Ian Lustick, "History, Historiography, and Political Science: Multiple Historical Records and the Problem of Selection Bias," *American Political Science Review* (1996).

20 Gary King, Robert O. Keohane, and Sidney Verba, *Designing Social Inquiry: Scientific Inference in Qualitative Research* (Princeton, NJ: Princeton University Press, 1994); David Collier and James Mahoney, "Insights and Pitfalls: Selection Bias in Qualitative Research," *World Politics* 49 (1996); Barbara Geddes, *Paradigms and Sand Castles: Theory Building and Research Design in Comparative Politics*, Analytical Perspectives on Politics (Ann Arbor: University of Michigan Press, 2003).

21 Note on spelling and transliteration: For the sake of simplicity and accessibility, I use contemporary spellings of German and Turkish words.

22 Lustick, "History, Historiography, and Political Science: Multiple Historical Records and the Problem of Selection Bias," 616.

supply-side approaches. Coalitional approaches explain institutional outcomes as consequences of the distributional conflicts among coalitions of social actors. I differentiate between two types of political coalitional theories: demand-side (bottom-up) explanations and supply-side (top-down) explanations.

Demand-side approach asserts that social actors such as merchants demand certain institutional changes in accordance with their objectively driven interests. If centralized and hierarchical institutions are in the interests of the merchants given the type of trade they are engaged in, then they demand such changes from the ruling elites. If the merchants are strong enough, then they ultimately obtain the desired changes. In contrast, supply-side explanations approach the issue from the side of the ruling elites who can supply new institutions. These arguments specifically theorize about the interests and strategies of the rulers.

Both approaches, as I show in Chapter 2, are one-sided and explain institutional outcomes only partially. My alternative explanation, in contrast, focuses on the strategic interaction between the demand- and supply-sides of the distributional conflict. Thus, my research offers a synthesis of the two hitherto isolated strands of explanation by endogenizing the preferences of rulers, nobility, and capital, and modeling the strategic interaction among them.

The second contribution of my research to the literature on state formation and economic development consists in offering a comparative-historical analysis of the key yet understudied cases of the Ottoman and Habsburg Empires. I show that the elites in these two cases acted differently in the face of a common problem, not because of their ideas or cultural predispositions but rather because they were responding to different structural constraints as self-interested, strategic actors. I also demonstrate that the differences in the elite strategies in turn shaped the long-term developmental prospects of the state.

What makes the puzzle of the "reversal of fortunes" of the Ottoman and Habsburg states interesting is that they are located on two sides of the historical gradient separating the East and the West. Each case contained elements of the other side. The Habsburg Empire, "the East of the West," displayed stark contrasts with the rest of Europe in terms of its economic and political features. The Ottoman Empire, "the West of the East," while Anatolian in origin, was an integral part of European affairs throughout its existence.

By providing a causal explanation of the divergence of developmental paths of these two states, and the *reversal of their fortunes*, this book sheds new light onto the age-old question of why and how the trajectory of the East got differentiated from that of the West. My explanation ultimately dovetails with the Weberian argument that multiple centers of power were initially more conducive to the emergence of the modern state and capitalism.[23] However, by focusing on the relations among elites and explicating the mechanisms governing the intra-elite conflict, I provide the micro-foundations of macro-level processes of economic and political change.

The book is structured as follows:

Chapter 2 explains the puzzle by discussing the causes and consequences of the seventeenth-century crisis and the differential responses by the Habsburg and Ottoman elites. I review the macro-structural theories of state formation that focus on culture, economy, and warfare as primary explanatory variables. Having established the limitations of existing approaches in accounting for the Habsburg and Ottoman cases, in the third section of this chapter I present my alternative explanation which stitches together the supply- and demand-sides of the intra-elite conflict.

Chapters 3 and 5 analyze the critical antecedent conditions in the Habsburg and Ottoman Empires, respectively. Each chapter traces the origin of the mode of imperial organization (horizontal vs. vertical) back to the earliest periods of imperial formation and analyzes how that particular type of imperial organization shaped the structure of intra-elite conflict in each case. These chapters also show why and how the crisis of the seventeenth century fundamentally shaped the intra-elite conflict by altering the distribution of power among elites, which, in turn, opened the space for elite realignment and determined the timing of the large-scale institutional change.

Chapters 4 and 6 focus on the explication of the dual causal mechanisms, which, combined with the critical antecedents in each case, account for the variation in the dependent variable. More specifically, these chapters explain (1) how the shifts in the dynamics of intra-elite conflict led to the inclusion or exclusion of capital in/from the new ruling coalition and (2) how the rulers strategically crafted a new set of institutions that transferred resources from their rivals to their allies. Chapters 4 and 6 also substantiate the variation in the dependent variable, i.e., the changes in the tax collection mechanisms and the extent to which the state contributed to economic development in each case.

---

23 D. Chirot, "The Rise of the West," *American Sociological Review* 50 (1985). Also see Hechter and Brustein's discussion of the relationship between the regional modes of production in Europe and the variation in the state types emerging in Europe. Michael Hechter and William Brustein, "Regional Modes of Production and Patterns of State Formation in Western Europe," *American Journal of Sociology* 85, no. 5 (1980).

Chapter 7, the final chapter, sums up the argument of the book and discusses its contributions to the literature.

Chapter 2 Elite Conflict, Political Coalitions, and Institutional Change

This chapter is divided into three main sections. The first section provides a closer look at the puzzle of the book: the divergence of the paths of the Habsburg and Ottoman Empires, "the reversal of fortunes." Since the seventeenth-century crisis is the critical juncture where the divergence occurred, this section starts with an overview of the causes and consequences of the crisis. The second section discusses existing explanations and their limitations. I review the major theories of state formation in Europe—economic, bellicist, and cultural approaches—with an eye on how and to what extent they could account for the Habsburg and Ottoman cases. The third section presents my alternative explanatory framework based on intra-elite distributional conflicts as the primary driver of institutional change.

1. The Seventeenth-Century Crisis

Empires are prone to economic crises. The limited infrastructural reach of the state forces rulers to adopt indirect means to administer distant localities, most notably by relying on native elites.[24] The bond between the imperial center and the periphery is weakened when intermediaries cut into the revenue flow from the imperial periphery to the core, paving the way for economic troubles.[25]

Starting as early as 1560, both the Habsburg and Ottoman states began to experience a steep decline in revenues and an unprecedented increase in expenditures, resulting in budget deficits. At the turn of the seventeenth century, the Ottoman state had a major budget deficit for the first time in its 300-year history. In the eighteenth and nineteenth centuries, however, budget deficits would become a chronic feature of the Ottoman state.[26] Similarly, the Habsburg rulers,

24 Nevertheless, empires vary in the extent to which they rely on indirect vs. direct mechanism. I will return to this point when I present my conceptual distinction between vertical and horizontal empires.

25 Karen Barkey, "Changing Modalities of Empire: A Comparative Study of Ottoman and Habsburg Decline."

26 Ömer Lütfi Barkan, "The Price Revolution in the Sixteenth Century," *International Journal of Middle East* (1975); Ömer Lütfi Barkan and M. A. Cook, "Research on the Ottoman Fiscal Surveys," in *Economic History of the Middle East* (London: Oxford

starting particularly with Ferdinand III (1608-1657), found themselves inheriting "empty treasuries."[27] In the early eighteenth century, the state owed to its domestic and external creditors around 50 million florins, which would almost double to 99 million florins in 1739.[28] Considering that when Maria Theresia ascended the Habsburg throne in 1740, the imperial treasury contained only 87,000 florins; the Habsburg state was practically insolvent.

Underlying the pressing fiscal troubles was a fundamental decline in the capacity to collect taxes and extract revenue. The crisis was structural and resilient rather than exogenous and transient; it ultimately threatened state survival. Yet at the same time, by forcing the elites to undertake fundamental changes in the core fiscal structures of the state, the crisis created an opportunity for reform for both Habsburgs and Ottomans.

Two sets of factors contributed to the crisis more than anything else: the turmoil in the world economy and the increasing financial burden of warfare, including but not limited to the high costs of the Habsburg-Ottoman rivalry in Central and Eastern Europe. In this section, I review these two sets of factors underlying the fiscal crisis.[29]

1.1 "The General Crisis"

Historians consider the seventeenth century an era of economic and political crisis that extended well beyond the boundaries of Western Europe.[30] Even

---

University Press, 1970); Gabor Agoston, Gaza David, and Pal Fodor, "The Costs of the Ottoman Fortress-System in Hungary in the Sixteenth and Seventeenth Centuries," in *Ottomans, Hungarians and Habsburgs in Central Europe. The Military Confines in the Era of Ottoman Conquest* (Leiden and Boston: Brill, 2000).

27 Konrad Kramar and Petra Stuiber, *Habsburgs Leere Kassen* (Wien: Verlag Carl Ueberreuter, 2001).

28 P. G. M. Dickson, *Finance and Government under Maria Theresa, 1740-1780*, 2 vols., vol. 1 (Oxford: Claredon Press, 1987).

29 For the role of the demographic trends on the economic decline, see Jack A. Goldstone, *Revolution and Rebellion in the Early Modern World* (Berkeley: University of California Press, 1991); Jack A. Goldstone, "East and West in the Seventeenth Century: Political Crisis in Stuart England, Ottoman Turkey, and Ming China," *Comparative Studies in Society and History* 30 (1988); Jon Komlos and Markus Heintel, "The Threat of a Malthusian Crisis in the Habsburg Monarchy," *Journal of Interdisciplinary History* 30, no. 1 (1999).

30 Christopher Hill, "Introduction," in *Crisis in Europe, 1560-1660, Essays from Past and Present* (London: Routledge & Kegan Paul, 1975). One of the earliest protagonists of the "general crisis" argument, Roland Mousnier, wrote, "The seventeenth century was

though there is a wide consensus regarding the ubiquity of the crisis, there is an ongoing discussion about its nature and causes.[31]

The origin of the seventeenth-century crisis is widely traced back to the price revolution of the sixteenth century. The rise of the prices in the second half of the sixteenth century first affected Britain but eventually reached Central and Eastern Europe. The price movements were initially triggered by the shifting of

---

a time of crisis which affected all mankind." Merriman examined six revolutionary incidents of the seventeenth century, including the Puritan Revolution in England, the revolt against the House of Orange in the Netherlands, the Fronde period in France, and the revolts against the King of Spain in Catalonia, Portugal, and Naples, and he argued that all six events constituted instances of a single anti-state revolutionary trend. Roger Bigelow Merriman, *Six Contemporaneous Revolutions* (Oxford: Clarendon Press, 1938). Roland Mousnier, *Les XVIe Et XVIIe Siecles. Les Progres De La Civilisations Europeenne Et Le Decline De l'Orient (1492-1715)* (Paris, 1954), quoted in Ivo Schoffer, "Did Holland's Golden Age Coincide with a Period of Crisis?," in *The General Crisis of the Seventeenth Century*, ed. Geoffrey Parker and Lesley M. Smith, 1978), 85. Contemporary observers of the seventeenth century were astounded by the peculiar character of the times they lived in. Parker and Smith cite several contemporary accounts emphasizing similarities between some of the revolts: the Dutchman Lieuve van Aitzema's comparative study of the 1647 Naples uprising and the 1648 Moscow revolt; the Italian Count Birago Avagaodro's multi-volume study of the revolts in Catalonia, Portugal, Sicily, England, France, Naples, and Brazil; and the French historian Robert Mentet de Salmonet's description of the "Iron Age" of the seventeenth century as "famous for the great and strange revolutions that have happened in it…Revolts have been frequent both in the East and the West," are only a few examples. Perhaps the most famous among the contemporary commentators on the crisis was Voltaire. In his *Essai sur les moeurs et l'esprit des nations,* he dealt with the political crises in England, France, Spain, Germany, Poland, and, most remarkably, in the Ottoman Empire, where Sultan Ibrahim had been deposed in 1648 after a violent upheaval. Voltaire observed that "this unfortunate time for Ibrahim was unfortunate for all monarchs" and that the seventeenth century "was a period of usurpations almost from one side of the world to the other." Cited in Parker, *Europe in Crisis, 1598-1648*, 3.

31 Geoffrey Parker, *Europe in Crisis, 1598-1648*, 2nd ed. (Oxford, UK; Malden, MA: Blackwell Publishers, 2001), 326; Geoffrey Parker and Smith Parker, eds., *The General Crisis of the Seventeenth Century* (London: Routledge & Kegan Paul, 1978); T. H. Aston, *Crisis in Europe, 1560-1660, Essays from Past and Present* (London: Routledge & Kegan Paul, 1975); Eric Hobsbawm, "The General Crisis of the European Economy in the seventeenth Century," *Past and Present* 5 (1954): 33-54; Niels Steensgaard, "The Seventeenth-Century Crisis and the Unity of Eurasian History," *Modern Asian Studies* 21 (1990).

the international trade routes in the sixteenth century and the injection of American silver into the European economy, boosting the money supply.[32]

This interpretation regarding the relationship between American silver and the price revolution has been disputed.[33] Gould notes that currency depreciation began in some instances decades before the influx of metals. He also underlines that demographic pressures might have contributed even more directly to the price revolution by exerting upward pressure on the prices of commodities in inelastic supply (e.g., grain).[34] Similarly, Pach notes that the prices were also affected by the endogenous changes in international trade, i.e. the shift in the commodity structures.[35] The disagreements among historians as to why prices rose notwithstanding, we know that the price increase halted in the seventeenth century. The widely accepted account of the price reversal is that the upward trend ended by 1640 and was followed by a period of decline and fluctuation until the early eighteenth century.

Trailing abrupt price fluctuations, interregional trade entered a period of contraction. The Mediterranean and the Baltic trade routes experienced a decline in volume. The Baltic trade, which connected the relatively urbanized economies of Western Europe to the Central and Eastern European agricultural production, was distressed by the replacement of foodstuffs by timber and metals as the dominant commodities. The volume of trade, measured by sound tolls, plummeted around 1620 and continued to decline until 1660.[36] Mediterranean trade was also affected by the changes in the commodity structure, notably the declining importance of the Eastern spice.[37] For instance, Hobsbawm reports that the French Levantine trade halved between 1630 and 1635 and contracted to zero around 1650, only to be partially recovered after 1670.[38]

---

32 Fernand Braudel, *The Mediterranean and the Mediterranean World in the Age of Philip II*, 1st U.S. ed. (New York: Harper & Row, 1972).

33 Immanuel Maurice Wallerstein, *The Modern World-System* (New York: Academic Press, 1974), 69-77.

34 J. D. Gould, "The Price Revolution Reconsidered," *The Economic History Review* 17, no. 2 (1964): 249-266, 252.

35 Pál Zsigmond Pach, "The Shifting of International Trade Routes in the 15th–17th Centuries," *Acta Historica* 14 (1968): 287-321.

36 Hobsbawm, *The General Crisis of the European Economy in the 17th Century*, 33-54; M. Malowist, "The Economic and Social Development of the Baltic Countries from the 15th to the 17th Centuries," *The Economic History Review* (1959).

37 F. C. Lane, "The Mediterranean Spice Trade," *The American Historical Review* (1940).

38 Hobsbawm, *The General Crisis of the European Economy in the 17th Century*, 33-54; Niels Steensgaard, "Asian Trade and World Market: Orders of Magnitude in the 'Long

The slowing interregional trade and declining prices put pressure on agricultural production. By the 1650s, major suppliers of agricultural commodities in the European periphery had to cut back their production for the market. Exacerbating the decay in agriculture was the secular decline in the average yield ratios throughout the seventeenth century,[39] which in turn led to rising real wages.

The economic crisis of the seventeenth century, as reflected in the price levels, trade patterns, and agricultural productivity, served as a key step in the transformation from feudalism to capitalism in Europe. Hobsbawm argues that the seventeenth-century transformation was different from the previous periods of large-scale change in social and economic structure. In his words, "There is a taste of 'bourgeois' and 'industrial' revolution about fourteenth century Tuscany and Flanders or early sixteenth century Germany. Yet it is only from the middle of the seventeenth century that this taste becomes more than a seasoning to an essentially medieval or feudal dish."[40] Wallerstein argues that the 1600-1750 period constitutes the *B-phase* in the capitalist long cycle, which contrasts with the expansion in the *A-phase* (1500-1600). He adds that the effects of the cyclical shift were equally important for outside of Western Europe, including the Central and Eastern European semi-periphery.[41]

We have multiple accounts of how the crisis was manifested outside Europe. Steensgaard discusses the extent to which the crises and the subsequent reforms in the large states of the seventeenth century, most notably the Chinese, Japanese, Ottoman, and Mughal Empires, can be construed as instances of an overarching crisis.[42] Reid argues that the recession in the international economy paved the way for the breakdown of the absolutist states in Southeast Asia.[43] Atwell focuses on China and Japan and observes that "after rapid economic growth in the late sixteenth and early seventeenth centuries, during the mid-seventeenth century both countries experienced severe economic problems that were at once interrelated and strikingly similar to those that were occurring in other parts of the

---

Seventeenth Century" In *Actes Du Colloque Franco-Polonais d'Histoire* (Nice: Laboratoire d'Histoire Quantitative: Univesite de Nice, 1981).

39 Charles Wilson, Geoffrey Parker and C. H. Wilson, *An Introduction to the Sources of European Economic History, 1500-1800* (Ithaca, NY: Cornell University Press, 1977), 256.

40 Hobsbawm, *The General Crisis of the European Economy in the 17th Century*, 33.

41 Wallerstein, *The Modern World-System II: Mercantilism and the Consolidation of the European World-Economy, 1600-1750*, chapter 1.

42 Steensgaard, *The Seventeenth-Century Crisis and the Unity of Eurasian History.*

43 Anthony Reid, "The Seventeenth-Century Crisis in Southeast Asia," *Modern Asian Studies* 24, no. 4 (1990), 639-59.

world."[44] Lastly, Goldstone asserts that the seventeenth-century crisis should be conceived as a "worldwide crisis of agrarian absolutist states that affected eastern empires in equal measure with western monarchies."[45]

1.2 The Costs of Warfare

Wars, like crises, are integral to empires as they are typically forged through conquest. From its inception as a frontier state in Western Anatolia in the early fourteenth century, the grand strategy of the Ottoman state involved western expansion.[46] This strategic vision originated at least partly from religious concerns.[47] Eastern Europe also had clear strategic importance in the defense of the northwest border of the Ottoman territories.[48] After the fall of Constantinople in 1453, and the conquest of Serbia in 1459 and southern parts of Bosnia in 1464, Ottomans turned their attention to Hungary.

The Habsburg rulers, who held the title of Holy Roman Emperor and considered themselves defenders of Europe, were naturally alarmed by the inroads the Ottomans made in Eastern Europe, which could eventually threaten Vienna, "the frontier post of Christendom."[49] The meeting of the two expanding imperial

44 William S. Atwell, "A Seventeenth-Century 'General Crisis' in East Asia?" *Modern Asian Studies* 24, no. 4 (1990), 661-82.

45 Jack A. Goldstone, "East and West in the Seventeenth Century: Political Crisis in Stuart England, Ottoman Turkey, and Ming China," *Comparative Studies in Society and History* 30 (1988): 103-42.

46 Halil İnalcık, "Ottoman Methods of Conquest," *Studia Islamica* 2 (1954); Stanford Shaw, "The Aims and Achievements of Ottoman Rule in the Balkans," *Slavic Review* 21, no. 4 (1962); John F. Guilmartin, "Ideology and Conflict: The Wars of the Ottoman Empire, 1453-1606," *Journal of Interdisciplinary History* 18 (1988); Heath W. Lowry, *The Nature of the Early Ottoman State*, Suny Series in the Social and Economic History of the Middle East (Albany: State University of New York Press, 2003).

47 Paul Wittek, *The Rise of the Ottoman Empire*, Vol. 23 (London: The Royal Asiatic Society of Great Britain and Ireland, and sold by its agents Luzac and co., ltd., 1958), 54; Mehmet Fuat Köprülü and Gary Leiser, *The Origins of the Ottoman Empire* (Albany, NY: State University of New York Press, 1992).

48 Pal Fodor, "Ottoman Policy Towards Hungary, 1520-1541," *Ada Orientata Academiae Scientia Scientiarum Hungaricae* 45 (1991): 271-345. Also see, Pál Fodor, *In Quest of the Golden Apple: Imperial Ideology, Politics, and Military Administration in the Ottoman Empire*, Vol. 45 (Istanbul: Isis Press, 2000), 105-71.

49 Jean Bérenger, *A History of the Habsburg Empire* (London; New York: Longman, 1994), especially Chapter 15. Also see Andrew Wheatcroft, *The Habsburgs: Embodying the Empire* (London: The Folio Society, 2004); Barbara Stollberg-Rilinger, *Das Heilige*

states along the Hungarian border led to one of the longest rivalries in European history.

Throughout the seventeenth century, both states had to spend their tax revenue almost exclusively on waging war against each other. The Ottoman central administration's expenditure on maintaining its military positions in Hungary far exceeded its total tax revenues from the wealthy province of Buda.[50] Even the historians of the time recognized the high burden that the maintenance of a permanent military presence in a distant locality placed on the treasury. The seventeenth-century Ottoman chronicler Ibrahim Peçevi wrote that the Porte had to transfer the tax revenue from Egypt to the Buda province to compensate for the deficit between local tax revenues and military expenditure.[51]

Thus, except for brief periods of extraordinarily successful administration (e.g., the reign of Uvey Pasha in the 1570s), attempts to maintain Ottoman rule in Hungary inflicted heavy losses on the treasury. The maintenance costs of the military force in peacetime were also far exceeded by the costs of actual campaigns, such as the 1593-1606 "Long War" between Ottomans and Habsburgs, which exhausted local resources.[52] The immediate need for cash to pay for the soldiers and supplies forced the rulers to expand the tax burden on the subject population (*reaya*), by turning irregular in-kind taxes (e.g., *avarız*) into regular in-cash payments.

Römische Reich Deutscher Nation Vom Ende Des Mittelalters Bis 1806 (Beck, 2006) for the self-perceptions of the Habsburg rulers as the Holy Roman Emperors.

50 Hungarian historian Agoston estimates that the annual payment made to the 10,328 soldiers stationed in the fortresses in Buda *sancak* (province) alone amounted to 23,046,862 akçe in 1558-9. This expenditure was well beyond the tax revenue extracted from Buda, 6,434,585, which covered only 28 percent of the expenses. Calculated in golden florins, for the sake of easier comparison with European figures, the deficit in 1558-9 was 225,506. Gabor Agoston, "The Costs of the Ottoman Fortress-System in Hungary in the Sixteenth and Seventeenth Centuries," in *Ottomans, Hungarians and Habsburgs in Central Europe. the Military Confines in the Era of Ottoman Conquest*, ed. Géza Dávid and Pál Fodor (Leiden and Boston: Brill, 2000).

51 Ibrahim Peçevi, *Tarih-i Peçevi* (Istanbul).

52 Finkel provides a very detailed study of the financial costs of the Ottoman campaigns in this period based on an examination of Ottoman "day books" of the Campaign Treasury (which record daily campaign revenues and expenditures). He estimates that only 17 percent of the local revenues of the Buda *sancak* had been driven from local sources. Finkel, *The Administration of Warfare: The Ottoman Military Campaigns in Hungary, 1593-1606*, 290-1.

The military revolution is another reason why the conflict between the Ottoman and Habsburg Empires turned out to be increasingly costly for both parties. The initial advantages that the well-trained and larger Ottoman army held over its rival declined as the Habsburg army introduced technological advances which arguably were "enough to equal out the numerical and logistical superiority of the adversary."[53] The rough equality of the two military forces resulted in a longer period of confrontation characterized by costly but mostly indecisive siege warfare.

Since the earliest days of the monarchy, the Habsburgs were involved in the dynastic conflicts of Europe. In addition to its enduring rivalry for continental hegemony with Bourbon Spain and France,[54] Habsburg monarchy faced formidable European rivals, most notably Sweden, which had become a major power in the seventeenth century after the reforms of Gustav II Adolf; and Prussia, which under Frederick aggressively sought to expand its influence in Central Europe in the early eighteenth century.[55]

The costliest of the Habsburgs' rivalries, however, was the confrontation with the Ottoman Empire. The Habsburgs, like the Ottomans, were motivated by ideological as well as strategic interests in confronting the Ottoman threat; they not only defended the strategically located Hungarian plane[56] but also used the very existence of the Islamic threat for legitimizing their position as Holy Roman Emperors.[57] The military competition, however, proved to be as expensive for the Habsburg Empire as it was for the Ottomans. As Wallerstein notes, "the Ottoman threat…made the Habsburgs suffer, more perhaps than any other sovereigns, in the seventeenth century, from an inability to raise sufficient money for their treasury, making them distinctively underendowed."[58]

---

53 Gabor Agoston, "Habsburgs and Ottomans: Defense, Military Change and Shifts in Power," *The Turkish Studies Association Bulletin* 22, no. 1 (1998): 126-41.

54 Kennedy, *The Rise and the Fall of Great Powers: Economic Change and Military Conflict from 1500-2000.*

55 Jeremy Black, *European Warfare: 1453-1815* (New York: St. Martin's Press, 1999); Peter Wilson and Jeremy Black, "Warfare in the Old Regime, 1648-1789," in *European Warfare, 1453-1815* (New York: St. Martin's Press, 1999).

56 Fodor, *In Quest of the Golden Apple: Imperial Ideology, Politics, and Military Administration in the Ottoman Empire.*

57 Maximilian Grothaus, "Zum Türkenbild in Der Kultur Der Habsburgermonarchie Zwischen Den 16. Und 18. Jahrhundert" In *Habsburg–osmanische Beziehungen*, ed. Andreas Tietze (Wien, 1983), 26-30.

58 Wallerstein, *The Modern World-System II: Mercantilism and the Consolidation of the European World-Economy, 1600-1750.*

A major source of military expenditure was the *Militärgrenze* (military frontier), a series of fortresses built in the latter half of the sixteenth century to prevent Ottoman advancement. The maintenance and provision of these fortresses in peacetime cost about 1 million florins a year. According to the official figures of *Hofkammer* (Court Chamber), another 1.6 million was paid to the soldiers serving in the *Militärgrenze*, which—combined with the upkeep costs mentioned above—well exceeded the 750,000 florins tax revenue obtained from the now shrunken territory of the Hungarian kingdom.[59] Thus, Habsburgs, like Ottomans, spent much more on the defense of the Hungarian border than the region generated in taxes and consequently accumulated a yearly debt that reached, according to *Hofkammer*, 10 million florins as early as 1578.

The economic consequences of the Habsburg-Ottoman rivalry are better understood when the rapid expansion of the Habsburg army is considered. The Habsburg monarchy did not have a standing army until the seventeenth century; its military force consisted mainly of seasonal mercenary troops, and the soldiers contributed by the provinces during wartime. The first attempt at creating a central standing army was made after the Battle of Mohacs in 1526.[60] The escalation of the Ottoman threat forced the Habsburg rulers to maintain unprecedented numbers of soldiers in the field between campaigning seasons, and these quasi-permanent units constituted the basis of the standing army. The first peacetime army of the monarchy was formally established in 1649 when Ferdinand III issued a decree announcing that the 52 regiments raised first during the Long War with the Ottomans (1593-1606) and later the Thirty Years' Wars (1618-1648) were to be kept as the permanent army of the *Erbländer* (hereditary lands).[61] The aggressive policies of Louis XIV and the resurgence of the Ottoman threat in the latter half of the seventeenth century led to a constant growth of this professional army, a trend that would continue well into the eighteenth century.

The increase in the size of the standing army put tremendous pressure on the treasury. The main reason was that the local estates prevented the court from mobilizing financial support for the regiments by retaining not only their traditional role in the recruitment of troops but also their right to assess and collect

59 Agoston, *The Costs of the Ottoman Fortress-System in Hungary in the Sixteenth and Seventeenth Centuries.*

60 John A. Mears, "Thirty Years War, the 'General Crisis' and the Origins of the Standing Professional Army in the Habsburg Monarchy," *Central European History* 21 (1988): 122-41.

61 Ibid.

the direct taxes for the maintenance of the army.[62] Even after 1654, when Leopold I deprived the Austrian estates of their right to refuse extraordinary taxes for military purposes, they could still bargain over the amounts as well as refuse ordinary taxes—taxes for court expenditures and civil administration. In practice, the *Landtage* resisted paying taxes even in such instances of immediate danger as the second Ottoman siege of Vienna in 1683.[63]

1.3 Divergent Responses to the Crisis

By the mid-seventeenth century, the ruling elites of the Habsburg and Ottoman states were dealing with similar economic troubles. The adverse effects of the downturn of intra-regional trade on the imperial revenues and the financial burden of warfare brought both states to the brink of a complete collapse. However, the decision-makers of these two states adopted opposite fiscal strategies in response to the crisis. These divergent elite choices, in turn, set these states onto opposite trajectories, which would prove resilient.

In the introductory chapter, I operationalized fiscal state through two empirically observable aspects: (1) the replacement of decentralized and indirect mechanisms of tax collection with a centralized and legal-rational tax collection apparatus, (2) the deployment of tax revenue toward the mobilization of market resources and promotion of economic growth. As I show in the following two chapters, by 1815 the Habsburg state achieved remarkable progress in both dimensions. By establishing administrative and tax-collection agencies, the state managed to transfer the power to collect taxes from the landowning nobility in the countryside to the central administration. The bureaucratic apparatus comprised well-educated officials employed on a meritocratic basis instead of noble descent. They were paid fixed salaries based on performance evaluations instead of traditional methods of "profit sharing."[64] This new bureaucracy allowed the central government to abate its reliance on intermediaries for resource extraction and to "reach into the deepest depths of the people."[65] The rebuilt fiscal

62 Ibid.

63 Thomas Mack Barker, *Double Eagle and Crescent; Vienna's Second Turkish Siege and Its Historical Setting* (Albany: State University of New York Press, 1967), 207-8.

64 Heindl, *Bureaucracy, Officials and the State in the Austrian Monarchy: Stages of Change since the Eighteenth Century*, 35-57.

65 Waltraud Heindl, "Bureaucracy, Officials and the State in the Austrian Monarchy: Stages of Change since the Eighteenth Century," *Austrian History Yearbook* 37 (2006): 35-57, 37.

state also permitted the Habsburg ruling elite to confront the privileges of the traditionally tax-exempt noble landowners and increase the contributions of the Habsburg *Länder*.[66] The Habsburg state then deployed its newfound institutional capacity to enlarge its tax revenue by promoting manufacturing and trade.

In the realm of agriculture, the state first reduced labor dues (Robot Patent) and then completely abolished forced labor (Emancipation Patent). The lifting of labor restrictions freed up a sizeable force that would later enter industrial sectors as wage labor. In commerce, as early as the 1750s, the Habsburg government made a determined effort to remove the barriers to trade by lowering intra-empire customs duties and protecting domestic merchants from outside competition. Lastly, in manufacturing, the state played a very active role by directly investing in key sectors that were not profitable enough for private business and by providing incentives, subsidies, information, and protection to domestic manufacturers and proto-industrialists.

The enhanced infrastructural power of the new state was the chief factor behind the sustained economic growth of the Habsburg territories throughout the nineteenth century. As early as the second half of the eighteenth century, manufacturing and proto-industry began to take off in the western regions (Bohemia and Moravia), followed by Hungary later in the nineteenth century.

Historians agree that fiscal centralization, particularly the reforms of 1740-1780, played a key role in the economic development of Habsburg regions. Klima asserts that the abolishment of serfdom directly contributed to the establishment of the textile, iron, and glass industries.[67] Berend argues that the reforms by Maria Theresia and Joseph II "laid the groundwork for capitalist transformation along western lines."[68] Good underlines the significance of the legislation in 1765 and 1780, which he asserts laid "the capitalist bases of Habsburg

---

66 P. G. M. Dickson, *Finance and Government Under Maria Theresia, 1740-1780* (Oxford: Claredon Press, 1987), especially 19-24.

67 Arnost Klima, "Industrial Growth and Entrepreneurship in the Early Stages of Industrialization in the Czech Lands," in *Economic Development in the Habsburg Monarch in the Nineteenth Century*, ed. John Komlos (New York: Columbia University Press, 1983), 82. Freudenberger calls the Moravian town of Brno, where a large fine-woolen factory was established in 1764, "the Manchester of central Europe." Herman Freudenberger, *The Industrialization of a Central European City: Brno and the Fine Woolen Industry in the Eighteenth Century* (Edington, Willts: Pasold, 1977).

68 T. Iván Berend, *History Derailed: Central and Eastern Europe in the Long Nineteenth Century* (Berkeley: University of California Press, 2003), 142.

agriculture,"[69] while Klima concurs that the "mercantilist theory of the second half of the seventeenth century and the economic activity developed out of mercantilist principles, mainly in the eighteenth century, laid the foundations for the manufacturing model of development."[70] Moreover, the reforms proved persistent and irrevocable, even during the reactionary rule of Francis I and Metternich from 1815 to 1848.

Like the Habsburgs, the Ottoman state underwent an institutional transformation in the seventeenth and eighteenth centuries. Yet the direction of the Ottoman transformation was quite the opposite. Instead of attempting to centralize the resource extraction process, the bureaucratic elite of the state opted for the privatization and decentralization of tax collection by expanding the scope of tax farming to new types of revenue as well as new geographic areas in the hope of tapping deeper into the agricultural revenue.

Tax farming had been utilized by the agricultural monarchies in Anatolia before the Ottomans. Anatolian Seljuk Empire employed the *iqta* method, and the Byzantine Empire collected taxes through the *pronoia* system. The Ottoman Empire inherited the basic structure of tax farming from these states and adapted it to its needs. Unlike its predecessors, however, Ottoman Empire did not utilize tax farming as its primary method of resource extraction. Indeed, before the seventeenth century, the use of tax farming (*iltizam*) was minimal in comparison to the ubiquitous *tımar* system.[71]

The *tımar* system was based on the assignment of agricultural revenues collected from independent peasant households to the troops stationed in the provinces. These troops, *tımarlı sipahi,* collected tax revenue in lieu of salary. From the inception of the Ottoman state in 1299, the *tımar* system allowed the extraction of agricultural surplus to remain firmly in the hands of the central elites by preventing the emergence of a privileged class in the countryside.

Throughout the seventeenth century, the central administration made several changes in the fiscal scheme of the empire that increased the share of tax farming

---

69 Good, *The Economic Rise of the Hapsburg Empire, 1750-1914*, 34.

70 Arnost Klima, "Mercantilism in the Habsburg Monarchy- with Special Reference to the Bohemian Lands," *Historica* 11 (1965), 199.

71 For a comprehensive account of the *tımar* system, Douglas A. Howard, *The Ottoman Tımar System and Its Transformation, 1563-1656* (Unpublished PhD Dissertation, Indiana University, 1987). Also, Halil İnalcık, "Land Problems in Turkish History," *The Muslim World* 45 (1955); Halil İnalcık, "1431 Tarihli Tımar Defterine Göre Fatih Devrinden Önce Tımar Sistemi," in *Osmanlı Imparatorluğu: Toplum Ve Ekonomi*, ed. Halil İnalcık (Istanbul: Eren, 1996).

vis-à-vis the *tımar* system. The turning point in fiscal decentralization came in 1695 when tax farming contracts, initially limited to 1-2 years, were extended to 3-5 years, and eventually became life-term contracts.[72]

The expansion of tax farming had significant long-term implications. One of the most important consequences was the rise of the tax-farming intermediaries known as the *ayan*.[73] In addition to monopolizing life-term contracts, the new provincial elites managed to consolidate their political power by combining their newfound wealth with military capacity. The most powerful local agents summoned their own armies by attracting local bandits, mercenaries, and disbanded soldiers of the central army: "By the eighteenth century, the central state had become so dependent on the provincial magnates not only for internal security but for protection from external aggression."[74]

The economic, political, and military power of the *ayan* reached its climax by the nineteenth century. After almost two centuries of fiscal decentralization, the Ottoman rulers attempted in the nineteenth century to re-centralize taxation by eliminating the provincial elites and reinstituting the state's authority in the countryside. The reforms initiated by Selim III and fully advanced by Mahmud II in the 1820s and 1830s ultimately failed, as discussed in Chapter 6.

The Ottoman bureaucracy, considered highly efficient and loyal to the central administration before 1700, had become inefficient and corrupt.[75] Even

---

72 Şevket Pamuk, *The Evolution of Fiscal Institutions in the Ottoman Empire, 1500-1914* (Paper Presented at the Thirteenth International Economic History Congress, Buenos Aires, 2002), 19.

73 Yücel Özkaya, *Osmanlı İmparatorluğunda Ayanlık* (Ankara: AUDTCF Yayınları, 1977); Halil İnalcık, "Military and Fiscal Transformation in the Ottoman Empire, 1600-1700," *Archivum Ottomanicum* VI (1980), 283-337; Kemal Karpat, "The Transformation of the Ottoman Empire, 1789-1908," *International Journal of Middle East Studies* 3, no. 2 (1972); Immanuel Wallerstein, Hale Decdeli, and Reşat Kasaba, "The Incorporation of the Ottoman Empire into the World-Economy," in *The Ottoman Empire and the World Economy*, ed. Huri Islamoğlu-Inan (CUP, 1987); Bruce McGowen, "The Age of the Ayan," in *An Economic and Social History of the Ottoman Empire, 1300-1914*, ed. Halil İnalcık and Donald Quataert (New York, NY: Cambridge University Press, 1994).

74 Abu-el-Haj, *Formation of the Modern State: The Ottoman Empire, Sixteenth to Eighteenth Centuries*, 17.

75 Carter V. Findley, *Bureaucratic Reform in the Ottoman Empire: The Sublime Porte, 1789-1922*, Princeton Studies on the near East (Princeton, NJ: Princeton University Press, 1980); Metin Heper, "The State and Public Bureaucracy," *Comparative Studies in Society and History* 27 (1985); Walter F. Weiker, "The Ottoman Bureaucracy: Modernization and Reform," *Administrative Science Quarterly* 13, no. 3 (1968).

though the wealthiest tax farmers were eliminated—through military force and coercion—the central administration did not have an institutional alternative to replace them. Consequently, small-scale tax farming continued to be the primary mode of tax collection until the early twentieth century.[76]

There is also considerable variation between the Habsburg and Ottoman cases in the second dimension of a centralized fiscal state, i.e., the deployment of the fiscal capacity of the state and the tax revenues toward the mobilization of market resources and the promotion of industrialization and economic development.

Unlike the Habsburg state which played a very active role in removing the barriers to trade and manufacturing, the involvement of the Ottoman state in the economy remained selective and limited throughout the nineteenth century. Instead of supporting local merchants and manufacturers, the Ottoman bureaucratic elite, desperate for additional funds, provided selective benefits to European merchants and indirectly undermined the competitiveness of domestic merchants and manufacturers. The state did not establish any industrial enterprises except for a few factories serving the needs of the court and the military. Without a well-developed banking sector, private entrepreneurs lacked access to capital. Lastly—and once again in stark comparison to the Habsburg state—the Ottoman state in the nineteenth century did not extensively invest in infrastructure, leaving the building of railroads exclusively to foreign direct investors.

Without state support, Ottoman merchants articulated into the world economy after 1830 mainly as suppliers of raw materials and foodstuffs. Exports remained limited to basic commodities and were eclipsed by the import of manufactured goods from Europe, creating a trade imbalance. Guild production, phased out in the Habsburg lands as early as the 1750s, remained prominent in the Ottoman Empire throughout the nineteenth century. Whereas several Habsburg regions climbed the ladder of industrialization from textiles to heavy machinery and steel production, Ottoman manufacturers were stuck at producing low-value textiles, which had to compete with cheaper and higher-quality European goods. Manufacturing declined, indefinitely delaying the arrival of industrialization.

By the end of the nineteenth century, the two largest and longest-standing empires of Europe, the Habsburg and Ottoman states, were standing at opposite ends of the path of political and economic development. The Habsburg state,

---

76 Şevket Pamuk, *Osmanlı-Türkiye Iktisadi Tarihi, 1500-1914* (Istanbul: İletişim, 2005); Mehmet Genç, "Osmanlı Maliyesinde Malikane Sistemi," in *Osmanlı'da Devlet ve Ekonomi*, ed. Mehmet Genç (Istanbul: Ötüken, 2003).

even though it suffered under the pressures of various nationalist movements,[77] had a centralized fiscal state presiding over a steady, if not very rapid,[78] industrialization. The Ottoman state, however, despite efforts in the first half of the nineteenth century, failed to centralize tax collection. The inability to extract resources combined with the decline of manufacturing and trade paved the way for even greater fiscal difficulties. After 1850, the Ottoman government borrowed heavily from European markets to pay for the expenses of the state. By the 1880s, the state could no longer pay the interest on its debts to European creditors. The establishment of the *Ottoman Public Debt Administration* in 1881, a multinational debt collection agency that practically took over the finances of the Ottoman state to ensure the repayment of outstanding balances marked the collapse of the Ottoman fiscal state.

The contrast in the institutional outcomes in these two cases becomes even more puzzling when the initial infrastructural and fiscal capacities of the two states are considered. As I show in Chapters 3 and 5, the Habsburg and Ottoman states displayed stark differences in their imperial organization from 1300 to 1600. More specifically, the Habsburg state before the seventeenth century was highly decentralized and lacked the infrastructural reach required for administering distant localities. The Ottoman state, on the other hand, had a much more centralized administrative structure that provided effective solutions to the problems of limited infrastructural power while at the same time preventing the state from relying on local elites.

How did the Ottoman state, which started with a more administrative and fiscal apparatus, end up with a decentralized state and eventually went bankrupt, while the Habsburg monarchy, which began with a much more decentralized state, transformed itself into a centralized fiscal state? In the next section, I review existing approaches in the literature on state formation and economic development. In the last section, I present my alternative causal explanation based on intra-elite conflict.

---

77 Oszkár Jászi, *The Dissolution of the Habsburg Monarchy* ([Chicago]: University of Chicago Press, 1961); Robert A. Kann, *The Habsburg Empire; a Study in Integration and Disintegration* (New York: Octagon Books, 1973); Rudolph and Good, *Nationalism and Empire: The Habsburg Empire and the Soviet Union*.

78 Rudolph and Komlos, "Social Structure and the Beginning of Austrian Economic Growth"; Richard L. Rudolph and John Komlos, "Economic Revolution in Austria? The Meaning of 1848 in Austrian Economic History," in *Economic Development in the Habsburg Monarchy* (New York: Columbia University Press, 1983).

2. Existing Theories and Their Limitations

2.1 Macro-structural Theories

By macro-structural theories, I mean the theories that posit causal links between two (or more) macro-level variables. I differentiate between three kinds of macro-structural theories of state formation based on their primary explanatory variable: culture, warfare, and economy. In the following three sub-sections, I review all three approaches and demonstrate why they fall short of solving the puzzle posed by the Habsburg and Ottoman cases.

2.1.1 Culture

Culture is an integral aspect of social change. Since all institutional change is ultimately the product of the actions of individuals and groups, it follows that the cognitive and affective beliefs of those actors shape the processes of institutional change, including state formation.[79] However, assuming rather than substantiating the primacy of cultural and/or ideational factors leads to incomplete causal explanations of the variation in institutional outcomes across time and space.

Historians and historically oriented social scientists working on the Habsburg or Ottoman Empires often highlight ideational factors such as religion as the primary driving force of their explanations.[80] This is partly a response to the crude interpretations of Marx's notion of the Asiatic mode of production. The tendency to explain the trajectories of social change with broad typologies of agrarian production and surplus extraction caused the "analysis of Asian transitions [to]

---

79 Gorski's study of the role of Calvinism in the emergence of modern state structures in reformed Protestant Europe is an excellent example of the culturalist approaches to state formation. He argues that Calvinist doctrines and practices facilitated the creation of a new infrastructure of social (and moral) control, which empowered the rulers to regulate various aspects of people's everyday lives for the first time in history. Philip S. Gorski, *The Disciplinary Revolution: Calvinism and the Rise of the State in Early Modern Europe* (Chicago; London: University of Chicago Press, 2003).

80 This is true even for the most analytical historians of Habsburg and Ottoman Empires, including Robin Okey, *The Habsburg Monarchy: From Enlightenment to Eclipse* (New York: St. Martin's Press, 2001); Alan Sked, *The Decline and Fall of the Habsburg Empire, 1815-1918* (Harlow, England; New York: Longman, 2001); Cemal Kafadar, "Between Two Worlds," (Berkeley: University of California Press, 1995).

become stuck in a rut."[81] Scholars of agricultural monarchies outside Western Europe began to highlight the unique features of these societies to differentiate them from both their European and non-European counterparts. While the emphasis on the uniqueness of each non-European case produced valuable historical data, it also paved the way for unwarranted cultural particularism.

Even though there is no systematic comparative study of the puzzle of the "reversal of fortunes" in the Habsburg and Ottoman states from a purely cultural perspective, historical narratives of the two cases place a heavy emphasis on the religious and ideational aspects of the institutional transformation. In explaining the revolutionary institutional reforms under the reign of Maria Theresia and her son/co-regent/successor Joseph II, many historians point to the effects of the enlightenment ideals and mercantilist thought, particularly French physiocracy.[82] It is argued that the reforms were driven by the notion of progress and an anti-church/secular agenda, particularly in the case of Joseph II who was even more radical than Maria Theresia.[83] Similarly, historians of the Ottoman Empire have traditionally held that the absence of mercantilist ideas in Ottoman society impeded institutional change along European lines.

The explanations that presume the causal primacy of ideas on institutional change, however, do not withstand careful empirical scrutiny of the preferences and motivations of actors. For instance, the great Habsburg reformer Maria Theresia who—as I discuss in Chapter 4—managed to partially revoke the traditional privileges of landed interests (including the church) was a very devout Catholic and a firm believer in the ancient régime. As revealed in her *Political Testament* as well as her private correspondences, she was highly suspicious of any form of rapid and fundamental change.[84] Why, then, did she undertake reforms that

---

81 Lachmann, *Capitalists in Spite of Themselves: Elite Conflict and Economic Transitions in Early Modern Europe*, 29. Also Anderson, "Asiatic Mode of Production," in *Lineages of the Absolutist State*, ed. Perry Anderson (London: New Left Books, 1974).

82 Grete Klingenstein and Charles W. Ingrao, "Between Mercantilism and Physiocracy: Stages, Modes and Functions of Economic Theory in the Habsburg Monarchy, 1748-63," in *State and Society in Early Modern Austria* (Indiana: Purdue University Press, 1994).

83 Saul K. Padover, *The Revolutionary Emperor: Joseph II of Austria* (London: Eyre&Spottiswoode, 1967).

84 Maria Theresia, "Political Testament," in *The Habsburg and Hohenzollern Dynasties in the Seventeenth and Eighteenth Centuries*, ed. C. A. Macartney (New York: Walker and Company, 1970); Ludwig F. Jedlicka, *Maria Theresia in Ihren Briefen Und Staatsscriften* (Wien: Bergland Verlag, 1955).

undermined the power of the main beneficiaries of the regime, putting the interests of the state beyond her personal predispositions?

The evidence regarding the ideational factors in the Ottoman case does not corroborate the initial expectations regarding their causal role. Historians usually evoke the role of the "Ottoman economic worldview,"[85] when explaining the provisionist[86] policies of the Ottoman state in the seventeenth and eighteenth centuries. Evidence for such ideational factors is limited to the anti-mercantilist policies of the state, which results in a vicious cycle of causality. However, evidence suggests that Ottoman rulers were indeed exposed to the mercantilist ideas of the time that swayed European states. For example, Naima, an early eighteenth-century Ottoman writer, publicized a set of ideas that openly advocated mercantilist thinking.[87] If the mercantilist ideas never gained prominence in Ottoman elite circles, then one must ask why not.

Even the more analytically rigorous iterations of the culturalist accounts fall short of providing adequate causal explanations. In his detailed comparative study of state reconstruction after agrarian and fiscal crises in Ming China, Tudor England, and the Ottoman Empire, Goldstone raises a question that is akin to the puzzle of this book: "[G]iven the structural similarities in the causes of state breakdown in all three cases, what differentiates their succeeding state reconstructions?"[88] Even though Goldstone asserts that the seventeenth-century crisis was a "multifaceted process" with many causal factors, he ultimately privileges ideology as the main factor that governed state reconstruction after the crisis.[89] He argues that the puritan ideology of the English was apocalyptic, whereas the Chinese and Ottomans had a cyclical worldview. He writes, "What appears in contemporary diagnoses of [Chinese and Ottoman] ills...was not the idea that the state should be redesigned for new challenges. Instead, all that was needed was a purging of corruption, a return to institutions as they had operated at the height of the empire."[90]

---

85 Mehmet Genç, "The Principle of Ottoman's Economical World View," *Sosyoloji Dergisi* III, no. 1 (1988).

86 Provisionism encouraged imports and discouraged exports. I discuss Ottoman provisionism in detail in Chapter 5.

87 Pamuk, "The Evolution of Fiscal Institutions in the Ottoman Empire, 1500-1914"; Naima, "Tarih- i Naima," (Istanbul: Danışman Yayınevi, 1968).

88 Goldstone, "East and West in the Seventeenth Century: Political Crisis in Stuart England, Ottoman Turkey, and Ming China," 131.

89 Ibid.

90 Ibid., 133.

In other words, when faced with the same crisis, the presumably backward-looking predispositions of the Chinese and Ottoman rulers pushed them in a regressive direction whereas the forward-looking ideology of the English elites brought about innovation and reform. Goldstone claims that these ideological differences governing state reconstruction after the seventeenth-century crisis have shaped the divergence of East and West.

There is much to praise in Goldstone's analysis. I concur with his observation that the post-crisis state reformation in the seventeenth century was a critical juncture for the Ottoman state (and the Habsburg monarchy), which set the empire on an institutional course that would prove extremely resistant to reversal. However, this ideational account is lacking in several aspects. First, Goldstone does not discuss *how* these ideational factors affected institutional outcomes. There are presumably certain *cognitive causal mechanisms* at work—mechanisms that link abstract religious/ideational factors to the processes of decision-making. However, such mechanisms are neither explicated nor substantiated with evidence.

Goldstone's ideational account also falls short of explaining the temporal variation within each case. Consider, for instance, the actions of the Ottoman ruling elites in the first half of the nineteenth century. The 1820s and 1830s were a period of reform and modernization in the Ottoman state. In this period, Ottoman elites acted very much like their Habsburg counterparts did a century ago: they tried to centralize taxation and administration along European lines instead of trying to re-institute the traditional order. As I discuss in Chapter 6, this was not due to an endogenous change in the cyclical nature of their belief system but because of the changes in structural constraints to which they were responding as rational actors.

Despite their strengths, cultural explanations—even the comparative ones—fall short of solving the puzzle posed by the Habsburg and Ottoman cases. In the last section of this chapter, I construct an explanatory framework based on distributional conflicts among elites that theorizes why the actors behaved the way they did at different points in time. In contrast to culturalist approaches, this framework is more dynamic and can explain a broader range of outcomes.

2.1.2 Economy

Economic theories of state formation operate at different levels of analysis. System-level explanations hold that the developmental trajectory of a state is primarily conditioned by its relative position in the international political economy, whereas unit-level explanations emphasize the local social and economic structures.

However, neither theory is adequately equipped to explain the puzzle posed by the Habsburg and Ottoman Empires.

Wallerstein's world-systems theory (WST) epitomizes systemic explanations. The basics of WST are well known: in the sixteenth century, Northwestern Europe established itself as the core of the emerging world economy. While Western Europeans specialized in high-value agricultural production with wage-labor, the rest of the world economy (periphery and semi-periphery) relied on exports of primary agricultural products and slavery/coerced cash-crop as modes of labor control. Thus, different zones benefited differentially from the expansion of the world economy. The surplus flow from the periphery to the core exacerbated the initial differences.[91]

System-level economic dynamics directly affected state strength and types. The initial slight differences in local conditions amplified by the workings of the world economy gave rise to unique constellations of interests in Europe, paving the way for the development of strong state mechanisms, whereas the periphery ended up with weak ones.[92] The result was the reproduction of the processes of surplus appropriation by the core from the periphery, mirroring and overlapping with the exploitation at the domestic level.

WST has been heavily criticized. In addition to the alleged empirical inaccuracies[93] and the reductionism of the theory,[94] the premise that there was only a slight difference between Western and Eastern Europe before the sixteenth century was disputed. Chirot wrote, "Eastern Europe was not just a little behind the West in 1500 or 1600, but very seriously so," and "the fundamental differences in agriculture existed very early and very decisively in creating a drastically different potential for

91 Immanuel Maurice Wallerstein, *The Modern World-System* (New York: Academic Press, 1974).

92 Wallerstein not only derives the relative differences in the strength of state machineries from system-level conditions but also asserts that the differences in the state capacities further exacerbated the inequality in the core-periphery relationship as the strong states of the core enforced their interests on the weak states of the periphery.

93 Economic historians argued that the export of agricultural surplus from Eastern Europe to the western core did not increase to the extent implied by the capitalist penetration argument. Similarly, the very timing of the "second-serfdom" which Wallerstein attributes to the growing demand from the West is a subject of debate. Jerome Blum, *Noble Landowners and Agriculture in Austria 1815-1848: A Study in the Origins of the Peasant Emancipation of 1848* (Baltimore: Johns Hopkins University Press, 1948).

94 Theda Skocpol, "Wallerstein's World Capitalist System: A Theoretical and Historical Critique," *The American Journal of Sociology* 82, no. 5 (1977).

economic growth by the late Middle Ages."[95] Whether it is due to the preponderance of pastoral economies in Eastern Europe[96] or the absence of a Roman legal tradition of private property,[97] critics considered Eastern Europe fundamentally different, to begin with.

This debate is pertinent to my analysis as it exemplifies the counterpart of Wallerstein's systemic approach: the unit-level explanations that underscore the autonomous role played by pre-existing local structures and institutions. Brenner criticized Wallerstein, among other things,[98] for reversing the causality between economic backwardness and dependency and argued that it was the historical backwardness of Eastern Europe that produced its dependency on Western Europe, not the other way around. This is based on the proposition that class structures and property relations are highly resilient to change. Once established, they continue to shape long-term outcomes without being significantly altered by demographic and commercial trends.[99]

---

95 Daniel Chirot, *The Origins of Backwardness in Eastern Europe: Economics and Politics from the Middle Ages until the Early Twentieth Century* (Berkeley: University of California Press, 1989). Similarly, Lampe and Jackson argue that Balkan economies from the eleventh to fifteenth century were characterized by a lack of urban markets and trade networks. John R. Lampe and Marvin R. Jackson, *Balkan Economic History, 1550-1950: From Imperial Borderlands to Developing Nations*, The Joint Committee on Eastern Europe Publication Series (Bloomington: Indiana University Press, 1982).

96 Fikret Adanır and Suraiya Faroqhi, "The Ottomans and the Balkans," in *Ottoman Empire and Its Heritage* (Leiden; Boston: Brill, 2002).

97 Peter Gunst, *Agrarian Development and Social Change in Eastern Europe, 14th-19th Centuries* (Varorium: 1996); Peter Gunst, Irene P. Winner, and Thomas G. Winner, "Some Characteristics of East European Economic and Social Development: Data and Reflections," in *The Peasant and the City in Eastern Europe: Interpenetrating Structures* (Schenkman, 1984); Peter Gunst, *Einige Probleme Der Wirtschaftlichen Und Sozialen Entwicklun Osteuropas* (Köln: Forschungsinst. fuer Sozial-u. Wirtschaftsgesch, 1977).

98 He criticized it for being a neo-Smithian explanation in disguise because it relied on unequal exchange rather than production. Robert Brenner, "Origins of Capitalist Development: A Critique of Neo-Smithian Marxism," *New Left Review* 104 (1977).

99 The emphasis on the relative autonomy and independent effects of unit-level variables on the outcomes of state formation processes is not peculiar to Brenner's arguments. Many theories of state formation, even those whose starting premise is the centrality of geopolitical competition, such as the theories of Perry Anderson, Charles Tilly and Thomas Ertman, ultimately place the source of the variation in the outcomes of state formation squarely at the domestic level. Anderson, *Lineages of the Absolutist State*; Charles Tilly, *Coercion, Capital, and European States, AD 990-1992*, Studies in Social Discontinuity (Cambridge, MA: Blackwell, 1992); Thomas Ertman, *Birth of the*

Despite its flaws, Wallerstein's explanation is ultimately on stronger ground than Brenner's analysis. The fundamental weakness of the latter is that it does not account for the origins and changes of interests of domestic social actors where these interests are externally generated. To be sure, Brenner does not deny that external economic forces can affect the processes of state formation. However, he only assigns a very limited influence to these factors by considering their effects as strictly contingent on pre-existing local conditions. Moreover, even this limited significance attached to external forces loses its weight in the actual analysis, and "class struggle appears, to all intents and purposes, as a *deus ex machina* with no presuppositions."[100]

This critique does not imply that unit-level economic factors lack causal significance. The coalitional framework proposed in the next section takes seriously such unit-level factors, most notably the structure of elite conflict. However, isolating the unit-level factors from the system-level variables yields at best incomplete explanations. If the unit-level factors themselves are generated by external factors, then explanations focusing exclusively on the unit-level could be erroneous to the extent they attribute causality to a set of (domestic) variables that are shaped by other (systemic) variables.[101]

Similarly, the most important shortcoming of the systemic explanations is the lack of attention to the processes at the domestic level. Even though the system-level framework is better suited to account for the macro-level social forces circumscribing unit-level dynamics, its failure to explicate the micro-dynamics of the macro-structural forces ultimately leads to functionalism.

Most historical narratives of the Habsburg and Ottoman state formation after the seventeenth century display these very shortcomings that stem from the gap between system- and unit-levels. The problem is more evident in the historical accounts of the Ottoman Empire that—as I discuss in Chapters 5 and 6—are roughly divided into two camps. First, some take their inspiration from Braudel and the Annales School and seek to explain the economic and political development of the Ottoman state, particularly in the nineteenth century, by

---

Leviathan: Building States and Regimes in Medieval and Early Modern Europe (Cambridge: Cambridge University Press, 1997).

100 Robert Denemark and Kenneth Thomas, "The Brenner-Wallerstein Debate," *International Studies Quarterly* 32 (1988): 56.

101 Herman Schwartz "Dependency or Institutions? Economic Geography, Causal Mechanisms, and Logic in the Understanding of Development." *Studies in Comparative International Development* 42 no. 1 (2007): 115–35.

exclusively focusing on the impact of the full integration of the empire into the world-economy.[102] Dissatisfied by the reductionism implicit in this approach, the later scholarship emphasized the *unique* aspects of the Ottoman social and economic structure, including the predominance of the independent peasantry, the historical weakness of the merchants, and the absence of a landholding class. However, just like Brenner, who neglected how the domestic class structures can be externally shaped, this approach to the Ottoman economic history fails to establish the connection between the system- and unit-level dynamics.

How can one adjudicate between these competing approaches given that neither the system-level explanations that lack any consideration of the domestic workings of the proposed systemic factors nor the unit-level theories that overemphasize the autonomous effects of domestic factors can provide adequate explanations? The intra-elite conflict framework I propose focuses on the interest of all relevant domestic actors while paying closer attention to the systemic factors that shape their interests, relative powers, and the resulting patterns of conflict.

2.1.3 *Warfare*

The common denominator of the bellicist explanations of state formation, ranging from the geopolitical theories of Hintze[103] to the fiscal-military theory of Ertman,[104] is the observation that state formation in late medieval Europe coincided with fundamental changes in the frequency, intensity, and technology of warfare, also known as the "military revolution."[105]

---

102 For a brief review of Wallerstein's thoughts on the place of the Ottoman empire in the world-economy, see Wallerstein et al., "The Incorporation of the Ottoman Empire into the World-Economy."

103 Otto Hintze, *The Historical Essays of Otto Hintze* (New York: Oxford University Press, 1975).

104 Ertman, *Birth of the Leviathan: Building States and Regimes in Medieval and Early Modern Europe.*

105 The essential text on the military revolution is Geoffrey Parker, *The Military Revolution: Military Innovation and the Rise of the West, 1500-1800* (Cambridge; New York: Cambridge University Press, 1996). Also see, Brian M. Downing, *The Military Revolution and Political Change: Origins of Democracy and Autocracy in Early Modern Europe* (Princeton, NJ: Princeton University Press, 1992); Geoffrey Francis Andrew Best, *War and Society in Revolutionary Europe, 1770-1870*, War and European Society (Montreal: McGill-Queen's University Press, 1998); Black, *European Warfare: 1453-1815.*

The first innovation in the art of war that paved the way for fundamental institutional change was the growing importance of massed infantry vis-à-vis heavy cavalry, partly due to technological developments such as the success of the longbow archers. The ever-increasing sizes of standing armies favored larger states that were capable of amassing and maintaining large numbers of infantry. The second crucial change was the widespread use of gunpowder. The siege cannon destroyed the strategic significance of castles, undermining the ability of the feudal nobility to resist the penetration by central governments. Additionally, the cannon (like the infantry) displayed economies of scale, privileging centralized states in the frequent and intense military conflicts of the period.[106]

Increasing costs of war pushed rulers to seek new means of resource extraction. Supplying standing armies required greater financial resources than seasonal campaigns. Widespread use of the siege cannon led to new and more expensive forms of defense such as the *trace itallienne*. Consequently, as Brewer shows, early states devoted most of their revenue to waging war.[107] The necessity for more efficient resource extraction, in turn, involved an expansion of the bureaucratic machinery at the disposal of rulers.[108]

The relationship between war making and state making was inherently reciprocal and mutually enforcing. Not only the act of building effective military machines contributed to the centralization of power and differentiation of the instruments of government (e.g., specialized tax collection agencies) but also

106 Bean, approaching the issue from the perspective optimal sizes of organizations, explains the birth of the modern state by a combination of initial economies of scale and decreasing returns to the growth of state sizes. Richard Bean, "War and the Birth of the Nation State," *Journal of Economic History* 33 (1973). Parker shows that the period between 1500 and 1700 was characterized by a largely unprecedented intensity of conflict among great powers in Europe. Parker, *The Military Revolution: Military Innovation and the Rise of the West, 1500-1800*; Geoffrey Parker, *Europe in Crisis, 1598-1648*, Blackwell Classic Histories of Europe (Oxford, UK; Malden, MA: Blackwell Publishers, 2001).

107 John Brewer, *The Sinews of Power: War, Money, and the English State, 1688-1783* (London; Boston: Unwin Hyman, 1989).

108 It is also important to underline that the institutional effects of warfare were not temporary and contingent on the presence of an external threat. Expanding states did not go back to their prewar scopes and capacities. The ratchet effect (states took "two steps forward in wartime but only one step back in peacetime") ensured that the institutional effects of war making were largely persistent. For the ratchet effect, see Mike Desch, "War and Strong States, Peace and Weak States?," *International Organization* 50 (1996): 243.

constant warfare tested the new institutions—weaker states did not survive. Some rulers were unable to extract resources efficiently enough, and their polities ultimately lost out in conflicts. Local structures directly shaped the strategies of resource extraction and state building. As Tilly wrote, "war made the state and the state made the war."[109]

Following the initial discovery of the war-state formation nexus, the second wave of research focused on the variation in institutional outcomes across regions. Tilly identified three paths of state formation, each contingent on the relative availability of capital versus coercion.[110] On the "coercion-intensive" path toward the modern state, rulers "squeezed" the means of war from the population and built massive state structures. Direct coercion was the only option available for effective resource extraction in areas where urbanization and commercialization were low and agriculture was dominant, as in Brandenburg and Prussia. In contrast, rulers relied on contracts with capital owners in capital-rich areas where cities and commerce were strong. In Italian city-states and urban trade federations, institutions ended up primarily reflecting the interests of the capital. The third, and in the long-run most salient mode of state formation, was based on "capitalized coercion." Rulers who enjoyed moderate levels of capital and means of coercion incorporated capital owners and extracted their resources while making sure that the new institutions did not simply reflect their interests. France and England followed this middle path toward centralization.

There are two major issues with bellicist theories. First, the exclusive focus on the costs of warfare in the sixteenth and seventeenth centuries neglects the macro-level changes in the European economy in this period. After all, the period of 1500-1700 was characterized not only by an intense conflict among European powers but also fundamental changes in the world economy: expansion in the sixteenth century, followed by a period of stagnation and crisis. Economic factors did play a critical role in the bellicist theories as evidenced by Tilly's argument. The accessibility of capital itself, however, is treated as an independent factor, disconnected from the dynamics of the international political economy.

Second, bellicist arguments do not fully substantiate the micro-foundational dynamics mediating between the macro-level variables of warfare and state formation. True, some bellicist theories deal with micro-dynamics when they

---

109 Charles Tilly, Gabriel Ardant, and Politics Social Science Research Council. Committee on Comparative, *The Formation of National States in Western Europe*, Studies in Political Development (Princeton, NJ: Princeton University Press, 1975), 42.

110 Tilly, *Coercion, Capital, and European States, AD 990-1992.*

theorize about the strategies of the domestic social actors: the capital-intensive, coercion-intensive, and capitalized coercion paths toward the national state reflect the variation in the resource extraction strategies of the state-builders. However, the micro-foundational dynamics remain incomplete since the strategies of resource extraction are entirely determined by domestic constraints, i.e., the prevalence of capital and coercion.

In Tilly's scheme, state-builders in the capital-poor areas opt for a certain extractive policy *not* as a matter of strategic choice but because of the lack of options. Tilly himself recognizes that the three paths to state formation "do not represent alternative 'strategies' so much as contrasting conditions of life."[111] As a result, Tilly's account ends up oscillating "between an explanation based on relative factor endowments and a coalitional explanation of political strategy."[112] In bellicist theories, economic factors play a decisive role in shaping institutional outcomes, not as class and/or elite relations but rather simply as concrete constraints on strategic behavior.

I demonstrated in this section that the explanatory capacity of macro-structural theories of cultural, economic, and bellicist varieties is limited to the extent that they neglect to theorize about the micro-dynamics of the macro-level processes. The cultural, economic, and warfare-related theories help us direct our attention to various elements of the institutional change in the Habsburg and Ottoman cases, yet they all fall short of adequately explaining the puzzle.

2.2 Coalitional Theories

Coalitional approaches explain institutional outcomes as products of distributional conflicts among coalitions of social actors with compatible interests.[113] By focusing on how the interests of main social actors are generated, how their relative powers shift, and how they enter and break alliances, the coalitional theories succeed where the macro-structural theories fail: provide the micro-level linkages between macro-structural factors.[114]

---

111 Tilly, *Coercion, Capital, and European States, AD 990-1992*, 30.

112 Hendrik Spruyt, "War, Trade and State Formation," in *The Oxford Handbook of Comparative Politics*, ed. Carles; Stokes Boix, Susan C. (Oxford: Oxford University Press, 2007), 6.

113 Jack Knight, *Institutions and Social Conflict* (Cambridge: Cambridge University Press, 1992).

114 The notion that coalitional arguments link macro- and micro-levels is based on Waldner, *State Building and Late Development*. Also see, D. Michael Shafer, *Winners and Losers: How Sectors Shape the Developmental Prospects of States*, Cornell Studies in

I differentiate between two analytically distinct ways to explain institutional outcomes through political coalitions among actors. Demand-side explanations see institutional change as a bottom-up process. Institutional outcomes are ultimately determined, at least in principle, by the objective interests of merchants and other market-oriented sectors that actively *demand* institutional arrangements that would further their interests. Supply-side explanations are similar in that they consider institutions as outcomes of distributional conflict, but they explicitly theorize about the interests of the ruler and other ruling elites who are in fact in a position to *supply* new institutions. I contend that existing theories treat the demand- and supply-side dynamics in isolation from each other. The isolation of the two sides of the intra-elite conflict is not only unwarranted but it ultimately results in incomplete explanations.

Spruyt's *Sovereign State and Its Competitors* is an excellent example of the demand-side approach.[115] Spruyt argues that the growth in long-distance trade in the late Middle Ages opened possibilities for institutional change by altering the interests of various social actors and shifting the balance of power among them. The key change was the rise of merchants in areas where cities expanded considerably. The merchants, whose interests were not best served under the existing institutional arrangements, formed coalitions with other actors to realize their interests. The variations in the composition of the coalitions between the kings, aristocracy, and merchants produced a spectrum of institutional outcomes. The alliance of the king and the burghers produced the territorial centralized states, whereas decentralized institutional arrangements materialized in cases where no such alliance was formed.

While Spruyt's emphasis on the coalitional dynamics is a significant improvement over previous theories,[116] I find the focus on the demands of merchants

---

Political Economy (Ithaca: Cornell University Press, 1994); Little, *Microfoundations, Method and Causation: On the Philosophy of the Social Sciences*; Michael Hechter, *The Microfoundations of Macrosociology* (Philadelphia: Temple University Press, 1983).

115 Hendrik Spruyt, *The Sovereign State and Its Competitors: An Analysis of Systems Change*, Princeton Studies in International History and Politics (Princeton, NJ: Princeton University Press, 1994).

116 First, while the bellicist literature explains the variation in state types by the differences in the local responses to the costs of preparing for and waging wars in an environment of intensified geopolitical conflict, Spruyt explains the variation by way of the exogenous growth in intra-regional trade in the earlier periods, the effects of which are mediated at the local level. Second, unlike the previous arguments, Spruyt's theory does not explain the selection among existing alternative institutional arrangements by their capacity to wage and survive costly wars. On the contrary, he argues that the

as the primary determinant of institutional outcomes incomplete. A closer look at the process of interest formation is necessary at this point, as it lies at the core of my critique of the demand-side explanations. The most important factor that shapes the composition of the ruling coalitions is the relative bargaining power of towns. Drawing on the neo-institutionalist premises,[117] Spruyt argues that towns had two competing preferences: independence and protection. In an ideal-typical free market, merchants would prefer a minimal degree of state involvement. However, market imperfections also warrant a stronger central authority to help reduce externalities, minimize transaction costs, and alleviate market imperfections. The choice between these two competing preferences is primarily contingent on externally generated objective factors, in Spruyt's case, the volume and level of trade.[118]

Supply-side dynamics, i.e., the interests and the strategies of other actors, most notably the king, are brought into the analysis only when the expected outcomes derived from the interests of towns do not fit with the observed outcomes. In *Sovereign State and Its Competitors*, the French and Italian towns' preferences perfectly overlap with the observed institutional outcomes. German case, however, poses a problem:

> Why did the German case turn out to be so different from the French? German towns, like the French, opposed domination by feudal lords and the church. Like the French, they would benefit from a central actor who could diminish feudal exactions and the incertitude caused by crosscutting jurisdictions. Given the high transaction costs and information costs involved in conducting long-distance trade...one might argue that they would benefit *even more* from an organization that could reduce such costs and uncertainty...So why did not the German king forge an alliance with the towns and create a sovereign state?[119]

---

very capacity to successfully engage in such conflicts is itself shaped by the efficacy of institutional arrangements.

117 North and Tomas wrote "during the era of mercantilism, merchants and entrepreneurs turned to government to open up markets, to break down monopolies and to provide naval and military protection for trade, in short to undertake the institutional innovations essential to internalizing externalities and reducing transaction costs." Douglass North, *The Rise of the Western World* (1973), 8.

118 Spruyt writes, "By measuring the volume and value of trade, we can conjecture what the towns' preferred political organization might have been." Spruyt, *The Sovereign State and Its Competitors: An Analysis of Systems Change*, 64.

119 Spruyt, *The Sovereign State and Its Competitors: An Analysis of Systems Change*, 111.

Based solely on objective interests, therefore, we expect the German merchants to prefer a centralized institutional arrangement. Why do they not realize their interest then? Spruyt's answer to this question underscores the independent effect of the "imperialist strategy" pursued by German kings, who sought to enhance their imperial reach instead of "concentrat[ing] on Germany and establish[ing] a sovereign, territorial state."[120] I do not contend that this explanation is historically inaccurate. However, I claim that it is insufficient to incorporate supply-side elements into the explanation only when there is a discrepancy between the expected outcomes of the theory and the observed outcomes in actual cases. There are several empirical and logical reasons why the supply-side dynamics should be specified and explained.

Consider once again the sources of merchants' competing preferences (independence vs. protection). The link proposed between the nature of the economic activity and the interest of the capital points to only the potential *gains* from seeking protection: if the merchants believe that they are to benefit from certain institutions, they demand it; if they are strong enough, they get what they demand. However, I contend that equally relevant are the expectations of the merchants concerning the *costs* of seeking state protection. These costs are in turn contingent on the strategies of the ruler. If the capital believes that the costs of protection are too high (in the case of a highly extractive strategy on the part of the ruler, for instance), then the capital might seek alternative, less costly, solutions to market imperfections or choose the exit option.[121]

There are additional reasons why a coalitional explanation should theorize explicitly about the interests and strategies of all actors involved in the conflict. The changes in the interests and relative bargaining power of the nobility, for instance, could directly shape the interests of all sides to the conflict as well as their capacities to realize those interests. Lachmann argues that urban autonomy—which was emphasized by Tilly and Spruyt as the most important factor shaping state types—was a function of the relative power of the emperor and nobles in Germany and Switzerland than the actual resources of the towns themselves. He shows that the German towns that had relatively high concentrations of capital had in fact very limited bargaining power. The towns were able to realize their institutional interests only after the nobles were divided amongst themselves.[122]

---

120 Ibid., 117.

121 Albert O. Hirschman, *Exit, Voice, and Loyalty; Responses to Decline in Firms, Organizations, and States* (Cambridge, MA: Harvard University Press, 1970).

122 Lachmann, *Capitalists in Spite of Themselves: Elite Conflict and Economic Transitions in Early Modern Europe*.

Lachmann's study of the transition from feudalism to capitalism in Europe between 1500 and 1800 is exemplary of supply-side theorizing in that it focuses on the question of how the structure of the intra-elite relations shapes the abilities of the monarchs to pursue a variety of state-building strategies.[123] The turning point in Lachmann's historical narrative is the Protestant Reformation which challenged the feudal elites' capacity to appropriate resources from non-elites. Elites moved toward a capitalist structure in an attempt to maintain their long-term capacity to appropriate resources. Consequently, sections of the feudal elite transformed themselves into capitalists "in spite of themselves."

Levi's *Of Rule and Revenue* offers a theory of institutional change that is squarely based on the strategic calculations of the rulers.[124] According to Levi, rulers are predatory; they are primarily interested in maximizing revenue accruing to the state. They devise those institutions that extract as much revenue as possible from the population. Rulers are constrained in their actions by three factors. First, their relative bargaining power[125] constrains their capacity to act upon their preferences. Second, the transaction costs of negotiating with other actors and the costs of implementing the decision are important. Third, discount rates shape the decision-making process; the lower the discount rate, the less an individual values the future relative to the present. All three variables, Levi adds, are themselves generated by antecedent variables: productive forces and economic structure, the international context, and the form of government. However, the investigation of such antecedent conditions is relegated to the margins of the analysis in Levi's work in favor of intermediate considerations of balance of power, transaction costs, and discount rates.

I contend that supply-side explanations curtail the validity of their causal arguments by discounting the weight of the antecedent conditions and focusing primarily on the immediate constraints. If factors like the economic structure, international context, and the pre-existing forms of institutions closely shape the balance of power among actors, then any theory that explains the outcomes based on the changes in balance of power should pay closer attention to such antecedents.

---

123 Ibid.

124 Margaret Levi, *Of Rule and Revenue*, California Series on Social Choice and Political Economy (Berkeley: University of California Press, 1988).

125 Bargaining power is defined as the degree to which they control coercive, economic, and political resources.

Given the limitations of explanations that treat demand- and supply-side dynamics in isolation, coalitional explanations should not exclusively focus on one side of the conflict among competing elites. Rather, they should explicitly theorize about the interests of the capital, ruler, and other relevant actors and thereby stitch together the demand- and supply-sides of distributional conflict. In Section 3, I construct an explanatory framework that focuses on both demand- and supply-sides of intra-elite conflict.

3. Intra-Elite Conflict and Institutional Change

3.1 Definitions, Assumptions, and Mechanisms

I define *fiscal state* as a state that efficiently collects taxes through a centralized revenue extraction apparatus and deploys the tax revenue to mobilize market resources and promote economic growth. The definition involves two analytically distinct aspects of fiscal states: institutional capacity and policy. In other words, fiscal states are institutionally capable to collect taxes *and* follow a developmental economic policy, which, in turn, will enhance economic resources available to the state through taxation.

As an ideal type, the fiscal state contrasts with the domain state, which collects its revenue directly from regalian properties and indirectly (i.e., through local intermediaries) from the peasantry. The tax revenue is then spent, almost exclusively, on court expenditures, upkeep of the military, and the maintenance of the state apparatus in general.[126] Dynastic empires of early modern Europe are—the differences in the sources of state revenue and tax collection methods notwithstanding—examples of the domain state.

The dependent variable of my research is operationalized by two empirically observable processes: (1) the replacement of decentralized and indirect mechanisms of tax collection with centralized, legal-rational bureaucratic tax collection agencies, (2) the extent to which the tax revenue was deployed toward the mobilization of market resources and economic growth, *either* through direct involvement of the state in manufacture and trade *or* through the provision of incentives for capital accumulation and production, *or* both.

126 For a general discussion of the evolution of the fiscal state in Europe, see Richard Bonney, *The Rise of the Fiscal State in Europe, C. 1200-1815* (Oxford; New York: Oxford University Press, 1999).

By elites, I mean "a group of rulers with the capacity to appropriate resources from non-elites and who inhabit a distinct organizational apparatus."[127] Elites have a monopoly over economic resources. Ruling elites, assumed to be rational and sufficiently cognizant of their interests, are primarily concerned about losing their capacity to appropriate revenue to rival elites. Their preferences are guided by their interest in maintaining their share of the revenue extracted from non-elites.[128] Consequently, various fractions of the elite (e.g., state bureaucracy vs. landed nobility) are in constant conflict with each other, and the institutional outcomes ultimately reflect the results of these conflicts.

Elites, however, are not always capable of prevailing in distributional conflicts. Consequently, elite fractions whose short-term interests are relatively compatible with each other form coalitions to bring about the institutional solutions that are most likely to consolidate their claims to resources. Institutions are created and sustained by such elite coalitions that manage to realize their interests. Similarly, institutions change when the composition of the existing elite coalition changes either by the inclusion of new elements, exclusion of the existing ones or by a shift in the distribution of power among various elements of the coalition.

The notion of redistribution is central to institutional analysis. Knight argues that institutions emerge from and offer solutions to distributional conflicts.[129] Similarly, the redistributive dimensions of state-building are well-established in the context of the political economy of post-colonial states. Examples of this approach include Geddes' argument that politicians will boost state capacity only when doing so is in their short-term political advantage,[130] Bates' study of the redistributive use of market institutions in African states,[131] Shafer's study of how economic sectors

---

127 Lachmann, *Capitalists in Spite of Themselves: Elite Conflict and Economic Transitions in Early Modern Europe.*

128 Institutional economics pays closer attention to similar elite dynamics underlying institutional change. Acemoglu and Robinson, for instance, argue that "political elites will block beneficial economic and institutional change when they are afraid that these changes will destabilize the existing system and make it more likely for them to lose political power and future rents." Daron Acemoglu and James A. Robinson. "Economic Backwardness in Political Perspective." *The American Political Science Review* 100, no. 1 (2006), 115.

129 Jack Knight, *Institutions and Social Conflict* (Cambridge: Cambridge University Press, 1992).

130 Barbara Geddes, *Politician's Dilemma: Building State Capacity in Latin America*, (Berkeley: University of California Press, 1994).

131 Robert H. Bates, *Markets and States in Tropical Africa: The Political Basis of Agricultural Policies*, (Berkeley: University of California Press, 2005).

shape the prospects of states[132] and Waldner's analysis of the origins of the developmental state.[133]

To explicate how exactly the distributional conflicts among elites produce the variation in institutional outcomes, I suggest two essential causal mechanisms: *balancing against threat* and *redistributive institution building*.

The first mechanism expands on the premise that elites are primarily concerned with maintaining relative positions vis-à-vis rival elites. If a rival elite group, e.g., landed nobility, benefits from the extant institutional order more than the ruling elites,[134] then the capacity of the ruling elites to reproduce their position diminishes. To prevent this, ruling elites will ally with other social actors whose interests are perceived as non-threatening.[135]

The second mechanism posits that rulers craft institutions that would provide side payments, or payoffs, to their new coalition partners while at the same time undermining their rivals by rechanneling access to economic resources. Hence, the incorporation of capital leads to centralized state structures not only because the capital demands such changes but also because the ruler, who can supply such changes, will benefit from them.

Institutional outcomes, in other words, are explained neither primarily as a product of the demands of the social actors (as in demand-side/bottom-up approaches) nor simply an extension of the strategic calculations of rulers operating under certain structural constraints (as in supply-side/top-down theories) but rather as a combination of both. These dual causal mechanisms jointly provide the key channels through which intra-elite conflict shapes institutional outcomes. While the first mechanism explains the coalitional outcomes of elite re-alignment by stipulating that elites form coalitions to minimize the threat to their capacity to extract revenue, the second mechanism posits that the same rationale leads the members of the resulting coalition to forge institutions to undermine their rivals by rechanneling access to revenue sources.

---

132 Shafer, *Winners and Losers: How Sectors Shape the Developmental Prospects of States*.

133 Waldner, *State Building and Late Development*.

134 I assume that elites have sufficiently *low discount rates*, i.e., in their strategic decision-making they value prospects more than short-term gains and losses. I substantiate the validity of this assumption in empirical chapters. For discount rates, see Levi, *Of Rule and Revenue*.

135 I borrow the term "balancing against threatf" from the international relations theory, particularly Stephen M. Walt, *The Origins of Alliances*, Cornell Studies in Security Affairs (Ithaca: Cornell University Press, 1987).

In explaining the variation in institutional outcomes in the Habsburg and Ottoman states, I combine these two causal mechanisms, which are essentially abstract and portable, with the historical analysis of the antecedent conditions in each case. By antecedent conditions, I mean the objective, structural constraints that precede institutional reform. The most critical among such conditions is the mode of imperial organization, which constitutes the starting point of my explanation of the puzzle posed by the Habsburg and Ottoman cases in the next section.

3.2 Main Arguments

Empires suffer from a chronic deficiency of infrastructural power.[136] Rulers are typically quite able to make decisions independently from society, but they cannot implement these decisions quite as easily throughout their realms. The primary reason is logistical: rulers can expand their territory through conquest but simply cannot govern the conquered territories from a central location.[137] In other words, there is an insolvable tension between conquest and rule: conquest through an army requires concentrating forces, whereas ruling such distant localities necessitates dispersing the available forces.[138]

Indirect rule, while providing rulers with low-cost security and administrative capacity without creating bulky apparatuses, inadvertently entails principal-agent problems. Imperial rulers cannot gather reliable information on and enforce compliance of their local agents—typically native elites and sometimes "foreign" rulers relocated by the imperial center.[139] These local intermediaries acquire independent interests and threaten the center by cutting into the resource flow from the periphery

---

136 Michael Mann, "The Autonomous Power of the State: Its Origins, Mechanisms and Results," *Arch. Europ. Sociol.* XXV (1984): 185-213. Michael Mann, *The Sources of Social Power* (Cambridge Cambridgeshire; New York: Cambridge University Press, 1986).

137 Mann calculates that in the pre-modern period the survival period of any self-equipped army was only three days.

138 Mann's discussion of imperial rule draws on a large body of scholarship on the historical sociology of empires, most notably Eisenstadt, Kautsky and of course Weber's discussion of the role of honoratories under patrimonial rule. S. N. Eisenstadt, *The Political Systems of Empires* (London [New York]: Free Press of Glencoe, 1963); John H. Kautsky, *The Politics of Aristocratic Empires* (Chapel Hill: University of North Carolina Press, 1982); Max Weber, Guenther Roth, and Claus Wittich, *Economy and Society: An Outline of Interpretive Sociology* [Wirtschaft und Gesellschaft.] (Berkeley: University of California Press, 1978).

139 Eisenstadt, *The Political Systems of Empires.*

to the center[140] and even revolting against the central authority by amassing their military force or allying themselves with an external rival of the central elites.[141]

Though logistical constraints on infrastructural power are ubiquitous, my research suggests that individual empires vary in the extent to which they rely on local intermediaries, resulting in distinct modalities of imperial rule. I differentiate between two subcategories of the imperial state.[142]

In *horizontally organized* empires, rulers are highly constrained in terms of the infrastructural reach of the state. Consequently, they are forced to rely on local intermediaries for basic governmental functions including tax collection, provision of law and order, and organization of military defenses. The Habsburg Empire before the eighteenth century is an example of the *horizontal mode of organization*. From its foundation in the late thirteenth century, the Habsburg monarchy operated under conditions of very low infrastructural power. In contrast, in *vertically organized* polities, central elites, while still subject to the logistical constraints on infrastructural power, have a relatively higher capacity to monitor and enforce compliance of rural elites. The Ottoman state, which had unique institutional solutions to the problem of infrastructural power at its disposal until the late seventeenth century,[143] was vertically organized.

The two logics of the imperial organization are not simply background conditions but rather critical antecedents.[144] Such antecedents have critical causal relevance as they contribute to generating the coalitional and institutional outcomes by providing the parameters within which the elites formed their institutional preferences and acted upon them. More specifically, within a horizontally organized imperial polity such as the Habsburg Empire, the ruling elite is typically divided between

---

140 Barkey, *Changing Modalities of Empire: A Comparative Study of Ottoman and Habsburg Decline.*

141 Mann, *The Sources of Social Power*, 143.

142 The dual categories of vertical and horizontal modes mirror similar distinctions made by Lachmann and Ertman. Lachmann, *Capitalists in Spite of Themselves: Elite Conflict and Economic Transitions in Early Modern Europe*; Ertman, *Birth of the Leviathan: Building States and Regimes in Medieval and Early Modern Europe*. Also see Cooley's distinction between U-Form and M-Form hierarchies. Alexander Cooley, *Logics of Hierarchy: The Organization of Empires, States and Military Occupations* (Ithaca: Cornell University Press, 2005).

143 I discuss the mechanisms of direct rule, particularly the institutions of *tımar* and *kul*, in detail in Chapter 5.

144 Dan Slater and Erica Simmons. "Informative regress: Critical antecedents in comparative politics." *Comparative Political Studies* 43, no. 7 (2010): 886-917.

central and rural elements. While mutually dependent on each other, these two fractions compete over the distribution of agricultural revenue through taxation.

In contrast, in the vertically organized Ottoman state, the sultan ruled (especially in Eastern Europe) without having to rely extensively on local nobility (which was eliminated and/or co-opted during imperial expansion). The bureaucratic elite of the Ottoman state ruled as a more-or-less unified elite that had a legally justified and militarily enforced claim to all revenue.

When the seventeenth-century crisis arrived, the Habsburg and Ottoman elites were operating under different constraints stemming from the distinctive structures of elite conflict. Moreover, the changes in the external economic conditions (e.g., shifting trade routes, and growing European demand) altered the balance of power among actors. In both cases, the intensity of the preexisting conflicts increased, paving the way for elite realignment.

The traditional coalition of the central ruling elites and the landed nobility in the countryside ended in the seventeenth century. The landowners expanded their relative power by completing the enserfment of their labor force as a response to the growing demand for agricultural goods in Western Europe. Threatened by the rise of the relative economic power and political influence of their coalitional partners, the Habsburg ruling elite enlisted the support of the capital (and sections of lesser nobility). Both the ruling elites and the capital holders had a shared interest in undermining the power of the landed nobility and formed a political coalition, which would survive until the end of the empire.

The Ottoman rulers had to deal with a similar revenue crisis in the seventeenth century but faced a different set of constraints and incentives. In the Ottoman case, it is harder to locate a strong landed elite in the countryside (before the eighteenth century) to challenge the power of the Porte. However, the central elites considered merchants and other holders of capital as the primary threat to their elite status. According to Ottoman elites, commercialization threatened their long-term capacity to appropriate revenue as it diverted resources away from the center.

As in the Habsburg case, the economic changes external to the empire had fundamentally affected the interests of the central bureaucratic elite and merchants engaged in long-distance trade. Taking advantage of the revitalization of markets in Europe, particularly after 1660, Ottoman merchants engaged in widespread contraband trade,[145] which intensified the conflict between the merchants and the bureaucratic elite.

145 Barkan, "The Price Revolution in the Sixteenth Century."

The intervening variable has two values: the ruling elite either incorporates capital into the ruling coalition, as in the Habsburg case or the merchants and other capital holders are excluded from the political process, as in the Ottoman case. The post-realignment coalitional outcomes are then linked to the institutional outcomes by way of the second causal mechanism: redistribution.

Why exactly did the ruler-capital coalition produce centralized fiscal institutions in the Habsburg case? The short answer is that such institutions satisfied the interests of both the merchants and the central elites. Centralized and hierarchical institutions help merchants deal with market imperfections. Merchants in the Habsburg Empire were demanding institutional changes that would remove what the mercantilist writers of the time called "unnatural barriers" to trade and industry, such as labor restrictions, guild privileges, internal tolls, etc.—barriers that were mostly erected by the landed elites in alliance with the Habsburg ruling elites in the fifteenth and sixteenth centuries.[146]

But why did the Habsburg ruler agree to supply these institutional changes? For two reasons: first, these institutional changes were essentially side payments to merchants whose economic vitality the ruling elite desperately needed. Second, and more importantly, these reforms would redistribute resources from the landed elites to the merchants and thus weakening the landed nobility.

Why did the exclusion of capital in the Ottoman state result in fiscal decentralization? When we look at the demand-side, the side of the Ottoman merchants, we see that such centralized institutions would have benefited them, just like the Habsburg merchants. Indeed, we have some evidence that the Ottoman merchants did demand such changes in the seventeenth and eighteenth centuries. However, the bureaucratic elite had little incentive to supply such institutional changes. Instead, the bureaucratic elite formed an implicit alliance with the local notables in the provinces. The expansion of tax farming, the institution of *malikane* (life-term tax farming contracts), and the privatization of tax collection were essentially side payments from the bureaucratic elite to the local notables. Even though such notables did not have any independent economic basis, they possessed some social and political capital, which the central elites could use to collect taxes and administer the countryside.

146 I discuss in Chapter 4 how exactly Habsburg rulers in this period helped landed elites consolidate their authority over agricultural lands and peasants, resulting in the spread of the so-called second serfdom. Jerome Blum, "The Rise of Second Serfdom in Eastern Europe," *American Historical Review* 62 (1957); Laszlo Makkai, "Neo-Serfdom: Its Origin and Nature in East Central Europe," *Slavic Review* XXXIV (1975); William E. Wright, "Neo-Serfdom in Bohemia," *Slavic Review* XXXIV (1975).

Lastly, my research also reveals that unlike the Habsburg case, where the post-crisis alignment between the ruling elites and merchants persisted until the end of the empire, in the Ottoman state there was a second realignment period in the early nineteenth century. The bureaucratic elite of the state, now threatened by the rise of tax farmers and export-oriented landlords, tried to incorporate the merchants into the political process by offering them a series of side-payments.

However, merchants did not respond positively to the central elites' move, because they now considered greater state involvement in economic affairs too costly. In fact, by then the Ottoman merchants were well integrated into the European economy as suppliers of raw materials and foodstuffs, and importers of manufactured goods into the Ottoman market. Given the predatory policies of the Ottoman state in the past, Ottoman merchants had very little to gain from a partnership with the state elite. Instead, the economic interests of the merchants were closely aligned with those of the export-oriented landlords of the period. Both sectors wanted faster and more direct integration of the Ottoman economy into the world-economy, and both considered the bureaucratic elite an impediment to this goal.

Charts 1 and 2 summarize the Habsburg and Ottoman cases.

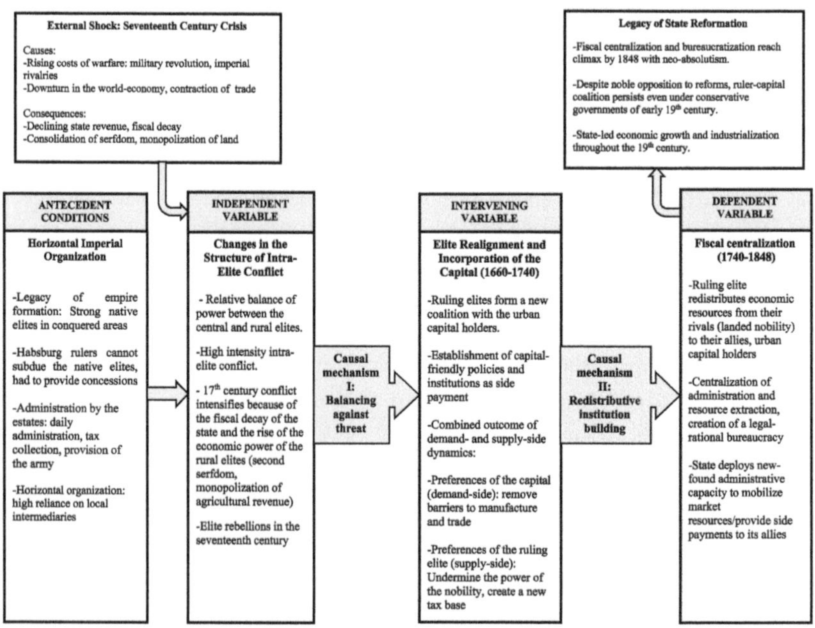

Chart 1: Summary of the Habsburg Case

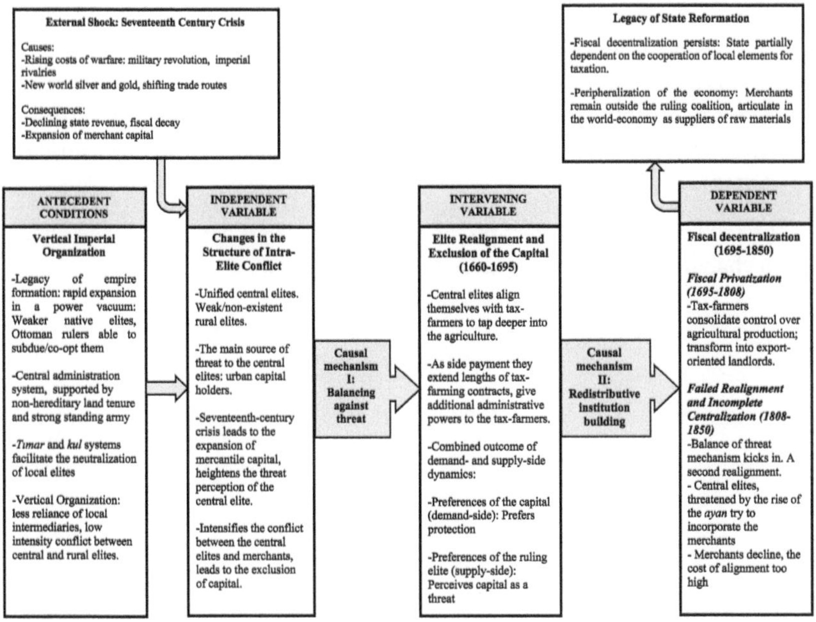

Chart 2: Summary of the Ottoman Case

4. Conclusion

This chapter accomplished three goals:

(1) It explored the causes and consequences of the seventeenth-century fiscal crisis in the Habsburg and Ottoman Empires. Two factors stood out: the adverse effects of the "general crisis" and the rising costs of warfare. I also briefly reviewed the post-crisis fiscal strategies of the two states facing similar crisis conditions. The variation in these fiscal strategies closely shaped the long-term developmental prospects of the two empires.

(2) It discussed the main tenets and limitations of the extant theories of state formation. In addition to their shortcomings, the purely cultural, economic, and bellicist theories of state formation are all lacking to the extent that they neglect the micro-structural dynamics underlying the macro-level processes. Theories that are centered on political coalitions are better equipped to address micro-dynamics as they focus on the formation of the interests of main social actors and the distributional conflicts among them. However, the coalitional theories could also be improved by bringing together the two

types of approaches that had hitherto typically remained separate: demand- and supply-side theories.

(3) The last part of the chapter provided the building blocks of a causal framework that combines the demand- and supply-side dynamics of intra-elite conflict. The framework was then briefly applied to the Habsburg and Ottoman cases.

The following four chapters provide a detailed causal narrative of the institutional change in the Habsburg and Ottoman Empires.

Chapter 3 Intra-Elite Conflict in the Habsburg Empire, 1278-1660

This chapter offers an analytic narrative of the origins and dynamics of intra-elite conflict in the Habsburg Empire. Reaching as far back as the formation of the Habsburg rule in Central Europe in the thirteenth century, I explain the relationship between the Habsburg rulers and the landowning nobility—a relationship based on mutual interdependence and balance of power.

The structure of the intra-elite conflict constitutes the antecedent conditions of the institutional transformation that took place in the eighteenth century, which produced a relatively centralized fiscal state in the Habsburg case and a decentralized fiscal apparatus in the Ottoman Empire. These antecedent conditions, however, are not simply background factors. They are *critical antecedents* in that they contributed to the generation of coalitional and institutional outcomes by providing the parameters within which the elites formed their institutional preferences and acted upon them.[147] This chapter elucidates the critical antecedents, laying the groundwork for the articulation of the dual causal mechanisms of *balancing against threat* and *redistributive institution building* in the following chapter.

The chapter is organized into two sections. The first section argues that the coalition between the elites in the imperial core and the nobility in the countryside is a product of the expansion of Habsburg rule in Central Europe from the fourteenth to the sixteenth century. The second section analyzes why the structure of the intra-elite relations was significantly altered in the seventeenth century, and how the conflict between the central ruling elites and the nobility intensified because of external factors, most notably the shifts in international trade.

After an overview of the rise of the Habsburg family to power from 1278 to 1291, the chapter moves on to the era of imperial expansion, roughly from 1291 to 1459, when the Habsburgs acquired territory through intricate diplomacy backed by military alliances. Because of this mode of imperial expansion, the Habsburg rulers had to deal with strong and well-entrenched landed interests. Unlike the Ottoman case, where the ruling elites were able to neutralize the native elites, Habsburg's imperial expansion left the local power bases in the newly

147 On critical antecedents, see Slater and Simmons, "Informative Regress: Critical Antecedents in Comparative-Historical Analysis."

acquired territories largely intact. The outcome was the coalition between the ruling elite and the nobility, a coalition of necessity.

I discuss in detail the specific arrangements between each region (Inner Austria, Hungary, and Bohemia) and the Habsburg state. I show that in each region, Habsburg rulers entirely depended on the rural elites that performed vital functions in three domains: local administration, tax collection, and defense provision. The nobles constituted the very infrastructural power of the state in the countryside by supervising the daily social and legal affairs in the countryside, collecting taxes from the peasantry, and financing/organizing military defenses of the imperial borders.

In the first section of this chapter, I also discuss the efforts of the Habsburg rulers to counterbalance the power of estates in the first half of the sixteenth century. Maximilian I (1459-1519) and Ferdinand I (1503-1564) sought to impose a common legal, financial, and administrative system upon the imperial lands, which would undermine noble estates' organizational capacity to pursue their independent interests. Even though such reforms produced short-lived archetypes of centralized institutions, they were of limited long-term consequence. Not only did the estates successfully resist change, but also the Habsburg rulers found themselves constrained by their reliance on local elites.

Thus, until the late sixteenth century, the structure of the intra-elite relations was characterized by relatively stable cooperation between the central and rural elites—an equilibrium that was only temporarily disturbed by the short-term fluctuations in the distribution of power. In the second section of the chapter, I discuss how this equilibrium shifted when the economic power of the landed elites increased dramatically by the seventeenth century. The cyclical dynamics of the world economy, the boom of the agricultural markets in Western Europe, followed by a decline in prices and contraction of intra-regional trade, resulted in the monopolization of agricultural lands in the hands of the largest landowners and the decline of lesser nobility.

Growing demesne production and the increasing enserfment of the peasantry throughout the seventeenth century enhanced the capacity of the rural elites to further cut into the flow of resources from the periphery to the center. The increasing power of the rural elites not only threatened the survival of the imperial state, which was already under severe fiscal strain due to increased costs of war and declining state revenues but also undermined the capacity of the Habsburg elite to perpetuate their rule. For the central elite, the costs of the dependence on rural elites for essential governmental functions started to outweigh the benefits of maintaining a coalition with them.

In terms of the explanatory framework of this book, the changes in the externally driven structural conditions altered the threat perception of the ruling elites: they started to view the rural elites as more of a detriment to their elite status than a necessary instrument of the state's infrastructural power. I document the empirical manifestations of the intensified intra-elite conflict, most notably the two major elite rebellions in the seventeenth century; the White Mountain in Bohemia, and the Bocskay Uprising in Hungary.

1. The Origins of Intra-Elite Relations in the Habsburg Empire

1.1 Horizontal Empire

Wer spricht von Siegen? Überste'n ist alles.[148]

The Habsburg Empire comprised the hereditary lands (*Erbländer*) of the Holy Roman Empire (i.e., the archduchy of Austria, the duchies of Styria, Carinthia, and Carniola, the county of Tyrol) and the kingdoms of Bohemia and Hungary. The sovereign of this multi-ethnic and multi-religious political entity held the title of the Holy Roman Emperor and the King of Germany, even though in the official acts of Hungary and Bohemia, he was simply the King.[149]

The conditions surrounding the Habsburgs' ascendance to power are crucial as they give us the first hints regarding the horizontal organization of the empire and the structure of the intra-elite relations. The House of Habsburg, a noble

---

148 "Who speaks of victories? Survival is everything." Adam Wandruszka, *The House of Habsburg; Six Hundred Years of a European Dynasty* (London: Sidgwick and Jackson, 1964), 74.

149 Jean Bérenger, *A History of the Habsburg Empire* (London; New York: Longman, 1994), 155-6. It was only in 1804 that Francis accepted the title of Austrian Emperor and in 1806, officially announced that the Holy Roman Empire was no longer. The ambiguities about the legal applicability of the concept of "empire" to the large multi-ethnic state ruled by the Habsburg dynasty for about seven centuries, however, do not diminish the fact that the Habsburg monarchy was one of the major empires of the early modern era in terms of its longevity and size. For a discussion of the relative place of the Habsburg in European history, see Andrew Wheatcroft, *The Habsburgs: Embodying the Empire* (London: Folio Sociert, 2004); Michael Erbe, *Die Habsburger (1493-1918): Eine Dynastie Im Reich und in Europa* (Stuttgart, Berlin, Koln, Kohlhammer: Urban-Taschenbuecher, 2000); Karl Friedrich Krieger, *Die Habsburger Im Mittelalter: Von Rudolf I. Bis Friedrich III*, Kohlhammer Urban-Taschenbucher (Stuttgart: W. Kohlhammer, 1994).

family whose origins are usually traced to Alemannic Switzerland and Upper Alsace,[150] first came to power in the region of Austria[151] in the thirteenth century. Frederich II of the ruling Babenberg family in Central Europe died in 1246, and the male line of the Babenbergs ended. Taking advantage of the interregnum that followed, Přemysl II Otakar, the king of Bohemia, outmaneuvered the rival Austrian noble families and claimed kingship over Austrian lands, allegedly in violation of laws of succession.[152]

As a response to the usurpation of the throne by the Bohemian King, the German princes blocked the candidacy of Otakar in the royal election of 1273, which would have legitimized his rule. The princes supported Rudolf of Habsburg, who was considered a neutral figure. Rudolf, the new king of Germany, summoned Otakar to obtain a legal right to hold Austrian lands as a fief in return for recognizing Rudolf's kingship. When Otakar refused, Rudolf defeated Otakar first at the Battle of Dürnkrut and then at Marchfeld in August 1278, and the Habsburg family consolidated their position as the kings of Germany and the Holy Roman Emperors.

For nearly 200 years following the foundation of the monarchy by King Rudolf I, the Habsburg rulers followed a restrained policy of territorial expansion.[153] In addition to Austria and Styria, which were acquired in 1278 under Rudolf I, Carinthia (1335), Carniola (1335) under Albrecht II, and Tyrol (1363) under Leopold III became part of the Habsburg domain.[154] In the late fourteenth century, the dynasty was temporarily divided between rival princes of the family; Albrecht II gained the core regions of Upper and Lower Austria, whereas Leopold

150 Bérenger, *A History of the Habsburg Empire*, chapter 8.

151 *Ostarrichi* in old German, as the "eastern mark" of the Roman Empire.

152 Steven Beller, *A Concise History of Austria* (Cambridge, UK; New York: Cambridge University Press, 2006), 26-37.

153 There was a great deal of variation and pragmatism in the imperial expansion policy. In certain regions, especially along the western border, the imperial policy was more geared towards maintaining the territorial status quo rather than expansion, in accordance with the so-called *Landfriedenspolitik* of King Rudolf. Christel Maria von Graevenitz, *Die Landfriedenspolitik Rudolfs Von Habsburg (1273-1291) Am Niederrhein Und Im Westfalen* (Koln, Weimar, Wien: Boehlau Verlag, 2003).

154 Despite these gains, the *domus Austriae* however was still far from being completely dominant in Central Europe in the fourteenth century. Among the chief rivals to the Habsburg family was the House of Luxemburg from western German lands, which was gaining power by acquiring lands on the western rim of the empire, challenging Habsburg supremacy. Beller, *A Concise History of Austria*, 29-30.

III ruled over the rest. The House remained divided for almost a century until Frederick V was elected king in 1440 and crowned emperor by the Pope in 1452.

The Habsburg strategy of territorial expansion combined the strength of arms with diplomacy, conducted through marriage alliances and mutual succession pacts. Rudolf, the founder of the monarchy, spearheaded the strategy by arranging a double wedding between his children and Otakar's. Frederick III (1415-1493) followed this policy by securing a marriage alliance with Burgundy. Marriage diplomacy as a tool of imperial expansion was perfected during the reign of Frederick III's son, Maximilian I. He arranged several marriage alliances in his time, stretching from England to Russia.

Two of these arrangements were crucial. The first was with the House of Castile in Spain and brought the Habsburg Spain, the New World, and much of Italy under Habsburg control.[155] In the east, Maximilian reinforced the historical claims to Bohemia and Hungary by securing a double marriage of his grandchildren to the children of Vladislav, Jagellon King of Bohemia and Hungary, in 1515. When Vladislav's son Louis II died in the Battle of Mohacs against the Ottomans, the estates elected Archduke Ferdinand the King of Bohemia and Hungary, realizing the Habsburg claims to the throne, which dated back to the reign of Rudolf I.[156]

However, the common notion that the Habsburgs forged their empire entirely through marriage diplomacy[157] is misleading. While marriage alliances provided the Habsburg dynasty with a legal pretext for acquiring the crowns and territories, in practice, the legal compacts were less than binding. Often the acquisition of new lands was contingent on larger strategic calculations and, most importantly, military enforcement of the legal arrangements. As Beller wrote, "[m]arriage as a strategy was only part of the secret to Habsburg success. Maximilian and his successors fought wars aplenty."[158] More importantly, the territorial claims of the

---

155 At least until 1556, when the so-called "Spanish" line of the Habsburgs, headed by Karl V, parted ways with the Austrian line ruled by Ferdinand.

156 Wandruszka, *Das Haus Habsburg: Die Geschichte Einer Europäischen Dynastie*. For a detailed account of the marriage alliances, see Paula S. Fichtner, *Ferdinand I of Austria: The Politics of Dynasticism in the Age of Reformation* (New York: 1982); Paula Fichtner, "Dynastic Marriage in Sixteenth-Century Habsburg Diplomacy and Statecraft: An Interdisciplinary Approach," *The American Historical Review* 81, no. 2 (1976).

157 The policy is best illustrated by what is known as the "unofficial family motto" of the Habsburgs in the fourteenth century: *Alli bella gerant/Tu, felix Austria, nube!* (Let others wage wars/You, happy Austria, marry).

158 Beller, *A Concise History of Austria*, 41-2.

Habsburg rulers, even when backed by military force, almost always needed to be reinforced by the votes and approval of the native estates.

The historical nations of Central and Eastern Europe, Bohemia, and Hungary had been ruled by strong families for centuries. Land tenure systems in Central and Eastern Europe evolved in a different trajectory and at a particularly slower pace compared to Western Europe. Unlike the highly fragmented political structure of the West, throughout Eastern Europe, stronger central powers ruled over a service nobility. By the thirteenth century, when Western Europe was already transforming from feudal to capitalistic relations, relations of vassalage were becoming increasingly more established in the East. Noble estates in Central and Eastern Europe retained and consolidated their influence, unlike their western counterparts, who were subordinated to monarchical authorities.[159]

One explanation for the differences in land tenures involves the differential legacies of the Roman Empire. It has been argued that the prevalence of a Greco-Roman legal tradition, combined with the early break-up of the common landed property, paved the way for an earlier emergence of feudal relations of production in the West.[160] Also relevant was that in Central and Eastern Europe the foundations of feudal society were laid by strong foreign families of often Germanic origin. These aristocratic families of foreign origin ruled jointly with the native Magyar elites in Hungary. Strong families also dominated Croatia, Slovenia, and Bohemia. The *Magnates* in Hungary, the *Herren* in the Austrian lands, and the *Pani Stavu* in Bohemia held sway in the countryside long before the Habsburg rule in these regions. In addition, the noble landowners also controlled private armies, often rivaling those of the monarchs.[161]

---

159 Gunst, *Agrarian Development and Social Change in Eastern Europe, 14th-19th Centuries*, R. J. W. Evans and T. V. Thomas, *Crown, Church and Estates: Central European Politics in the Sixteenth and Seventeenth Centuries* (1991); Otto Brunner, *Land and Lordship: Structures of Governance in Medieval Austria* (Philadelphia: University of Philadelphia Press, 1992); Florin Curta, *East Central & Eastern Europe in the Early Middle Ages* (Ann Arbor: University of Michigan Press, 2005).

160 Gunst, Winner, and Winner, "Some Characteristics of East European Economic and Social Development: Data and Reflections."

161 Gabor Agoston, "Habsburgs and Ottomans: Defense, Military Change and Shifts in Power," *The Turkish Studies Association Bulletin* 22, no. 1 (1998); Pal Fodor and Gaza David, *Ottomans, Hungarians, and Habsburgs in Central Europe: The Military Confines in the Era of Ottoman Conquest*, Ottoman Empire and Its Heritage (Leiden; Boston: Brill, 2000).

Facing these constraints, the Habsburgs were compelled to build the administrative skeleton of the empire on the cooperation of local elites, which required granting them concessions and side payments through recurrent bargaining. As a political concession, Habsburg rulers had to go through the royal election by local noble families, even though both crowns were legally hereditary.[162] Rulers also allowed the nobles to preserve their hold over the lower estates and towns. Perhaps the most consequential concessions were the exemption from direct taxation and widespread discretion that allowed landowners to manage agricultural relations.

Despite the political and economic concessions granted to the estates, the Habsburg kings still benefited from an alliance with the nobility. First, rulers used the distribution of land and other benefits to build a political patronage network. For instance, Ferdinand I maintained close relations with the leading aristocratic families and even replaced dying noble families with new ones.

The other reason why "cooperation of local intermediary powers was in some ways far more crucial for the Habsburgs than for those whom they ruled"[163] concerned the limits of the infrastructural reach of the former's administrative capacity. In Chapter 2 I discussed, drawing on Michael Mann's work,[164] that the logistical constraints to the exercise of infrastructural power necessitated reliance on indirect means of rule. In the Habsburg Empire, where such constraints were formidable, the cooperation of nobility was essential for basic functions of the state including border defense, tax collection, and the administration of the countryside. Below I take a closer look at the military, fiscal, and administrative roles of the estates in imperial lands.

1.2 Administration by the Estates and Royal Reforms in the Sixteenth Century

1.2.1 Bohemia

By the time Ferdinand I acquired the Bohemian crown in 1526, the Bohemian state—which in a geographic sense denoted Bohemia proper as well as the four Lands of Moravia, Silesia, and the two Lusatias—had been in existence for almost half a millennium. The Land of Bohemia was the most privileged among

---

162 Fichtner, *The Habsburg Monarchy, 1490-1848: Attributes of Empire*, 15.

163 Ibid., 20.

164 Michael Mann, "The Autonomous Power of the State: Its Origins, Mechanisms and Results," *Arch. Europ. Sociol.* XXV (1984).

all Habsburg lands. The Bohemian elites held the authority to elect a new king and control the key agencies of the crown, i.e., the Royal Council, the Bohemian Chancellery, the Aulic Court (*dvorský soud*), and the Chamber Court (*komorni soud*).[165] The Bohemian estates retained *de jure* authority to elect the king, despite succession having gained a *de facto* hereditary character.[166] Yet the real basis of the estates' power rested with their chief political apparatus, the diet.

The organization of the diet, *sněmy*, differed in each Land of Bohemia, yet the overall structure remained similar. The nobility formed the first two colleges: the barons (*páni*) and the knights (*rytíři*). Barons could afford to attend diet personally, whereas the less wealthy knights held local congresses in the local administrative units called circuits (*kraje, Kreise*) and elected two to six persons to represent the circuit at the diet. About 1,400 noble families were represented in the diet at the end of the sixteenth century.[167]

Royal towns were entitled to representation, but their influence was limited compared to the noble estates. Bohemian royal towns, which numbered around 40 in the sixteenth century, were represented in the third college of the *sněmy*, where each town held only a single vote even if they could send two to three representatives at a time. In the other lands of the Bohemian crown, there were much fewer royal towns (six each in Moravia and Upper Lusatia and four in Lower Lusatia) and they shared the third college with the estate of prelates, which further undermined their capacity to influence outcomes. Even though the legislative procedure required important measures to be obtained by a unanimous vote of all colleges, in practice, the first two colleges dominated the decision-making by being able to set the agenda and dictate the outcomes.

The diet was charged with formulating and enacting policy primarily in three areas: collection of taxation, provision of defense, and administration of local social and legal affairs. Administrative functions were performed through the top administrators and judges in each land, the "highest officials" (*nejvyšší úředníci zemští*). These officials represented the estates; even when the Habsburg kings

---

165 The most comprehensive account of the role of estates in the administration of imperial lands is Robert A. Kann and Zdenek David, *The Peoples of Eastern Habsburg Lands, 1526-1918* (Seattle: 1984).

166 The successors to Ferdinand I were always accepted by the diet during the lifetime of the preceding king, and the instances where the estates asserted their right of free royal election, such as in 1619, were rare.

167 Kann and David, *The Peoples of Eastern Habsburg Lands, 1526-1918*, 26-7.

asserted their right to make appointments for such positions, the estates were to approve these appointments.[168]

The administration of the Bohemian countryside was organized into 14 circuits. Two captains, a baron, and a knight, were in charge of each circuit and were responsible for maintaining law and order. In addition to performing a wide range of duties, from enforcing wage rates to arresting criminals, the circuit captains assisted with tax collection and organization of military levy. As the main instruments of state infrastructure in the countryside, the circuits were "centers of local autonomy and strongholds of the political influence of the estates."[169]

Royal towns were not subject to any local seigneur. The head of the town government (*purkmeister*) was technically elected, but the council was to be confirmed by the officials of the Land. Thus, the royal towns, despite their *de jure* jurisdictional and administrative autonomy, were not outside the control of the noble estates. Additionally, royal authorities frequently enlisted the help of estates in collecting taxes from royal towns, which, combined with the infeasibility of monitoring the agents' misconduct, subjugated the towns to the unchecked authority of the nobility.

Noble estates were exempt from ordinary taxes collected to meet the expenses of the imperial court and civil administration. Thus, the state revenue was limited to a few sources: royal estates, royal towns, and ecclesiastical estates, especially taxes imposed on the sale of beer, salt, and livestock, as well as regalian rights applied to mining. The collection of the extraordinary taxes (*dica, subsidium, contributio*) from the estates was reserved primarily for military purposes and was contingent on the approval of the diets, which rarely agreed to grant them. Even as late as 1654, when Leopold I managed to impose some ordinary taxes on the estates and made it illegal to refuse extraordinary taxes, the estates were still able to bargain over the amount and timetable of payments.[170]

An even more striking aspect of the taxation of the estates was that the Bohemian estates were in charge of collecting and distributing the extraordinary taxes they were subject to. The extraordinary taxes were collected by the estates

168 Ibid., 31. They were selected among members of the nobility, barons, and less frequently wealthier knights.

169 Ibid.

170 Thomas Mack Barker, *Double Eagle, and Crescent; Vienna's Second Turkish Siege and its Historical Setting* (Albany: State University of New York Press, 1967), 207-8. Barker reports that the estates resisted paying taxes even during the second Ottoman siege of Vienna in 1683.

themselves, not by a royal organ like the Bohemian Chamber, which collected the ordinary revenue only. The diet performed this function in Bohemia by appointing three tax collectors (*berníci zemští*) in each Land. In addition, even after the sixteenth-century reforms, the Bohemian estates retained the power to decide how to distribute tax revenue for "state purposes," usually to maintain troops and fortresses along the Hungarian military frontier.[171]

This takes us to another critical function performed by the estates: the provision of the army. The Habsburg Empire did not have a peacetime standing army until 1649 when Ferdinand III issued a decree announcing that the regiments raised for the Long War with the Ottomans (1593-1606) and the Thirty Years Wars (1618-1648) were to be transformed into a permanent army of the hereditary lands.[172] Before 1649, and partially after then, the wartime army of the Habsburg lands was controlled by the estates, which raised, paid for, and administered it.[173]

The Habsburg rulers depended not only on the estates for the provision of soldiers, but they also needed the estates' approval to use military forces. Regiments raised with the support of the Bohemian estates, for instance, could not be deployed outside Bohemian Lands without the estates' permission. The king even had to negotiate special agreements with the estates to secure the use of Bohemian troops in Hungary against the Ottomans. Thus, in addition to political dominance in the diets and economic power through the monopoly over agricultural revenue, the estates wielded considerable military power, which they used, in times of escalated tension with the Habsburg rulers, to serve their interests either by revolting against the central administration or allying themselves with an external rival of the empire.

1.2.2 The Slovene Lands

The Slovene regions of Styria, Carniola, and Carinthia were among the earliest acquisitions of the Habsburg monarchy, conquered between 1282 and 1335. However, the early Habsburg presence did not translate into a more favorable

---

171 W. E. Wright, *Serf, Seigneur and Sovereign. Agrarian Reform in Eighteenth Century Bohemia* (Minneapolis: 1966), 6-27.

172 John A. Mears, "Thirty Years War, the 'General Crisis' and the Origins of the Standing Professional Army in the Habsburg Monarchy," *Central European History* 21 (1988): 122-41.

173 Kann and David, *The Peoples of Eastern Habsburg Lands, 1526-1918*, 36.

position within the intra-elite balance of power for the central elites. The diets were powerful, especially after the early fifteenth century.[174]

Slovene diets consisted, minor differences among individual lands aside, of four colleges (*curiae*): the prelates, the higher nobility, the lower nobility, and the towns. The towns did not have any officially recognized right to representation until the late sixteenth century. The change in the towns' representation mainly came from the noble estates' strategy to enlist their support in the escalating tension between the Protestant nobles and the Catholic Habsburg rulers.[175] The towns, however, did not provide a powerful ally for the Protestant cause at this time mainly because of their declining economic stance. The disruption of trade in the Slovene regions following the Turkish conquests and the shifting of the major long-distance trade routes from the Mediterranean to the Atlantic contributed to the economic decline of towns.

Like their Bohemian counterparts, the noble estates in the Slovene regions controlled nearly every aspect of the administration of the lands. The main administrative official of each land (*Landeshauptmann*) was nominated by the estates and appointed by the Habsburg king. He was assisted by the Committee of the Land, also elected by the diets. Implementing the decisions of the estates and the committees was the responsibility of the chancelleries, who were paid by and held accountable to the diets.

The Slovene estates performed vital functions in local administration, tax collection, and organization of military defenses. As in Bohemia, the Slovene estates were mainly in charge of the daily affairs in manors and towns through the seigniorial officials in the former and the judges and councils in the latter. These officials provided police protection and distributed civil and lower criminal justice. Matters of higher criminal nature were the responsibility of the Courts of the Land, which consisted of the Captain of the Land and his assessors, all of whom were elected from within and by the noble estates themselves.

Tax assessment and collection were also strictly controlled by the diets. The noble estates were exempt from ordinary taxes. One key difference between the Slovene and Bohemian regions was that due to the former's proximity to the

174 A critical difference between the Slovene and Bohemian diets was that the estates of Carniola, Carinthia, and Styria tended to maintain good relations with each other and cooperate on key issues, especially while bargaining with the Habsburg kings over the payment of taxes or organizing joint defense forces against the Turks.

175 Kann and David, *The Peoples of Eastern Habsburg Lands, 1526-1918*, 44.

Ottoman threat,[176] the Slovene estates were able to exploit even more effectively the king's reliance on them. Thus, the Slovene estates not only retained their authority to approve extraordinary annual taxes for military purposes but also maintained complete control over how the tax revenue would be spent.

The Slovene lands were among the best defended of all the territories under Habsburg sovereignty. The Ottoman incursions into the Slovene lands, particularly intense in the 1520s and 1530s, forced the estates to assume responsibility for protecting the border. The organization of the military forces in the Slovene regions was feudal, where each noble was expected to supply one rider and a certain number of foot soldiers for every 100 or 200 florins of income from his estate. Nobles were also responsible for raising able-bodied peasants during wartime. The lands were organized into military quarters (*Viertel*), each being governed by a captain responsible for calling out the "insurrection" in case of an incursion. [177]

The strategic position of the Slovene regions also necessitated a network of fortifications, which served as an early warning and defense system by covering all of Carniola, Styria, and Gorizia.[178] The costs of soldiers' provisions, weaponry, and the upkeep of the fortifications were borne directly by the estates. Kann and David report that the military expenditure of the estates increased from 10,000 florins in the 1520s to 300,000 by mid-century, and eventually to 550,000 florins around 1578.[179]

The estates bore the financial and organizational responsibility of defending the empire's eastern borders; in return, they retained complete authority over the military and, indirectly, fiscal matters. All army officers had to be local nobles. The estates were even authorized to appoint their officers to command the Habsburg ruler's troops when they entered the Slovene lands.

---

176 Sixteenth-century campaigns had brought the Ottomans within 15 km of the Slovene lands. Ibid., 46.

177 Ibid. For a detailed discussion of the impact of the Habsburg-Ottoman rivalry on the Slovene regions, see, John R. Lampe, *Yugoslavia as History: Twice There Was a Country*. 2nd ed. (Cambridge: Cambridge University Press, 2000), 9-39.

178 The construction of the fortifications was rapid in the mid-sixteenth century: there were only seven such fortresses in 1522 but their number increased to 60 by the 1570s.

179 Kann and David, *The Peoples of Eastern Habsburg Lands, 1526-1918*, 48-9. For a detailed discussion of the network of fortresses in Hungary, as well as in Slovenia, see Agoston, David, and Fodor, "The Costs of the Ottoman Fortress-System in Hungary in the Sixteenth and Seventeenth Centuries."

1.2.3 Hungary

By the time the Habsburgs became the rulers of Hungary in 1526, the Hungarian state, like the Bohemian kingdom, had existed for more than 500 years. Hungarian magnates were dominant in the countryside throughout the long reign of the native Magyar dynasties from the tenth to the early fourteenth century. The reformist Magyar rulers Sigismund of Luxemburg (1387-1437) and especially Matthias Corvinus (1458-1490) attempted to reassert the royal authority against the magnates, albeit with minimal success. The royal authority declined considerably under the Jagiellonian rulers (1490-1526).[180] When Ferdinand I became the king of Hungary, the Hungarian nobility was at the peak of their power.

Of all the imperial lands, Hungary, or the Habsburg-controlled portions of it to be precise,[181] contained the best fortified local elites. The Hungarian diet (*országgyűlés, Reichstag*), unlike the Bohemian and Slovene diets, consisted of two chambers only. The superior chamber, the Table of Magnates (*tabula superior, felső table*), housed the magnates and the highest ecclesiastics (bishops and abbots). Although superior in number, the lower nobility was not entitled to full representation in the diet. The traditional practice, which also received legislative sanction in 1608, limited the lower nobility's participation to elected delegates who sat in the Lower Table (*tabula inferior, alsó table*). Thus, the very structure of the Hungarian diet reflected the predominance of the magnates over other elite groups within the highly rigid social hierarchy.

The lesser nobility was further divided. Propertied nobles constituted the top layer of lesser nobles. Nobles with at least twenty serfs were considered propertied and were obliged to attend county assemblies, where votes were weighed according to wealth and prestige. The propertied nobles were also entitled to hold county offices.[182] The non-propertied nobles had to work the land themselves, and consequently, their lifestyle differed significantly from serf-owning

---

180 For the early history of the Hungarian state, see Janos Hauszmann, *Ungarn* (Regensburg: Friedrich Pustet, 2004), 28-89.

181 The rivalry between the Habsburgs and Ottomans in Hungarian lands had resulted in the division of historic Hungarian kingdom into three parts, which lasted for about 150 years. Habsburgs controlled the western and northern Hungary, which contained large German minorities as well as the native Magyar population, Slovaks and Ruthenians. Western parts of Croatia were also under Habsburg rule. After 1541, Ottoman Empire intermittently ruled central Hungary, including Buda. Transylvania became a semi-autonomous tribute-paying vassal state of Ottoman Empire.

182 Kann and David, *The Peoples of Eastern Habsburg Lands, 1526-1918*, 57-8.

lesser nobility. Unlike magnates and propertied lesser nobility, they were subject to ordinary taxes.

Royal towns can be considered the third estate in Hungary, yet they did not wield any significant political power. The Hungarian royal towns enjoyed a "noble" status as collective units but not as individual entities. After the fifteenth century, they gained regular participation in the diet, not in a separate chamber but as a part of the Lower Table, along with the delegates of the lesser nobility. Even more importantly, towns were not entitled to cast individual votes; instead, the representatives of towns voted collectively. Lastly, all royal towns were subject to heavy taxation.

Even before the establishment of Habsburg rule in Hungary, the diet had been the chief legislative organ of the nominally constitutional order of the Hungarian state. The king would unilaterally formulate policy and issue ordinances in minor matters, but he could not promulgate general laws without the approval of the diet. Approval of foreign treaties, the election of the king, and the *palatin* (the chief official of the kingdom) were subject to the consent of the diet. The estates also had strict control over the right to collect extraordinary taxes even though Ferdinand I's centralist reforms forced the Hungarian nobles, unlike their Bohemian counterparts, as I discussed above, to partially relinquish their authority over the expenditure of tax revenues.

The Hungarian countryside was organized into counties (*comitatus, megye*). When the administrative reforms of Sigismund (1387-1437) inadvertently resulted in the devolution of chief administrative and judicial functions from royal officials to the local nobility, the counties practically became units of provincial self-government. Even during the centralizing efforts of the sixteenth century, "the county governments maintained and even increased their significance as power bases of the estates."[183]

The self-government in counties was in the hands of the community of nobles, who exercised their authority through the county assemblies. The chief official in the countryside was the *főispán* (*Obergespan*), in principle appointed by and accountable to the king. In practice, the power of appointment meant little since the chosen official had to be a property-owning *persona grata* in the county. Moreover, before commencing his term, the *főispán* was expected to swear an oath to observe the county's autonomous rights. On the surface, the most important official in the countryside was loyal to both the nobility and the king. In practice, since the king could neither monitor efficiently nor enforce compliance

183 Kann and David, *The Peoples of Eastern Habsburg Lands, 1526-1918*, 64.

of his agent, the *főispán* mostly sided with the interests of the local nobles. Local nobles had minimal difficulty enforcing compliance; through regular monitoring via the county assemblies, the local notables would hold főispán responsible for any "misuse of power," which denoted any policy that went against the interests of the estates.

Further down the hierarchy of county governments were county judges (four in each county) and jurors (twelve in each county), all of whom elected by the county assembly and from within the propertied nobles. In addition to participating in sessions of the county court, the judges were charged with assisting with military registration, raising the levy, and assessing and collecting taxes. The official directly in charge of taxes was the royal tax collector. Yet, he could not act without the authorization of the county assembly. Enforcement of tax collection and punishment of tax evaders were solely the responsibility of local governments. By the seventeenth century, local governments were often able to completely dispense with the royal tax collector, transferring his authority to a tax collector elected from within the local nobles or the *alispán* himself.

Even in periods when the legal authority of the local nobles subsided, their practical control over the means of administration enabled the estates to retain their dominance in the countryside. For instance, when the Habsburg rulers limited the legal discretion over how the tax revenue could be spent, the Hungarian nobles replaced the royal tax collector with their agents, who retained even greater portions of the extraordinary taxes in county treasuries for internal administrative expenses.

The last domain where the nobles held autonomous power vis-à-vis the central administration was the military. The traditional Hungarian military organization was based on the *banderial* system. The *banderium* was a relatively permanent and coherent army unit. The largest *banderium* was the royal *banderium*, and it consisted of at least 1,000 cavalrymen, financed by the royal income and the proceeds of the estates. However, the greatest proportion of the Hungarian army consisted of the *banderia* raised by the prelates and secular magnates, who were charged with raising full (four hundred cavalrymen) or partial *banderia* depending on their income and stationing them either in their manors or in border fortresses. To compensate for the expenses of these regular units, the magnates were permitted to retain the proceeds of the war tax collected on their manors instead of turning them over to the county officials. Combined with the decentralized tax collection mechanisms riddled with ambiguities and split loyalties, the banderial system systematically favored the noble estates in their attempts to divert resources away from the imperial center.[184]

Even before the acquisition of the Bohemian and Hungarian crowns, Habsburg rulers were searching for ways to limit the estates' influence in hereditary lands. Maximilian I (1459-1519), considered the second founder of the Habsburg state after Rudolf I in the thirteenth century, was the first of these reformers. As part of his effort to build the grand Austrian state as a universal monarchy that would reanimate the Holy Roman Empire, Maximilian I sought to unite the hereditary lands under a single administrative framework.[185] In 1490, he instituted two regencies, one for Tyrol and the *Vorlände*, and the other for Lower and Inner Austria, which were later united under Vienna's rule. In Vienna, he founded new institutions, including a court tribunal, a chamber of accounts (*Ratkammer*), and a court chamber (*Hofkammer*).

These changes encountered the "vehement opposition" of the estates.[186] Maximilian I, knowing that the reforms went against the privileges of the estates, quickly offered concessions at the local level in return for their compliance.[187] For instance, while seeking to centralize decision-making through the new executive organs in Vienna, Maximilian granted new rights and administrative autonomy to diets in the lands.[188] Ultimately, the estates restored the pre-reform *status quo* by having the court tribunal and the court chamber dismantled in 1510, leaving the chamber of accounts the only surviving element of Maximilian's reforms.[189]

The territorial expansion of 1526 and the rising Ottoman threat along the eastern border allowed Ferdinand I to reassert the royal authority on the imperial lands, old and new. To that end, the king issued an executive order (*Hofstatsordnung*) in 1527, which established the core elements of a new centralized government: Privy Council (*Geheime Rat*), which was entrusted with foreign affairs; the Aulic Council (*Hofrat*), which was to function as the supreme court of justice; and a Court of Chancellery (*Hofkanzlei*) in charge of administrative matters. A

184 Kann and David, *The Peoples of Eastern Habsburg Lands, 1526-1918*; János M. Bak and Béla K. Király, *From Hunyadi to Rákóczi: War and Society in Late Medieval and Early Modern Hungary* ([Boulder][New York]: Brooklyn College Press 1982).

185 Konrad Edith, "Absolutismus Der Habsburger Im 16. Und Beginnenden 17. Jahrhundert," (Salzburg: Paris-London Universitaet Salzburg, 1987).

186 Bérenger, *A History of the Habsburg Empire*, 130.

187 Ibid., 130-6.

188 Ibid.

189 Beller, *A Concise History of Austria*, 42.

late addition was the Aulic War Council (*Hofkriegsrat*), which was specifically established to coordinate the Hungarian campaigns centrally.[190] Branches of these new institutions were established in Prague, Pozsony, and Innsbruck all of which were directly tied to the seat of Ferdinand.

The *Hofstaatsordnung* of 1527 was the most important imperial decree to date, and it officially remained in effect until the mid-eighteenth-century reforms of Maria Theresia.[191] However, in practice, the effects of the order were relatively short-lived. As early as 1537, both the Bohemian and Hungarian lands had already managed to exclude themselves from the purview of the Aulic Council and the Court Chancellery, rolling back the royal progress in the domains of justice and administration.

The main asset in the hands of the estates when bargaining with the Habsburg crown was their power over the collection of taxes. The rising costs of military defenses in Hungary and the campaigns against the Ottoman forces put a tremendous strain on the imperial budget and forced Ferdinand to seek additional tax revenues. Despite the short-term increases in the tax revenues that the 1527 reforms brought about, as of 1542, the military expenditures (625,000 florins) and the court expenditures (530,000) exceeded the total royal revenues (1 million florins at most).[192] Through issue-linkage and bargaining, the estates used the financial dependence of the royal authority on them to constantly renegotiate and consolidate their autonomous powers.[193]

Ferdinand I took several measures to curb the organizational capacity of the estates to oppose future reforms collectively. For instance, the king sought to establish joint congresses of the Bohemian and Hungarian diets with the Austrian hereditary lands, where he had relatively stronger control over the agenda-setting and decision-making process. The Bohemian and Hungarian estates successfully defeated this measure.[194] Ferdinand I also intervened with the inner workings of the diets of the individual lands and local assemblies. He insisted that only the king could invoke the diets. He further targeted the right of the legislative initiative by demanding that the royal proposals be discussed first and that the diets are dissolved immediately after the acceptance of the proposals. Once again, the estates refused to vote for extraordinary taxes before their proposal

190 Ibid., 51.

191 Fichtner, *The Habsburg Monarchy, 1490-1848: Attributes of Empire*, 19.

192 Bérenger, *A History of the Habsburg Empire*, 168.

193 Beller, *A Concise History of Austria*, 51-2.

194 Fichtner, *Ferdinand I of Austria: The Politics of Dynasticism in the Age of Reformation*.

was discussed.[195] Lastly, Ferdinand I attempted, with limited success, to suppress the circuit assemblies in Bohemia and Hungary by changing the rules governing how frequently and under what circumstances they could be convened.

Even though several of the institutions created by the 1527 imperial decree persisted in name, the net effects of Ferdinand's reforms proved to be ultimately short-lived and reversible. Especially after the death of Ferdinand in 1564, estates were on the rise again, recuperating any losses and consolidating their winnings from their previous bargains with the royal authority.

In sum, until the late sixteenth century, the elite conflict structure within the Habsburg Empire's horizontal organization reflected a relatively stable equilibrium between the noble estates in the countryside and the ruling elites of the state. The rulers sought to impose their authority on the nobility, who, in turn, constantly renegotiated their position as the chief agents of the state in the countryside. The nobles were also the primary source of state revenue, paying extraordinary taxes and lending money to the crown directly or buying lands that the kings sold and pawned to them in times of budgetary distress.[196] In return, rulers not only gave the nobility a free hand in their dealings with the peasantry but also supported the nobility against the towns.

Thus, the mutual interdependence of the ruler and the nobility ensured that the intensity of the intra-elite conflict remained stable until the seventeenth century. In the last instance, the nobles had the upper hand in this conflict for the simple reason that "cooperation of local intermediary powers was in some ways far more crucial for the Habsburgs than for those whom they ruled."[197] Nevertheless, the intensity of the intra-elite conflict reached a *higher* level only after the changes in the world economy dramatically altered the interests of the ruler and the nobility and how they perceived each other.

---

195 Kann and David, *The Peoples of Eastern Habsburg Lands, 1526-1918*, 27.

196 Kramar and Stuiber, *Habsburgs Leere Kassen*, especially 67-89 and 125-143. For a more detailed study of the financial policy, especially with regard to borrowing from nobles, see Werner Watzenig, "Die Finanz- Und Wirtschaftspolitik in Den Erblaendern Und Im Reich Unter Maximilian I in Den Jahren 1493 Bis 1507" (Karl-Franzens Universitaet, 1983).

197 Fichtner, *The Habsburg Monarchy, 1490-1848: Attributes of Empire*, 20.

2. The Changes in the Structure of Intra-Elite Relations

2.1 Shifts in the European Economy and Monopolization of Agricultural Lands

This section explains how external economic developments in the seventeenth century altered the intra-elite balance of power and fundamentally changed the structure of conflict. I focus on the growing demand in Western Europe for agricultural products and the corresponding growth of serf-based production in Central and Eastern Europe.[198]

The main consequence of the re-emergence of serf-based agricultural production in Central and Eastern Europe is that it tipped the intra-elite balance of power toward the nobility. Given the scarcity of capital and the landowners' broad discretion over the labor force, the least costly way for the landowning nobility to increase production for the market was to further squeeze the peasantry by increasing labor dues and enlarging demesnes. The growing demesne production, in turn, enhanced the capacity of the nobility to cut into the flow of resources from the peasantry to the state.

In terms of the theoretical framework advanced in this book, the growing economic power of the landowners enhanced their capacity to divert resources from the imperial center. As a result, the ruling elites started to perceive the nobility no longer as a necessary instrument of governance but rather as a detriment to the capacity of the elites to extract revenue from the population, and ultimately a threat to their very elite status. Accordingly, after the seventeenth century, Habsburg rulers systematically sought to counterbalance the nobility with a less-threatening ally, the urban capital holders. Before discussing the effects of the second serfdom on the structure of the elite conflict, let us take a closer look at the dynamics in the agrarian relations of Central and Eastern Europe.

Serfdom, understood as the social arrangement where the "lord had legal jurisdiction over his peasants to the complete, or nearly complete, exclusion of the state,"[199] was commonplace throughout Europe until the early thirteenth century. However, following the relative prosperity of the High Middle Ages in the West and the German colonization in Central and Eastern Europe, the conditions of the peasants to the east of Elbe (roughly speaking, East Germany, Moravia,

198 Blum, "The Rise of Second Serfdom in Eastern Europe."; Makkai, "Neo-Serfdom: Its Origin and Nature in East Central Europe."; Wright, "Neo-Serfdom in Bohemia."; Bela K. Kiraly, "Neo-Serfdom in Hungary," *Slavic Review* 34, no. 2 (1975).

199 Blum, "The Rise of Second Serfdom in Eastern Europe," 809.

Bohemia, Silesia, Poland, and even parts of Hungary and Russia) improved dramatically. Throughout the thirteenth and fourteenth centuries, serfdom declined in the East, and the peasants, much like their western counterparts, attained greater freedom of movement and improved living conditions.[200]

However, after the sixteenth century, the paths of the peasantry in the West and East diverged.[201] While the peasantry in the West continued the path toward fewer labor obligations and a contractual relationship with the landlords, Central and Eastern European peasants once again faced deteriorating conditions. The landlords managed to reinstate the critical components of serf-based agricultural production by limiting the peasants' movements, raising the weekly labor dues (*robot*), and increasing the demesne sizes. As a result, the relatively free peasants of the *Grundherrschaft* system were transformed into dependent serfs under *Gutherrshaft*.[202]

There is considerable variation concerning the timing, degree, and exact nature of serf-based economies that (re-)emerged across Central and Eastern Europe.[203] For instance, rent obligations and money-based exchanges persisted in some areas, whereas other parts were dominated by demesne-robot farming. In some other areas, as in Poland-Lithuania, a form of serfdom emerged that involved all the conventional restrictions regarding robot labor but not a rigid system of large demesne farming.[204] As historian Makkai notes, *Grundherrschaft* and *Gutherrschaft* are both "ideal types" and neither ever existed in a "pure" form in history.[205]

The way to the consolidation of serfdom was long and gradual, and there is no consensus as to when exactly the process began. Some historians trace the reemergence of serfdom to the late fifteenth-century legislation in Bohemia. In 1487, a series of laws were passed that restricted peasant mobility and increased

---

200 Makkai, "Neo-Serfdom: Its Origin and Nature in East Central Europe."

201 Wallerstein, *The Modern World-System.*

202 Makkai, "Neo-Serfdom: Its Origin and Nature in East Central Europe," 227. *Grundherrschaft* refers to production in large feudal estates where the landowner earned his income from his peasants whose obligations were either in kind or in case. *Gutherrschaft*, in contrast, entails that the lords' lands were worked with the help of forced labor and tools supplied without remuneration by dependent serfs.

203 Wright, "Neo-Serfdom in Bohemia." Also see W. E. Wright, *Serf, Seigneur and Sovereign. Agrarian Reform in Eighteenth Century Bohemia* (Minneapolis: 1996).

204 Andrzej Kaminski, "Neo-Serfdom in Poland Lithuania," *Slavic Review* XXXIV (1975): 256.

205 Makkai, "Neo-Serfdom: Its Origin and Nature in East Central Europe," 227.

labor dues; the codes of 1500 further granted far-reaching controls to the noble landowners over the peasants.[206] Laws to the same effect were passed in Poland in 1495, Silesia and Brandenburg in 1526, and Upper Austria in 1539.[207] Blum argues, for instance, that by the beginning of the sixteenth century, the peasants in the lands to the east of Elbe were well on their way to losing their status as free peasants and becoming serfs.[208] Throughout the seventeenth century, the restrictions and obligations became progressively heavier and the legal framework of enserfment was nearly completed.

The rise of serfdom to its peak in the seventeenth century can be partially explained by the adverse social and demographic effects of the Thirty Years' War (1618-1648).[209] These historical accounts emphasize the devastation caused by prolonged religious conflict, which exacerbated labor scarcity, pushing the landlords toward burdening the serfs with additional labor services.[210] War drove peasants from their villages, simultaneously enlarging both the landless population *and* the cultivable land available to enclosure by noble landowners.[211]

While the long-term social and demographic trends and the cataclysmic events such as the Thirty Years' War played a vital role in the re-emergence of serfdom in Central and Eastern Europe, a more critical factor is the growing demand for agricultural products in Western Europe and the steady increase in agricultural prices, which incentivized the landowners in the East to establish large-scale agrarian export businesses, particularly grain exports.[212]

Responding to the market signals, the landlords stepped up grain production by increasing their demesne sizes. Large manorial farms emerged in Bohemia, Moravia, Lower Silesia, Lower Austria, Saxony, and Western Hungary. The estates grew by absorbing abandoned peasant lands and forcibly carving parts of peasant homesteads.[213] Landlords lacked the credit to engage paid workers for large-scale grain production and instead resorted to gradually increasing weekly

---

206 Wright, "Neo-Serfdom in Bohemia."
207 Makkai, "Neo-Serfdom: Its Origin and Nature in East Central Europe," 232.
208 Blum, "The Rise of Second Serfdom in Eastern Europe," 821-2.
209 Mears, "Thirty Years War, the 'General Crisis' and the Origins of the Standing Professional Army in the Habsburg Monarchy."
210 Arnost Klima, "Agrarian Class Structure and Economic Development in Pre-Industrial Bohemia," *Past & Present* 85 (1979): 51.
211 Wright, "Neo-Serfdom in Bohemia."
212 Makkai, "Neo-Serfdom: Its Origin and Nature in East Central Europe," 237; Gunst, *Agrarian Development and Social Change in Eastern Europe, 14th-19th Centuries*, 68.
213 Kann and David, *The Peoples of Eastern Habsburg Lands, 1526-1918*, 70.

labor dues. By the mid-century, the legal limit of one day to work on the demesne lands was replaced with two, and in some regions (like Hungary), three days per week.

Noble landowners took advantage of their close ties with the king and secured new legal arrangements, further limiting the free movement of peasants, and increasing labor obligations.[214] In 1680, the imperial Feudal Labor Service Decree (*Robotpatent*) legally obliged peasants to perform labor services on their lord's demesne for at least three days a week. The decree also stipulated that the number of days could be increased by the lord "at will," practically giving the lords a free hand in managing serf labor. In most areas, peasants lost their traditional right to seek redress beyond the manorial courts, aggravating their vulnerability against the arbitrary demands of landowners.[215]

The exact nature and degree of coerced crash-crop labor production for the European market depended on several factors, most notably proximity to European markets via established trade routes. Well-connected regions such as Bohemia experienced the harshest enserfment. In Central Hungarian lands, where the main river of the Carpathian region, the Danube, did not allow a direct articulation to the European grain trade, large, manorial, grain-producing farms were not nearly as widespread. The Hungarian nobility, however, managed to consolidate their monopolies in other products that were high in demand, especially wine and spirits, as well as cattle.[216] Despite the differences in the processes of enserfment across regions, the conditions of enserfment remained similar.

While it is evident that there is a link between the changes in European agricultural markets and the proliferation of manorial production based on *corvée labor*, the causality is not entirely deterministic. First, increased demesne production was not the only feasible response to the shifting market conditions. The challenge to expand production for the market was initially met in two different ways. The first option was farming large demesnes with coerced labor, as discussed above. The second possible trajectory was the development of farming and production for the market by wealthier peasants. Wallerstein argues that there was a fierce domestic conflict between these two modes of production,

---

214 Blum, "The Rise of Second Serfdom in Eastern Europe," 828.

215 Kann and David, *The Peoples of Eastern Habsburg Lands, 1526-1918*, 40.

216 Pal Zsigmond Pach, "The Shifting of International Trade Routes in the 15th-17th Centuries," *Acta Historica* 14 (1968): 314.

and the conflict ended by the early seventeenth century with the victory of *Gutherrschaft*.[217]

The effect of the changes in the structure of the world market on the strategies of landlords was not linear. More specifically, while increased participation in the emerging European market as suppliers of agricultural products gave the noble landowners an incentive to enclose more lands and impose higher labor dues, the reversal of the market conditions in the latter part of the seventeenth century brought about further consolidation of enserfment. Pach analyzes these opposing trends in the development of the modern world economy in two separate stages. When the world economy began to expand in the sixteenth century, largely as a result of the shifting of international trade routes (from the Mediterranean to the Baltic region) and the change in the commodity structure of trade (from luxury to bulk goods), the Central and Eastern European regions, not the overseas colonies, were initially articulated into the modern market as exporters of primary goods.[218]

The second stage of the expansion of the world economy witnessed rapid growth and transformation of transatlantic trade, and the American colonies began to attach to West European economies. In other words, while in the first stage of the development of the world economy, the West European economies rested largely on Central and Eastern European agricultural exports; in the subsequent stage of development, they began to depend almost exclusively on the overseas colonial markets.[219] As a result, the export of Polish grain, Hungarian wine and cattle, and Bohemian rye to Western Europe plummeted.[220]

The steep decline in the relative share of Central and Eastern Europe in the intra-European trade paved the way for the stagnation of agricultural production

217 Immanuel Wallerstein, *The Modern World-System II: Mercantilism and the Consolidation of the European World-Economy, 1600-1750* (New York: Academic Press, 1980), 135. Other economic historians also warn us that the tendency to look at the origin and development of the demesne-robot system exclusively through the prism of grain production might ultimately be misleading, given such facts as the dual role of peasants as sellers and buyers in the domestic market. Wright, "Neo-Serfdom in Bohemia," 264-65.

218 Pach, "The Shifting of International Trade Routes in the 15th-17th Centuries"; F. C. Lane, "The Mediterranean Spice Trade," *The American Historical Review* (1940).

219 Pal Zsigmond Pach, "Diminishing Share of East-Central Europe in the 17th Century International Trade," *Acta Historica* 16 (1970): 300.

220 Eric Hobsbawm, "The General Crisis of the European Economy in the 17th Century," *Past and Present* 5 (1954).

by the middle of the seventeenth century. In the previous chapter, I discussed the "general crisis."[221] The aspect of the crisis that is pertinent here is how it affected the labor strategies of landowners. Facing the decline in market demand and profits, the landowners opted for cost cutting, which involved further increasing the pressure on the peasantry farming the demesnes. Thus, despite the reversal of market conditions for agricultural products increase in the weekly labor dues of the peasantry as well as the demesne sizes continued throughout the seventeenth century. Second serfdom reached its peak around 1680, at the same period when the economic crisis was in full swing.

To compensate for the contraction in the extra-manorial markets, the landlords began to rely on domestic markets, especially compulsory purchases by their subjects.[222] Serfs' production was almost exclusively destined for local consumption in the latter half of the seventeenth century,[223] allowing the lords to siphon out any capital assets that the peasantry might have.

The concentration of agricultural lands also indicates that the economic crisis inadvertently increased the power of the landlords. The manorial farms grew in the seventeenth century by absorbing abandoned (by choice or by force) peasant lands and acquiring the properties of bankrupt lesser nobility. As noted earlier, the lesser propertied nobles in Bohemian, Slovene, and Hungarian regions had fewer peasants. Thus, when the decline in European trade hit agricultural production in Central and Eastern Europe, it hit the lesser nobles the hardest. Unable to minimize production costs to withstand the contracting market and declining prices, lesser nobles continued to amass debts throughout the seventeenth century.

Habsburgs' tax policy indirectly contributed to the decline of the lesser nobility. Even though the nobility was exempt from ordinary taxes, both higher and lesser nobles were subject to a specific tax on their fortunes (*Vermögensteuer*): 1.2 percent of capital or 24 percent of revenue. In the seventeenth century, higher

221 T. H. Aston, *Crisis in Europe, 1560-1660, Essays from Past and Present* (London: Routledge & Kegan Paul, 1975); Roper Trevor, "The General Crisis of the Seventeenth Century," in *Crisis in Europe, 1560-1660. Essays from Past and Present* (London: Routledge & Kegan Paul, 1975); Geoffrey Parker and Smith Parker, *The General Crisis of the Seventeenth Century* (London: Routledge & Kegan Paul, 1978); Niels Steensgaard, "The Seventeenth-Century Crisis and the Unity of Eurasian History," *Modern Asian Studies* 21 (1990).

222 Kann and David, *The Peoples of Eastern Habsburg Lands, 1526-1918*, 116.

223 Klima, "Agrarian Class Structure and Economic Development in Pre-Industrial Bohemia," 60-1.

nobility largely escaped the adverse effects of the economic crisis as far as tax obligations were concerned, primarily because their properties were undervalued, allowing them to pay less than 50 percent of the required tax. In addition, the lesser nobility was much less organizationally capable of opposing royal advances for more taxation. As early as the late sixteenth century, numerous small and medium-sized property owners were unable to pay taxes and faced foreclosures.[224]

Thus, the economic crisis of the seventeenth century led to the monopolization of agricultural lands in the hands of the largest landowners. At the end of the fifteenth century, 49.9 percent of the total arable land in the Polish regions was in the hands of those nobles whose possessions were smaller than 1,600 hectares; by the eighteenth century, however, the same group had only 9.8 percent of this land.[225] In contrast, the proportion of the land owned by nobles holding more than 9,000 hectares increased from 13.3 percent in the sixteenth century to 41.9 percent in the eighteenth century.[226] Even in Bohemia where the biggest landowners already owned the majority of the land, the lesser nobility lost over one-third of their lands to the upper nobility from 1656 to 1757.[227] In Lower Austria, the number of knightly families (*Ritterstand*) declined by one-third (from 197 to 128) while the upper nobility (*Herrenstand*) grew by about one-half (56 to 86).[228] In 1789, the estimated total worth of the 952 estates in Austrian lands was 239 million florins, of which 162 million florins (67 percent) belonged to the *Herrenstand* alone, and the remainder to the crown, church, and lesser nobility.

The decline of the economic fortunes of the lesser nobility adversely affected their already limited political influence. Throughout the seventeenth century, numerous knights left the country, vacating their seats in the diet and their positions in the bureaucratic administrations of the countryside. The power vacuum left by the lesser nobles was filled by large landowners and clergy, i.e., bishops,

224 Bérenger, *A History of the Habsburg Empire*, 207.
225 Kaminski, "Neo-Serfdom in Poland Lithuania," 263.
226 Ibid.
227 Klima, "Agrarian Class Structure and Economic Development in Pre-Industrial Bohemia," 53. The exact land distribution in 1656 is as follows: Upper nobility 59 percent, lower nobility 9.6 percent, towns 13.1 percent, church 12.3 percent, and the crown 5.0 percent; in 1757: upper nobility 62.4 percent, lower nobility 6.1 percent, towns 12.2. percent, church 13.6 percent, and crown: 5.0 percent.
228 Machardy Karin J. MacHardy, "The Rise of Absolutism and Noble Rebellion in Early Modern Habsburg Austria, 1570 to 1620," *Comparative Studies in Society and History* 34, no. 3 (1992): 413.

abbots, and deans of chapters, who were also recruited from the ranks of the higher nobility. Consequently, the diet truly became "a manifestation of lords."[229]

The economic crisis of the seventeenth century also led to the decline of towns. From the thirteenth to the sixteenth centuries, the free and royal towns of Central and Eastern Europe participated in the long-distance European trade. They were the sole sites of non-seigniorial economic activity. Royal towns, however, were subject to heavier taxes, tariffs, and other limitations, which served the anti-urban interests of the nobility, who, in coalition with the Habsburg rulers, sought to keep the towns on a tight leash. Imperial and local regulations guaranteed, for instance, that the nobles were given favorable tariff provisions for their shipments, which gave them a price advantage over the urban merchants.

The towns were hit particularly hard when the share of Eastern Europe in the intra-regional trade declined in the second stage of European market expansion.[230] Combined with the devastation of the Thirty Years' War, the decline in intra-regional trade brought urban manufacturing to a complete halt. At the same time, the nobility increased the pressure on towns. They were particularly concerned with ending the towns' practice of harboring peasants running away from the increasingly harsh conditions. As a result of the contracting trade and the increased noble pressure, Central and Eastern European urban centers progressively declined in the seventeenth century and became "sleepy provincial towns."[231]

In sum, the economic crisis of the seventeenth century profoundly affected the structure of intra-elite conflict in Habsburg lands. The cyclical trends of the European agricultural market—the rapid growth of the demand for agricultural products followed by a period of contraction—directly contributed to the consolidation of the largest landlords' economic power. At the same time, both the lesser gentry and the towns declined.

2.2 The High-Intensity Intra-Elite Conflict

With the decline of these lesser social actors, which had served as a buffer zone between the big landlords and the ruler, the distributional conflict reached a higher level of intensity. The intensification of the conflict culminated in rebellions in the seventeenth century. Let me take a closer look at two major incidents: the

229 Bérenger, *A History of the Habsburg Empire*, 297.

230 Pach, "Diminishing Share of East-Central Europe in the 17th Century International Trade."

231 Blum, "The Rise of Second Serfdom in Eastern Europe," 834-5.

1620 noble revolt in Bohemia, which resulted in the infamous White Mountain massacre, and the Bosckay movement in Hungary, followed by decades of conflict between the Habsburg king and the Hungarian *magnates*.

The conflict between the nobles and the king reached a critical stage when the estates revolted in 1618. Lords, claiming their rights were violated, took up arms against the emperor, by the medieval law of feud.[232] Ferdinand II's army defeated the rebels at the White Mountain in 1620. The king capitalized on this victory and moved on to eradicate the rebellious members of the estates. No less than 27 Czech and German members of the Bohemian diet were condemned to death and executed in Prague on June 21, 1621.[233] Those rebel families that escaped persecution lost their estates and social privileges and were forced into exile.[234]

Historians underline the role of the intra-elite rivalry over the distribution of economic resources as the critical factor in the 1620 noble rebellion. MacHardy writes, "Demographic change and inflation led to increased competition over resources. This intensified rivalry and factionalism within the nobility exacerbated the longstanding political conflict between crown and nobles."[235] According to this view, the reformation only strengthened this underlying dynamic by pitting a Lutheran nobility against the Catholic emperor. Indeed, after eliminating the rebellious members of the diet, Ferdinand II sought to replace the old Bohemian nobility with his clientele. The estates of the dispossessed old nobility were transferred to the new nobility, which was almost exclusively Catholic and presumably more loyal to the king.[236]

Post-1620 Habsburg rulers strategically deployed the religious tensions of the reformation period to eliminate the Protestant nobles that survived the White Mountain. By modifying the traditional rules of acceptance into nobility, Ferdinand II restructured the nobility in a way that ultimately equated Catholicism with loyalty and service to the ruler.[237] After 1620, nearly half of the members of

---

232 Brunner, *Land and Lordship: Structures of Governance in Medieval Austria*.

233 Bérenger, *A History of the Habsburg Empire*, 265-6.

234 Beller, *A Concise History of Austria*, 61; Hans Sturmberger, *Aufstand in Böhmen; Der Beginn Des Dreissigjährigen Krieges* (München: R. Oldenbourg, 1959).

235 MacHardy, "The Rise of Absolutism and Noble Rebellion in Early Modern Habsburg Austria, 1570 to 1620," 410.

236 Wright, "Neo-Serfdom in Bohemia," 246.

237 MacHardy, "The Rise of Absolutism and Noble Rebellion in Early Modern Habsburg Austria, 1570 to 1620," 416.

the *Herrenstand* were new arrivals, and the overall number of the noble families increased by more than one-half.[238]

The royal victory at the White Mountain is considered a turning point in the emergence of the Habsburg "royal absolutism" in the seventeenth century. Ferdinand II required the submission of new lords to the loyal government and managed to pass several legal measures that strengthened royal authority. Chief among them was the establishment of an automatic process of royal election. With the passing of the historical *Verneuerte Landesordnung* (Renewed Land Ordinances) for Bohemia in 1627 and Moravia in 1628, the king practically eliminated opportunities for the noble estates to extort concessions before recognizing the new king of the Bohemian Lands.[239]

While the White Mountain allowed the king to reverse some of the privileges of the estates, the royal gains came at a very high price. The new nobles of Bohemia relinquished some of the authority that the older Protestant noble families enjoyed; in return, they acquired new privileges, especially concerning their dealings with the peasantry. The document that established some gains for the royal authority (e.g., the automatic process of royal succession) introduced new legal arrangements that abandoned the peasants entirely to the lords' governance.[240] Both labor dues and demesne sizes continued to expand after 1620, and the process of enserfment reached its peak in Bohemia only in the mid-seventeenth century.

In addition to expanding their economic power after 1620, the estates retained their function as the main instruments of state infrastructural power in the countryside and even acquired some new administrative functions.[241] As Kann and David put it, "[d]espite the Absolute power, which the king had acquired in the seventeenth century, he could not entirely dispense with the cooperation of the estates, since he lacked an adequate bureaucratic apparatus of his own…He still depended for the exercise of his authority on a governmental machinery that was to a large degree staffed and operated by the estates."[242]

Neither did the estates relinquish their control over fiscal matters. The kings still needed the estates' approval for the extraordinary taxes, and the nobility often granted less than demanded. The power of the estates over taxation not

---

238 Ibid., 421.

239 Kann and David, *The Peoples of Eastern Habsburg Lands, 1526-1918*, 104-5.

240 Wright, "Neo-Serfdom in Bohemia," 246.

241 Fichtner, *The Habsburg Monarchy, 1490-1848: Attributes of Empire*, 38.

242 Kann and David, *The Peoples of Eastern Habsburg Lands, 1526-1918*, 104-5.

only remained intact throughout the seventeenth century but also grew until the first decades of the eighteenth century.[243] As a consequence, neither Ferdinand II nor his successors had complete authority over legal or fiscal affairs throughout the empire.[244]

In sum, despite the significance attributed to the royalization process following the incident at White Mountain, the efforts of the Habsburg rulers had minimal success in tipping the balance between the royal authority and the noble landowners in favor of the former. White Mountain allowed the replacement of the Protestant nobility with a Catholic one, or an "old-new oligarchy."[245] However, the state, still lacking infrastructural power, continued to rely on the nobles for administration and resource extraction.

The long-term effect of White Mountain was, in fact, the further intensification of the intra-elite conflict over the distribution of economic resources: the nobility retained and consolidated their control over agricultural production and managed to divert the resources from the center even more efficiently within the newly formed network of royal patronage. Fichtner wrote, "While Habsburg [religious] policies would change the names of Bohemia's nobility, they did not alter the economic position or the social preeminence of that class…[W]hoever the great lords and knights of Bohemia were, they would still control about 80 percent of the land not directly held by the crown."[246]

The power of the Hungarian magnates grew considerably throughout the seventeenth century as demesne lands disproportionately increased at the expense of the serfs' rustical land. The Hungarian estates frequently revolted against the Habsburg rulers in the seventeenth century. An early example was the infamous Bocskay movement from 1604 to 1606, where István Bocskay waged a successful war of independence against the Habsburgs.[247] The Peace of Vienna (1606) ended the rebellion but at the cost of enlarging the privileges of the estates by granting them even wider discretion in serf-lord relations.

The decades following the Peace of Vienna witnessed further tensions between the Hungarian magnates and the Habsburg rulers. The treaties of Mikulov

243 R. J. W. Evans, *Austria, Hungary and the Habsburgs: Essays on Central Europe, C. 1683-1867* (New York: Oxford University Press, 2006), 85.

244 Fichtner, *The Habsburg Monarchy, 1490-1848: Attributes of Empire*, 38.

245 Evans, *Austria, Hungary and the Habsburgs: Essays on Central Europe, C. 1683-1867*, 85.

246 Fichtner, *The Habsburg Monarchy, 1490-1848: Attributes of Empire*, 37.

247 Leopold Toifl and Hildegard Leitgeb, *Ostösterreich Im Bocskay-Aufstand, 1605*, Militärhistorische Schriftenreihe (Wien: Bundesverlag, 1990).

(1622) and Pozsony (1626) essentially safeguarded the estates' privileges in return for minor concessions and thus achieved little to alter the *status quo*. Shortly after Pozsony, the Habsburg king launched a campaign of attrition against the Hungarian nobility, which primarily intended to accomplish what the Habsburgs had done in Bohemia: replace the rebellious (Protestant) nobles with more loyal (Catholic) families. In the early 1660s, the Viennese government made one last significant effort to uproot the Hungarian nobility and subvert the Hungarian constitution. Kann and David argue that Habsburgs' rather uncompromising stance against Hungary was intentionally geared toward inciting the Hungarian nobility to revolt and then using the suppression of the rebellion "as an occasion for annihilating the estates' political power."[248]

The efforts to eradicate autonomous Hungarian elites ultimately failed. After the 1660s, the Habsburg king had to withdraw the pressure, partly due to the re-escalating Ottoman threat and the vital strategic importance of the Hungarian plain for defense. A compromise was reached between the king and the Hungarian estates at Sopron in 1681. The nobility's traditional rights and privileges were once again affirmed.[249]

Taxation remained the primary source of conflict between the nobility and the king after the Sopron Compromise. The pressing fiscal crisis and the lingering Ottoman threat had made the king even less tolerant of the Hungarian nobles' tax privileges. Habsburg Emperor Leopold I envisaged a comprehensive reform program in the 1690s. The most important aspect of this program, known as Kollonich's project, was the annulment of the tax privileges of the nobility, not only in Hungary but also in Bohemia and Inner Austria. The Viennese government also proposed that the war tax be made permanent. The imperial proposition invoked a gathering of the representatives of imperial lands in Vienna in 1693, but the convention produced no compromise.

With unprecedented unilateralism, the central government attempted to establish a permanent war tax without the approval of the diets. Monarchy's bold attempt was met with yet another major rebellion in Hungary in 1703 under the leadership of magnate Francis Rakoczi, who managed to seize some of the territory freed from the Ottomans. Once again, the nobles secured a formal

---

248 Kann and David, *The Peoples of Eastern Habsburg Lands, 1526-1918*, 137. Also, the sales taxes, recently imposed by a royal decree and opposed by the magnates, were abolished. The Hungarian chamber pledged to cooperate with the Viennese court, but not to be subordinate to it in all matters.

249 Ibid., 139.

compromise with the monarchy after the rebellion. The Szatmár compromise confirmed the rights and privileges of nobles in Hungary and Transylvania and even offered amnesty to the rebels.[250]

3. Conclusion

This chapter argued that since the establishment of the imperial state, the Habsburg rulers lacked the resources and organizational capacity to administer distant localities effectively. By surveying the functions of estates in Bohemian, Slovene, and Hungarian lands, I documented that the ruling elites exclusively relied on the rural elites in the administration of social and legal affairs, collection of taxes, and the provision of warfare. I showed that the royal efforts at curbing the power of the estates in the early sixteenth century proved to be of very limited impact and only served to intensify the conflict between central and rural elites.

The second part of the chapter posited that the cyclical changes in the European economy, the growth of the agricultural demand, and the rise of agricultural prices incentivized the landowners to produce for the European market by enlarging their demesne holdings. The reversal of the market conditions, the contraction in the European agricultural markets, and the decline of intra-regional trade in the seventeenth century further consolidated the economic power of the largest landowners who responded to the shifted external conditions by monopolizing agricultural production.

The effect of the economic changes in the seventeenth century on the structure of the intra-elite relations was the rise of the largest landowners in Bohemian, Slovene, and Hungarian regions and the decline of the lesser nobility and towns. The state, already under tremendous strain due to the rising costs of warfare and declining tax revenues, slid into a fiscal crisis. The intensity of conflict between the central and rural elites reached a higher level, as manifested by the elite rebellions in Bohemia and Hungary in the seventeenth century.

Despite the apparent rise of the absolutist state in the seventeenth century, the rural elites retained their power. The noble lords still controlled the majority of the land. The crown was also financially dependent on the landowners who made large loans to the crown, collecting very high returns. Among the largest landowners who made fortunes loaning to the crown were Prince Ferdinand Schwarzenburg of Lower Austria, the famous Prince Esterházy, the palatine of Hungary in 1681, and Prince Lobkowitz of Bohemia, all of whom loaned

250 Ibid., 144.

considerable sums to the crown in the 1680s alone.[251] As Camille Freschot (a monk from France-Comte) remarked in 1701, "[t]he Emperor [was] hardly the master in his states."[252]

As a result of these changes, the ruling elites started to perceive the nobility in the countryside as a direct threat to the resource extraction capacity of the state and the central elites rather than a necessary instrument of state power within the horizontally organized structure of imperial governance. In the following chapter, I show how the changes in the structure of conflict led to realignment in intra-elite relations after 1660.

---

251 Bérenger, *A History of the Habsburg Empire*, 342.
252 Cited in Ibid.

Chapter 4 Elite Realignment and Institutional Change in the Habsburg Empire, 1660-1848

The seventeenth century was a period of crisis for the Habsburg lands. Following the economic boom and the price inflation of the sixteenth century, agricultural productivity declined, and intra-regional trade contracted in Europe roughly from 1560 to 1660. At the same time, the costs of warfare increased throughout the seventeenth century. The provision of the standing imperial army established in 1649, and the upkeep of the fortifications along the eastern border put additional strain on the treasury. My argument is that while the fiscal decay paved the way for institutional restructuring, the nature of the elite response to the crisis was shaped by the structure of the intra-elite conflict.

Having explicated the critical antecedents of institutional change (horizontal imperial organization) and the independent variable (the structure of intra-elite relations) in the previous chapter, I now turn to the analysis of:

(1) The realignment in intra-elite relations after 1660. I show that the mechanism of balancing accounts for the incorporation of urban capital holders into the ruling coalition. In line with my assertion that a complete explanation of long-term institutional outcomes should theorize about both supply- and demand-sides of the intra-elite conflict, I focus on the coalitional and institutional preferences of the ruling elites and the capital holders and explain how their interests converged.

(2) The building of a centralized fiscal state through a series of reforms between 1740 and 1790. I explicate how the second mechanism, redistributive institution building, links the intervening variable (the post-crisis coalition between the ruling elites and urban capital holders) to the dependent variable (fiscal state). I show that the reforming elites of the eighteenth century, in their efforts to undermine the power of the nobility and deliver side payments to new allies, ended up with a centralized fiscal state.

(3) The mobilization of market forces, which would in turn facilitate industrialization and economic development throughout the empire. I extend the historical narrative into the nineteenth century and show that despite the nobility's opposition to the institutional changes, the coalition between the ruling elites and the urban capital holders survived. The legacy of the reform period remained largely intact as the dual processes of centralization

and economic development reached their peak after the mid-nineteenth century.

1. The Realignment and Incorporation of the Capital

What do capital holders expect from the state? As discussed in Chapter 2, let us assume that they have two alternative sets of preferences. They may prefer a centralized, hierarchically organized structure that would enable them to deal with market imperfections. This option entails greater state involvement in the economy. Alternatively, capital holders might value their independence from any extra-market interference and prefer a state that stays out of the market. The choice between these two alternative sets of preferences would depend on several factors. The nature of the economic activity (the volume/type of trade) determines the preferences of the capital.[253] Some forms of trade might involve greater risk and information costs, necessitating a stronger hierarchy. Similarly, capital accumulation requirements of productive activities might differ.

While this reasoning considers the potential *benefits* of seeking state protection, the capital's preferences could also be based on the potential *costs* of protection. If the costs of protection outweigh the benefits, then the merchants will seek alternative solutions to market imperfections or choose the exit option. In either case, the preferences of the capital cannot be solely derived from objective conditions and should be empirically substantiated. In this section, I show that the capital holders in the Habsburg Empire in the latter half of the seventeenth century preferred state protection to independence and actively demanded a hierarchically organized market.

The evidence indicates that in the latter half of the seventeenth century, merchants, manufacturers, and other urban capital holders demanded greater state involvement in the economy. As early as 1653, a burgher of the town of Brno, Pavel Hynek Morgenthaler published a book advocating a grand state-led economic development scheme. Morgenthaler later authored a proposal addressed to Charles VI where he impressed upon the emperor that the government was weakened by spending large sums on importing goods that could be produced domestically. He suggested that the government support and protect local manufacturers.[254] He criticized owners of large demesnes for monopolizing

253 Spruyt, "Institutional Selection in International Relations: State Anarchy as Order." Spruyt, *The Sovereign State and Its Competitors: An Analysis of Systems Change*.

254 Woolen cloth production in Bohemia and Moravia, linen and lace in Silesia, metal goods in Upper Austria, and silk production in Styria and Corinthia. Herman

manufacture and distorting prices, which he argued impeded development and undermined state revenues. Morgenthaler was not alone in his advocacy of the so-called cameralist principles.[255] Prominent merchants and proto-industrialists such as Schröder, Hörnigk, and others urged the state to facilitate local manufacturing actively.

Throughout the 1660s, mercantilist proposals resonated strongly among elite circles. Malisky, owner of a woolen cloth manufacturing business in Moravia, sent a lengthy memorandum to the emperor in 1663, criticizing the restrictive guild practices and limitations imposed by the landowners on agricultural production. He proposed that the state protect domestic agricultural manufacturers and promote the export of manufactured goods. He did not neglect to note, "The emperor would be the first to feel the beneficial results of this as his revenue would rise."[256] Malisky's proposal generated genuine interest in Vienna. Emperor Leopold I issued a letter the following year to the Moravian Tribunal urging the preparation of an expert report on Malisky's proposal. In 1666, J.J. Becher, one of the leading Austrian entrepreneurs, came to Vienna at the request of emperor Leopold I. He would later establish a state-supported manufacturing company and a government agency to promote commerce and industry (*Kommerzienrat*).

It would be misleading to consider the demands of Morgenthaler, Malisky, Schröder, Hörnigk, Becher, and others "individual phenomena without any real basis in the actual conditions of the country."[257] Their voice represented a general feeling of discontent among the commercial sectors with the state policies that had hitherto been favoring the interests of the landowning nobility.

The seventeenth century was devastating for most towns in Central and Eastern Europe. Even before the crisis, Habsburg towns were not well placed within the European trade networks, as several major trade routes bypassed them. Nonetheless, they still were a part of the European intra-regional trade in the Late Middle Ages. The situation worsened in the seventeenth century

---

Freudenberger, "An Industrial Momentum in the Habsburg Monarchy," *Journal of European Economic History* 12 (1983): 340-1; Klima, "Mercantilism in the Habsburg Monarchy- with Special Reference to the Bohemian Lands," 96-7.

255 Fichtner, *The Habsburg Monarchy, 1490-1848: Attributes of Empire*; Klima, "Mercantilism in the Habsburg Monarchy- with Special Reference to the Bohemian Lands "; Klingenstein and Ingrao, "Between Mercantilism and Physiocracy: Stages, Modes and Functions of Economic Theory in the Habsburg Monarchy, 1748-63."

256 Klima, "Mercantilism in the Habsburg Monarchy- with Special Reference to the Bohemian Lands," 98.

257 Ibid., 101.

as the major trade routes shifted westward.[258] Germanic towns of central Europe directly connected to the Baltic trade gained importance, while Bohemian, Moravian, and Austrian towns became entirely dependent on inferior indirect connections.[259]

In addition to the shifting trade routes, the seventeenth-century crisis indirectly increased the pressure on towns by tightening the hold of the landowning nobility over them. Chartered and royal towns were detrimental to the interests of the landowning nobility as they protected peasants fleeing from the rough working and living conditions in the manors. Landowners frequently pressured the towns to stop harboring runaway peasants and serfs.

There were other, less direct, yet consequential, ways in which the landowning nobility stifled non-manorial manufacture and trade. Within the country-based putting-out system of manufacturing prominent after the sixteenth century in Bohemia, Moravia, and Austrian lands, trading firms were required to obtain permissions from the landlords to put out work to the peasants.[260] In return for the permission to do this work, the lords exacted dues from their serfs, which decreased the profitability of the putting-out firms. The entire system of manufacturing was contingent on the landlords' profits from the production of their serfs.[261]

Yet another mechanism through which the noble landowners hampered non-manorial production involved control over raw materials. Under feudal legal practices, town merchants and craftsmen were not able to buy raw materials directly from producers. Instead, they had to go through country middlemen who used this monopoly to dictate prices. The intermediaries between the agricultural producers and urban manufacturers were particularly difficult to circumvent as they had the full support of the nobility.[262] Merchants (particularly in

---

258 Pach, "The Shifting of International Trade Routes in the 15th-17th Centuries."; Pach, "Diminishing Share of East-Central Europe in the 17th Century International Trade."

259 Nachum T. Gross and John Komlos, "Austria-Hungary in World Economy," in *Economic Development in the Habsburg Monarchy in the Nineteenth Century* (New York: Columbia University Press, 1983), 7.

260 Arnost Klima, "Industrial Development in Bohemia, 1648-1781," *Past and Present* (1957): 91.

261 Gale Stokes, "Social Origins of East European Politics," in *The Origins of Backwardness in Eastern Europe: Economics and Politics from the Middle Ages until the Early Twentieth Century* (California: University of California Press, 1991), 213-15.

262 Arnost Klima and John Komlos, "Industrial Growth and Entrepreneurship in the Early Stages of Industrialization in the Czech Lands," in *Economic Development in*

royal towns) were also subject to additional taxes and fees that were not exacted from landowners. Yet the towns were in no position to defend their interests politically, as they were severely underrepresented in local and national diets.

The urban capital holders demanded that the government redress the imbalances in political representation. In a series of memoranda directly addressed to the emperor, Christian Julius von Schierendorff proposed that burghers (and peasants) be granted greater representation in the diets so that they could create a more uniform tax system.[263] He suggested changes in the legal framework facilitating the leasing of demesnes by the lords to the peasants.[264] Mercantilists of the late seventeenth century, primarily manufacturers and traders, were essentially advocating an overhaul of the existing system of production. As Klima states, "the mercantilists, whilst they were theorizing about the wealth of the nation and the state, were, in reality, carrying into the effect the interests of the capitalists."[265]

The turning point in the relations between the ruling elites and the urban capital holders was the publication of the *Deputy Governorship Report* in 1699, which signified the forging of a coalition between the capital holders and the ruling elites. The detailed report surveyed (i) the current state of production, (ii) the barriers to the development of production and trade, (iii) the reasons for credit insufficiency, and (iv) how money flows into the country and production could be increased. It included an in-depth analysis of the textile industry in Bohemia, which was unsuccessfully competing with Dutch producers importing raw materials from Bohemia and exporting back finished goods.

The report made several concrete proposals that mirrored the writings of mercantilists like Becher, Morgenthaler, and Malisky, including the change of policies protecting craft guilds which the reporters explicitly denounced as "harmful to manufacturers and are a hindrance to them." Heavy taxes and labor dues imposed by the landlords were also criticized. The authors of the report concluded, "[R]evision of all privileges, orders, statutes and guild rules

---

the Habsburg Monarch in the Nineteenth Century (New York: Columbia University Press, 1983).

263 Alfred Fischel, *Christian Julius Von Schierendorff: Ein Vorlaufer Des Liberalen Zentralismus Im Zeitalter Josefs I Und Karls VI* (1906).

264 Peter Arend Jan van den Berg, *The Politics of European Codification: A History of the Unification of Law in France, Prussia, the Austrian Monarchy and the Netherlands* (Groningen: Europa Law Pub., 2007), 89; Ernst Wangermann, *The Austrian Achievement, 1700-1800* (New York: Harcourt, Brace & Jovanovich, 1973), 44.

265 Klima, "Mercantilism in the Habsburg Monarchy- with Special Reference to the Bohemian Lands," 109.

was necessary because the prosperity of towns must be of great concern to the emperor."[266]

Beginning with the late 1660s, the Habsburg government enacted several policies favoring merchants and manufacturers. In 1665, a *Commercial Council* was established in Vienna. The Council was explicitly charged with encouraging the foundation of manufacturers, banks, warehouses, and other commercial establishments. The governments offered several initiatives including tax breaks, preferential customs on importing raw materials, and partial exceptions from guild restrictions. As a result, the number of state-sponsored manufacturers increased throughout the 1670s.

Besides providing incentives for private firms, the state was increasingly involved in the economy by investing in manufacturing and trade entities. A critical development in this period was the establishment of the first *Oriental Trading Society*. The society, founded in 1660 to compete with English and Dutch products in the eastern markets, expanded its activities under Becher's leadership. In 1670, the society obtained privileges and subsidies from the state to establish manufactories to produce woolen cloth. In 1666, the first state-owned silk production facility was established in Lower Austria. It was followed by the establishment of two fine woolen cloth factories, both under the direct control of Becher, in Linz in 1672 and in Vienna in 1676.

While the change in the economic policy after 1660 does not yet suggest a complete revolutionization of economic relations—this would have to wait until the latter half of the eighteenth century—it does signal that the ruling elites were beginning to favor urban capitalists vis-à-vis the landowners. Merchants and manufacturers demanded greater state involvement in the economy, and the government responded positively.

However, the policy and institutional changes cannot be considered solely a consequence of the demands of the capital. Rather the changes in the preferences of the ruling elite made it possible for the demands of the capital holders to be taken seriously. The incorporation of capital was a combined product of the preferences of the ruling elite and the capital. There are two reasons why.

First, urban capital holders in the Habsburg empire were not strong enough to unilaterally dictate preferences. A key indicator of the weakness of the commercial sectors is the low degree of urbanization. Towns with populations of above 10,000 in the early eighteenth century accounted for 4.4 percent in Austria,[267]

266 Ibid., 115.

267 Gross and Komlos, "Austria-Hungary in World Economy," 8.

while 70 percent of towns had 1,000 inhabitants or fewer.[268] The two largest towns were Prague and Vienna. In the latter half of the eighteenth century, Prague had a population of 50,000 (1754 census), whereas Vienna's population was around 175,000.[269]

Second, and more importantly, if the demands of the urban capital holders for greater state protection were sufficient to bring about drastic changes in government policy toward them, we should have observed a similar outcome in the Ottoman Empire. As will be discussed in the following two chapters, in the Ottoman case, where the strength of the commercial sectors was comparable to that of the Habsburg case,[270] the outcome is the opposite: the exclusion of the capital holders from the ruling coalition. Thus, the demand of the capital holders for institutional change is necessary yet insufficient to produce the observed outcomes in either case. We should also consider the preferences of the ruling elites to explain whether and to what extent the capital's preferences can be realized.

The primary determinant of the Habsburg elite's preferences was the intensity of their conflict with the landed nobility. While the intensity of the conflict increased steadily throughout the seventeenth century, the critical point in the conflict was reached at the end of the seventeenth century as the rising costs of warfare clashed with the nobility's resistance to the state's efforts to tax them.

At the turn of the century, the Habsburg state was involved in several costly conflicts. After the Great Ottoman War (1683-1699), which had resulted in the reacquisition of the greater part of Hungary by the Habsburgs, the Ottoman threat subsided, but only partially, as evidenced by the recurring wars between the Habsburgs and Ottomans first in 1714-1718 and then again in 1735-1739. Besides their rivalry with the Ottomans, the Habsburgs were deeply involved in dynastic struggles. To counter the expansion of France under Louis XIV and defend the Habsburg claim to the Spanish throne following the death of Charles II of Spain, Emperor Leopold I decided to fight the superior French army. With

268 Dickson, *Finance and Government under Maria Theresa, 1740-1780*, 50.

269 It should be noted that both cities grew considerably after 1754 under Maria Theresia's rule. According to the 1774 census, Prague's population had reached 74,874 and Vienna's 202,729.

270 For the purposes of illustration, the population of Istanbul and its surrounding areas is estimated to be around 700,000 in the early seventeenth century. For the development of market towns in the Ottoman Empire, see Suraiya Faroqhi, *Towns and Townsmen of Ottoman Anatolia: Trade, Crafts, and Food Production in an Urban Setting, 1520-1650*, Cambridge Studies in Islamic Civilization (Cambridge, Cambridgeshire; New York: Cambridge University Press, 1984).

the entrance of other major players, The War of Spanish Succession became a major European conflict that lasted from 1701 to 1714. Even though the coalition led by the Habsburgs succeeded in containing Bourbon expansionism, the war was financially devastating for the Habsburgs.[271] As Prince Eugene lamented during the War of Spanish Succession, "if the monarchy's survival depended on its ability to raise 50,000 florins at once, it would nonetheless be impossible to save it."[272]

Another source of military and financial trouble for the Habsburg state was Prussia, which was becoming a major European power under Frederick II's reign. Prussia defeated the Habsburgs thrice between 1733 and 1748, amounting to a significant territorial loss.[273] The most crucial loss was, without a doubt, Silesia, "the most prosperous and industrialized province" of the Habsburg empire.[274] The loss of Silesia was a "staggering blow" to Habsburgs, "not only because of Silesia's industrial output, but because it was the 'principal commercial intermediary' of the Habsburg monarchy with the outside world."[275]

The great reformer of the eighteenth century, Maria Theresia, ascended the Habsburg throne under the most adverse conditions. To finance the wars in the first half of the century, Charles VI was forced to borrow heavily from domestic and external creditors. Nonetheless, the most important source of domestic credit for the Habsburg state well into the 1770s was the landowners, the church, and the religious houses. In 1740, the biggest domestic lenders to the crown were in Bohemia: the Estates[276] (870,000 fl.), Count Gallas (160,000 fl.), Society of Jesus (150,000 fl.); in Moravia: the Estates (290,000 fl.), Prince Lichtenstein (145,000 fl.), *Prälatenstand*[277] (72,000 fl.); and in Austria: *Prälatenstand* (437,000

271 Thomas Mack Barker, *Army, Aristocracy, Monarchy: Essays on War, Society, and Government in Austria, 1618-1780*, East European Monographs (Boulder; New York: Social Science Monographs; Distributed by Columbia University Press, 1982).

272 Charles W. Ingrao, *The Habsburg Monarchy, 1618-1815*, New Approaches to European History (Cambridge, UK; New York: Cambridge University Press, 2000), 159.

273 Ibid.

274 Anderson, *Lineages of the Absolutist State*, 317.

275 Wallerstein, *The Modern World-System II: Mercantilism and the Consolidation of the European World-Economy, 1600-1750*, 236. One of the main trading arteries linking the heartland to the west, the *Oder*, was in Silesia. Also see Maria Theresia's political testament for the effect that the loss of Silesia had on the monarchy and the empress. Theresia, "Political Testament."

276 Not including individual lenders.

277 The estate of highest clergy. Headed by members of high nobility.

fl.).[278] Next to the nobility and clergy, the private financiers in Vienna, the so-called *Hofjuden* (court Jews) played a critical role. Prominent figures like Lemle Moses, Marx Schlesinger, Low Sinzheim, Abraham Ulm, Wolf Wertheimer, and Emanuel Oppenheimer, who held key nodes in the network of credit and exchange in Central and Eastern Europe, provided the essential sinews of war.[279]

Jewish firms, while powerful, were not the only private financiers that made large loans to the government. Under Charles VI, Christian financial firms in Vienna were also quite active. During the reign of Maria Theresia, the relative importance of the Jewish financiers declined as Christian Viennese merchants (*Bürgerlicher Handelstand*) crowded out their competitors. The number of Christian merchants and financiers increased in Vienna; there were only 24 Christian warehouses in Vienna in 1740, which increased to 46 by 1748.[280]

Due to the extensive domestic and external borrowing, the state debt had reached 52.1 million florins in 1714, 70 million in 1718, and 99 million in 1739.[281] Considering the fact that the imperial treasury contained only 87,000 florins in cash credit in 1740, Maria Theresia was hardly exaggerating when she said that upon ascending the throne, she found herself "*ohne Geld, ohne Kredit, ohne Armee*."[282]

---

278 P. G. M. Dickson, *Finance and Government under Maria Theresia, 1749-1780*, 2 vols., vol. 2 (Oxford: Claredon Press, 1987), 418. Maria Theresia openly complains of the dependency of the crown on such lenders when she writes "When I found myself forced to ask for this purpose [supplying a few regiments against Prussia] for some hundreds of thousands as loans or urgent grants in aid from private persons, I could not but see that the 'big men', and even the Ministers themselves, were plainly trying to spare their own pockets." Theresia, "Political Testament," 102.

279 Dickson, *Finance and Government under Maria Theresia, 1749-1780*, 418.

280 It should be also noted that neither Christian nor Jewish capital in the first half of the eighteenth century made extensive long-term investments in trade and industry. Rather, both groups were almost exclusively involved in banking and government finance. Exceptions included a few Christian warehouses in Austrian lands (Bozenhard, Fachiny, Fried, Gaillard, Puthon among them) that had investments in manufacturing, and the Jewish financiers in Bohemia who had invested in textile.

281 Moreover, after 1730 most of the external loans had to be charged on the contribution revenue intended for military purposes, which undermined the financing of the army. Maria Theresia wrote: "So credit was hampered in every province, and yet credit was necessary to cover requirements of the state: the exchequer had no more funds or resources to draw or on pledge, so that everything had to be raised on the credit of the provincial war tax, which brought little or no profit to the prince or the paying common man." Theresia, "Political Testament," 113.

282 "Without money, without credit, without army." Ibid., 100.

Maria Theresia and the members of her close circle, Bartenstein (Secretary of the State Conference), Koch (Cabinet Secretary), and her most prominent adviser Haugwitz, were convinced that the survival of the monarchy was contingent on creating a "more assertive and efficient central government, one that was capable of raising sufficient funds and troops to defend itself without having to rely on voluntary domestic or foreign support."[283] They were certain that the main source of the problem was the "unwillingness and inability of the provincial estates to provide adequately for the payment and supplies."[284]

The ruling elites' discontent with the nobility was evident in Maria Theresia's biographies,[285] letters,[286] and perhaps most clearly in her *Political Testament*, where she provided a candid account of, in her own words, "the situation of the monarchy…as [she] found it when [she] began her reign," "the abuses which had gradually kept into the monarchy," "the measures [she] introduced" and the "necessity of the maintaining the institutions so established."[287] The empress observed, "the prime cause of the decay of [her] hereditary lands l[ay] in the overgreat freedom the estates gradually usurped."[288] She mentioned on multiple occasions the danger that "the whole essence of the Prince's authority, the whole material condition of its existence [could become] dependent on the pleasure and arbitrary disposition of the estates."[289]

Throughout the costly wars of the previous decades, the provincial estates had made clear that their "principal and consistent concern had been to minimize

283 Ingrao, *The Habsburg Monarchy, 1618-1815*, 160.

284 The noble estates had avoided paying extra taxes even during the Siege of Vienna in 1683, when the very survival of the monarchy was in peril. Thomas Mack Barker, *Double Eagle and Crescent; Vienna's Second Turkish Siege and Its Historical Setting* (Albany: State University of New York Press, 1967), 207-8.

285 Edward Crankshaw, *Maria Theresa* (New York: Viking Press, 1970); G. Mraz, *Maria Theresia Als Koenigin Von Ungarn* (Eisenstadt: 1984); Adam Wandruszka, *Maria Theresia: D. Grosse Kaiserin* (Göttingen; Zürich; Frankfurt [Main]: Muster-Schmidt, 1980).

286 A. von Arneth, *Maria Theresa Und Joseph II. Ihre Correspondenz* (Vienna: 1868); Jedlicka, *Maria Theresia in Ihren Briefen Und Staatsscriften*, Theresa Maria, Antoinette Marie, and Alfred Arneth, *Maria Theresia und Marie Antoinette: Ihr Briefwechsel Während Der Jahre 1770-1780* (Osnabrück: Biblio Verlag, 1978); Maria Theresia and Alfred Arneth, *Briefe Der Kaiserin Maria Theresia an Ihre Kinder Und Freunde*, 4 vols. (Osnabrück: Biblio Verlag, 1978).

287 Theresia, "Political Testament," 97.

288 Ibid., 123.

289 Ibid., 120.

the burden on themselves and on their particular province."[290] Partially since the estates were "abetted in this concern by officials and ministers whose local and class loyalties outweighed all other considerations," they successfully resisted the state's attempts to extract greater resources from them.[291]

As Maria Theresia observed, the ministers were the biggest landowners in the provinces they represented, which divided their loyalty and created major principal/agent problems for the crown. She wrote, "Ministers almost always, in any province, enjoyed a free hand dealing with the estates; the minister in charge of any province was usually the biggest landowner in it and thus enjoyed the greatest respect and authority among the estates, and for that reason, many of them received large annual remunerations from the estates."[292] The empress also complained that "the heads and presidents [of the Bohemian and Austrian Chancelleries] were paid and remunerated by the estates at their pleasure" and "remained in a state of constant dependence on the estates."[293]

The empress' contempt for the administration by estates was neither motivated by nor framed in terms of any ideological reasoning that intrinsically glorified the rights of the crown over those of the estates. Contrary to what one might expect, Maria Theresia was *not* a political revolutionary. Indeed, as many biographers of Maria Theresia noted, the empress herself was a highly religious and conservative person who held the preservation of the *ancien régime* above everything. Yet, her beliefs in tradition inevitably clashed with the objectively driven interests of the state. As she writes in her *Testament*,

> I cannot repeat often enough that if I had found their privileges so clear, or if they had conducted the administration more justly than I or the crown, I should not merely have hesitated to submit and abrogate my authority entirely to them; I should rather myself have diminished and renounced or limited it for my successors, because I should always have placed the welfare and prosperity of the provinces before my own or that of my family and children. But neither my interest nor that of my successors, and the least of all the public interest, can be sacrificed have taken root…This applies above all to the supervision of the Estates' domestic funds and the management of them, which should be conscientiously undertaken in the interest of justice and of the general welfare.[294]

---

290 Wangermann, *The Austrian Achievement, 1700-1800*, 60.

291 Ibid. Dickson provides additional evidence that the estates freely bribed the ministers in Vienna to get what they wanted. Dickson, *Finance and Government under Maria Theresa, 1740-1780.*

292 Theresia, "Political Testament,“ 108.

293 Ibid., 112.

294 Ibid., 124.

For all these reasons, following the Treaty of Aix-la-Chapelle that ended the War of Austrian Succession, Maria Theresia decided to raise the Contribution (war tax) from the provinces to the level required for the maintenance of a larger permanent military. The additional burden would be met by subjecting seigniorial land to direct taxation.[295] The plan was designed by Theresia's chief advisor Haugwitz.[296]

In 1747, Haugwitz prepared a lengthy memorandum of fourteen "axioms." The main contention was that the survival of the monarchy depended on the reduction of the role of the estates in local administration and tax collection. Haugwitz warned that the Habsburg monarchy was in grave danger of losing Bohemia and Moravia to Prussia. The only way to prevent it was to ensure that the estates that were normally exempt from taxes assumed the tax burden in peacetime. Haugwitz's plan envisaged a permanent army of 108,000 men, which would cost at least 14 million florins annually.[297] The finance of this new army would require the Contribution of the Bohemian and Austrian lands to be nearly doubled, from 5.61 million to 10.39 million. The new Contribution scheme would be renewed every 10 years.

To ensure the efficient collection of taxes, the empress launched a series of administrative and fiscal reforms which historians called "more substantial than any previously attempted in a single historical period"[298] and "without parallel in the monarchy's history."[299] In fact, Maria Theresia was not the first ruler to attempt to try to centralize the administrative and fiscal institutions. Maximilian I (1459-1519) and Ferdinand I (1503-1564) had already undertaken a series of reforms.

However, as argued in the previous chapter, such attempts at centralization were inevitably limited as the rulers were unwilling to break their coalition with the estates decisively due to the very limited infrastructural reach of the central government. Consequently, the reforms of Maximilian I and Ferdinand I were

---

295 Wangermann, *The Austrian Achievement, 1700-1800*, 60.

296 Ingrao, *The Habsburg Monarchy, 1618-1815*, 160.

297 Maria Theresia writes: "I instructed Koch to have Haugwtiz draw up a plan for the maintenance of a force of 100,000 men with all possible economy." Theresia, "Political Testament," 119.

298 Wangermann, *The Austrian Achievement, 1700-1800*, 18.

299 Ingrao, *The Habsburg Monarchy, 1618-1815*, 160. The most comprehensive coverage of the institutional reforms can be found in Dickson's two volume study, Dickson, *Finance and Government under Maria Theresa, 1740-1780*.

ultimately part of the ongoing bargaining between the central and rural elites rather than a rupture in the relationship of mutual dependence.

In contrast, the mid-eighteenth-century reforms initiated by Maria Theresia and then further developed by her son Joseph II were directly aimed at undermining the power of the nobility and *redistributing* benefits to the new allies of the ruling elites, urban capital holders. In the next section, I analyze how the administrative and fiscal reforms worked toward realizing these objectives.

2. Building the Fiscal State

The first wave of Theresian reform was administrative; the objective was the standardization of the internal structure of the monarchy[300] and transforming it into "a whole."[301] Up to that point, the structure of the imperial state was akin to a "confederation in which various territories were connected only by a loose union, with each territory largely ruled by powerful elites."[302] The central location of the economic policy was the *Hofkammer* council which formally oversaw the collection of the contribution through the chancelleries. Yet in practice, the chancelleries had little authority. Everything from the preparation of the cadastral records on which the Contribution was based to the actual collection of the levy was carried out by the estates under minimal supervision of the royal authorities.

Theresia's advisor Haugwitz was convinced that the monarchy's defective system of finance and governance constituted an enemy "as dangerous to the crown and as the more obvious enemies from without."[303] He openly advocated that "political power, currently in the hands of the chancelleries, with their close links with the estates, must be seized and untied with the crowns' financial claims, inadequately promoted by the *Hofkammer*."[304]

The first step toward the goal of transferring power from the estates to the crown was the creation of central agencies seated in Vienna, the *Hofstellen*. The *Hofstellen* were headed by a newly formed highest central authority *Directorium*

300 Waltraud Heindl, "Bureaucracy, Officials and the State in the Austrian Monarchy: Stages of Change since the Eighteenth Century," *Austrian History Yearbook* 37 (2006): 37.

301 Wangermann, *The Austrian Achievement, 1700-1800*, 18.

302 Heindl, "Bureaucracy, Officials and the State in the Austrian Monarchy: Stages of Change since the Eighteenth Century," 37.

303 Dickson, *Finance and Government under Maria Theresa, 1740-1780*, 223.

304 Ibid.

in Publicis et Cameralibum. With the formation of the *Directorium*, the administrations of the Bohemian and Austrian lands were, for the first time, brought together under a single royal authority.[305] Maria Theresia relates the reasons behind the abolition of the *Hofkammer* and the institutions of the *Directorium* in the following way:

> Having perceived that the root cause of my monarchy's troubles lay in the fact that each minister and his staff was always satisfied to play the advocate and protector of the province in which he is in charge—often with only half-hearted regard to the general welfare and to the interests of the crown...I abolished altogether all the Cameral agenda of the former *Hofkammer* in the Austrian and Bohemian Provinces... and transferred all administrative and Cameral agenda, with the non-technical military, to the newly established Directorate.[306]

Several related institutional changes accompanied *Directorium*. In the main *Länder*, except Hungary (more on this below), a new type of provincial government, *Gubernium*, was instituted.[307]

Another institutional innovation brought about by 1749 reforms was the subdivision of the crown lands into district offices (*Kreisamter*). Each office would be headed by an administrative officer appointed by the royal government. This new administrative subdivision was important as the district administrators were intended to supervise the execution and enforcement of all laws. They were charged with overseeing the manors and protecting peasants and the burghers from noble infringements on their rights. The new district offices boosted the infrastructural power of the state, which, for the first time, in the words of a contemporary observer, "reached into the deepest depth of the people."[308]

While the *Kreisamter* undermined the estates' role in administration and justice, another institutional innovation, the small executive committees called

---

305 Beller, *A Concise History of Austria*, 89-90. Heindl, "Bureaucracy, Officials and the State in the Austrian Monarchy: Stages of Change since the Eighteenth Century," 37-8; P. G. M. Dickson, "Monarchy and Bureaucracy in Late Eighteenth Century Austria," *The English Historical Review* 110 (1995): 328.

306 Theresia, "Political Testament," 128.

307 The new provincial governments were called *Staathalterei* in Bohemia, *Tribunal* in Moravia, *Oberamt* in Silesia, *Regierung* in Lower Austria, *and Geheimer Rat und Kanzlei* in Inner Austria. They were directly subordinate to the empress and oversaw the daily administration and the maintenance of law and order, which were previously within the jurisdiction of the estates.

308 Heindl, "Bureaucracy, Officials and the State in the Austrian Monarchy: Stages of Change since the Eighteenth Century," 37.

Deputationen, took away their fiscal authority. The Deputations were first established in the Bohemian and Austrian lands and were directly accountable to the crown.[309] The main task of these new committees was to control the cadasters on which the Contribution was based, supervise the levy of the tax as well as oversee its local partition. The deputations were now assigned the task of ensuring that the tax revenue "came to the Estates' chest and out again to the army and other uses."[310]

The new administrative instruments of the crown achieved their short-term objectives. The establishment of *Deputationen* marked a decisive breach with the past in terms of the balance of power in the fiscal domain because it showed, for the first time, that the fiscal demands of the state could be enforced upon the estates.[311] The 1749 reforms, however, only marked the beginning. While the increase in the tax revenue was enough to cover ordinary peacetime expenditure, it could barely meet half the costs of war.[312] The Seven Years' War particularly revealed the limitations of the first wave of Theresian reforms. Despite the nominal increase in tax revenue, the government was still very much in debt at the close of the war.[313]

Underlying the insufficiency of the initial wave of reforms was the formidable opposition of the nobility. The representatives of the provincial nobility in the imperial government, the ministers about whom Maria Theresia constantly complained in her memoirs and letters, deliberately slowed the reform process by engaging in lengthy negotiations and using their veto powers. For instance, the Supreme Chancellor, Count Friedrich Harrach, submitted a plan that stipulated that the increased subsidies be accompanied by a proportional increase in the political influence of the estates.[314] Except for her close circle of advisors,

---

309 Maria Theresia writes: "In each of the provinces I appointed a Deputation whose sole business it should be to collect and report on all material relevant to the system." Theresia, "Political Testament," 127.

310 Dickson, *Finance and Government under Maria Theresa, 1740-1780*, 264. Regular payment of soldiers under arms and the provision of military supplies to the army were also among the responsibilities of the deputations.

311 Walter, *Die Geschichte Der Oestterichischen Zentralverwaltung Unter Maria Theresia*, 117-23.

312 Wangermann, *The Austrian Achievement, 1700-1800.* Dickson notes that by 1760 expenditure in the central lands was met as to 53 percent by direct taxes and 20 percent by subsidies from allies.

313 Dickson, *Finance and Government under Maria Theresa, 1740-1780.*

314 Wangermann, *The Austrian Achievement, 1700-1800*, 61.

who were of a primarily non-noble origin, Maria Theresia found very little support among the nobility.

In the end, the opposition of the estates proved very difficult to circumvent entirely. In the regions where the reforms were most effective (hereditary crown lands and Bohemia), the increased provincial contribution was to remain in effect only for 10 years, after which it would be subject to renewal by local diets. Moreover, the territories in which the monarchy had the slightest authority—Lombardy and the Austrian Netherlands in the west and Hungary in the east—remained virtually unaffected by the reforms.[315] Lastly, the initial changes accomplished little in terms of asserting the state power vis-à-vis the church, which was among the largest taxpayers and lenders to the crown.[316]

The limits of the first batch of reforms compelled the government to undertake an even more comprehensive series of changes in 1762. The second wave of reforms was led by Kaunitz, the new chief adviser of the empress.[317] One of the initial changes in government was the dissolution of the Privy Conference, which was one of the sites where the nobility voiced their opposition to the reforms. The Privy Conference was replaced by a new administrative organ, *Staatsraat*, to advise the empress on all the monarchy's internal matters, including agriculture, trade, credit, and manufacturing. Beneath this nominal shift from one advisory council to the other was a more significant transformation: the receding influence of the high nobility in the central government.

A closer look at the composition of the Privy Conference of 1749 and the *Staatsrat* by 1770 reveals the decline of the nobility. The ministries and financial officers of the Privy Conference were occupied by hereditary counts from established families of Austria and Bohemia, such as Althann, Batthyany, Harrach, Kinsky, Kuefstein, Starhember, and others. This contrasts markedly with the origins of the members of the *Staatraat*, which included professionals from early on. Even the formally noble members of the council (Binder, Borie, Gebler, König, Löhr, Stupan, and others) owed little to noble descent and much to merit.[318]

315 Beller, *A Concise History of Austria*, 88.

316 Evans and Thomas, *Crown, Church and Estates: Central European Politics in the Sixteenth and Seventeenth Centuries.*

317 Franz A. Szabo, *Kaunitz and Enlightened Absolutism, 1753-1780* (Cambridge: Cambridge University Press).

318 The Court contained only one Count, Blümengen, who came from a newly ennobled family. Most members of the court were of a professional character, such as Blanc, Martini, Perdacher, Riegger, and Zencker who "were eminent lawyers of modest

In 1762, the major institutional innovation of the previous round of changes, *Directorium*, was renamed Bohemian and Austrian Court, which, in combination with the Hungarian Chancellery and Siebenburgen Chancellery, constituted the central administrative apparatus of the monarchy. Once again, the ebbing influence of the nobility was evident in the new Bohemian and Austrian Court.[319]

One final key change from the previous reforms in 1749 was the revival of *Hofkammer* (which Haugwitz's legislation had replaced with *Directorium*). However, unlike the traditional *Hofkammer*, the newly instituted apparatus was entirely in charge of all cameral revenue and less susceptible to the influence of the estates.

Beneath the seemingly endless cycles of abolishing institutions and creating new ones, which to a certain extent reflected the short-term outcomes of the constant bargaining between the crown and the estates, the process of bureaucratization was marching on. The reforms of Maria Theresia and her successor Joseph II created a legal-rational bureaucracy along the Weberian lines. The establishment of a *Beamtenstaat*, a bureaucratic state, was a lengthy process. The rapid changes in the late eighteenth century would come to a stall (but never completely cease, as I discuss later) under the reactionary post-1790 governments. Bureaucratization would once again gain momentum and reach its climax with the reintroduction of absolutism in 1848.[320]

The process of bureaucratization in the Habsburg monarchy in the eighteenth century can be analyzed in two related dimensions: first, the qualitative changes in the rules and regulations governing the officialdom; second, the drastic changes in the composition and social origins of the new bureaucracy.

Weber defined legal-rational bureaucracy in terms of several characteristics: temporal continuation in the offices, creation of documentary records, transparent distribution of competence, a solid hierarchical order, specialized education, pre-structured career paths rewarding merit and hard work, and a salary scheme.[321] Habsburg reformers, who—like Weber himself—were inspired

---

origin, who had earned their places by brains and hard work." Dickson, *Finance and Government under Maria Theresa, 1740-1780*, 381.

319 Ibid.

320 For a general history of bureaucratization in the Habsburg Empire, see Walter Heindl's work: Waltraud Heindl, "Burokratie Und Verwaltung Im Österreichischen Neoabsolutismus," *Oesterreichische Osthefte* 22, no. 3 (1980); Heindl, "Bureaucracy, Officials and the State in the Austrian Monarchy: Stages of Change since the Eighteenth Century."

321 Max Weber, *Economy and Society: An Outline of Interpretive Sociology* (Berkeley: University of California Press, 1978).

by the fabled, if perhaps exaggerated,[322] efficiency of the Prussian bureaucracy, aimed to achieve these essential characteristics in their new bureaucratic machinery.

To begin with, reformed law faculties and universities provided instruction and specialized practical training on laws and statutes. Once the graduates entered officialdom, a high degree of discipline and impersonal dedication were expected of them.[323] Reformers rewarded hard work and discipline by changing the rules governing career advancement and salaries. A new order of ranks, titles, and decorations was introduced. In place of the highly inefficient mechanism of profit-sharing, a fixed salary structure was instituted. In 1781, a new method for performance evaluation, the "conduit lists," was created. These lists determined salary increases based on "merit and skillfulness."[324]

Another key change in the Habsburg officialdom after 1762 was the systematic compilation of rules and regulations. For the first time in Habsburg history, detailed and orderly records of all government decrees and policies were kept and published. Accurate keeping of official records, a defining feature of Weberian legal-rational bureaucracy, was to a certain extent a corollary of the sheer volume of government activity. The number of government decrees issued annually increased steadily from 1730 to 1780 and exploded thereafter.[325] The expansion of the central government after 1749 led to a proliferation of imperial decrees and orders, which generated a "real risk of administrative chaos unless an accurate record could be kept."[326]

The expansion of the scope of government activity leads us directly to the second key aspect of the process of bureaucratization: the growth of the bureaucratic apparatus. The number of officials employed by the crown, both in

322 Hans Rosenberg, *Bureaucracy, Aristocracy, and Autocracy: The Prussian Experience, 1660-1815* (Boston: Beacon Press, 1966).

323 Heindl, *Gehorsame Rebellen: Burokratie Und Beamte in Österreich 1780 Bis 1848*, 103-15, "Bureaucracy, Officials and the State in the Austrian Monarchy: Stages of Change since the Eighteenth Century," 39. Joseph II remarked in the Pastoral Letter of 1783 addressed to the public officials, "whoever wants to serve and serves the state has to disregard his own interest entirely."

324 Even though the conduit lists were abolished in 1790 by Leopold II, they were later reintroduced and reformed under Francis II and remained a key component of Habsburg bureaucratic apparatus in the nineteenth century. Ibid.: 40-1.

325 Dickson, *Finance and Government under Maria Theresa, 1740-1780*, 319.

326 Ibid., 316.

the central administration and the regional governments, rose after 1749.[327] By the time the second wave of administrative reforms was launched in 1762, the number of government officials had reached 10,000.[328]

The drastic changes in the social origins of the new bureaucrats were similarly impressive. Before the 1750s, most administrative posts, both in the central and provincial offices, were staffed by members of the highest nobility and clergy. With the reforms of Haugwitz in 1749 and Kaunitz in 1762, the relative importance of noble status declined, and bureaucratic posts became increasingly filled by members of the lesser nobility and urban middle class.

Lesser nobility was adversely affected by the crisis of the seventeenth century. While propertied, the lesser nobles did not have large numbers of enslaved peasants, which had sheltered the larger landowners from the effects of the declining demand for agricultural goods. Unable to cut production costs, lesser landowners lost not only their estates but also their administrative posts in the provincial offices and diets. Under these circumstances, the creation of a centralized bureaucratic apparatus provided "a much-needed field of honorable employment for the lesser nobility."[329]

The new bureaucratic norms and the widespread university education also allowed the members of the urban middle class to enter bureaucracy. For many burghers with professional backgrounds (lawyers, entrepreneurs, etc.), ennoblement was the most direct method of mobility. From 1741 to 1780, at least 1,449

327 It is difficult to gauge the rate of growth as the data before 1749 are sketchy at best. Mikoletzky estimates that under Charles VI, there were approximately 2,175 court employees and central government officials. There is no comparable data for the number of personnel in the provincial governments, which were under the control of the estates. Dickson estimates that there were approximately 3,300 court personnel by the time the first wave of Maria Theresian reforms was being launched in 1749. Including the personnel of the Vienna City Bank and some other agencies in the central lands, he places the total number of government officials in 1749 around 6000 at most. Heindl, "Bureaucracy, Officials and the State in the Austrian Monarchy: Stages of Change since the Eighteenth Century"; Dickson, *Finance and Government under Maria Theresa, 1740-1780*, 306.

328 Beller, *A Concise History of Austria*, 89. This growth rate is perhaps doubly impressive given the concern of the empress, who reportedly was keen on keeping the numbers of the bureaucracy constant. Dickson, "Monarchy and Bureaucracy in Late Eighteenth Century Austria."

329 Wangermann, *The Austrian Achievement, 1700-1800*, 63; Fichtner, *The Habsburg Monarchy, 1490-1848: Attributes of Empire*, 75.

aristocratic titles[330] were conferred, representing an increase of over 100 percent compared to the 40 years preceding 1740.[331] Moreover, as Dickson's genealogical analysis of the ennoblements shows, the new titles "did not call a new aristocracy into existence in this period."[332] The *arriviste* families mainly remained loyal to the crown.

While Maria Theresia and Joseph II authorized unprecedented numbers of ennoblements, it was Joseph II who "went out of his way to encourage middle-class entrepreneurs."[333] The number of burghers ennobled doubled under Joseph II. Joseph II showed the significance he attached to merit and competence over lineage and social status when he argued in his memoirs that it was "no longer rich, landowning noblemen but rather poor commoners who would serve as officials."[334]

Evaluated based on their initial goal, i.e., increasing state revenue, it is "beyond question" that "the reforms, on the whole, achieved their objective."[335] Evidence indicates that the centralizing reforms enabled the state to extract resources more efficiently than before: peacetime ordinary revenue increased steadily from 1740 to 1782. Indeed, in 1775 the monarchy achieved the first balanced budget in its history.[336] Growing revenue also allowed the state to maintain a larger military force. Haugwitz's plan had envisaged a peacetime army of over 100,000 men, which was about twice as large as the state was able to maintain in 1740. After 1763, the army of the crown lands numbered around 300,000 men.[337] In wartime, the monarchy was able to mobilize a military force that was "comparable to those of the armies of France."[338]

The reforms, however, proved insufficient to significantly alter the intra-elite balance of power in favor of the ruling elites. Despite the royal gains in taxation and the decline of the political authority of the estates, the nobility continued to dominate agriculture, manufacturing, and trade. In turn, the economic power of

---

330 Adel, Ritter, Freiherr, Graf, and Fürst.

331 Dickson, *Finance and Government under Maria Theresa, 1740-1780*, 80.

332 Ibid., 82.

333 Okey, *The Habsburg Monarchy: From Enlightenment to Eclipse*, 57.

334 Heindl, "Bureaucracy, Officials and the State in the Austrian Monarchy: Stages of Change since the Eighteenth Century," 38.

335 Wangermann, *The Austrian Achievement, 1700-1800*, 63.

336 Beller, *A Concise History of Austria*, 90.

337 Wangermann, *The Austrian Achievement, 1700-1800*, Ingrao, *The Habsburg Monarchy, 1618-1815*.

338 Dickson, *Finance and Government under Maria Theresia, 1749-1780*, 123.

the nobility provided them with the organizational capacity needed to roll back some of the royal gains.

In the following section, I discuss how the central elites of the empire deployed their newfound administrative capacity toward undermining the rural elites' power by redistributing economic resources from large landowners to capital holders.

3. Reforms in Agriculture, Trade, and Manufacturing

Throughout the seventeenth century, the landlords in Austria, Bohemia, and Hungary gradually solidified their control over agrarian labor. The process of enserfment reached its peak by 1648 when the economic and social devastation of the Thirty Years' War allowed the landowners to employ displaced peasants and enclose the cultivable lands abandoned by the free peasantry and lesser nobles.[339] Throughout this process, the landowners had the support and cooperation of the crown, which, through a series of royal decrees, provided the legal framework of the enserfment of the peasantry.[340]

Following at least 200 years of policy and legislation favoring the nobility at the expense of the peasantry, the Habsburg crown began to intervene heavily in agrarian relations, protecting the interests of the peasantry against the nobility. The main instrument for implementing the new policy was the *Robot Patents* (imperial labor decrees) promulgated in all imperial lands: Silesia in 1768 (amended in 1771), Lower Austria in 1772, and Bohemia and Moravia in 1775. With these new arrangements, labor dues were limited to two days per week. Any increase of labor dues on manors where customary services had been less than the new maximum was also prohibited.[341]

In addition to reducing excessive *robot*, lifting major limitations to peasant mobility, and prohibiting the incorporation of peasant land into demesne, the labor decrees brought about several other regulations targeting more subtle mechanisms of peasant exploitation. For instance, almost all decrees included a clause forbidding landlords to force peasants to buy the product of lords' demesnes at fixed prices.[342] The list of forbidden lordly premises also included

---

339 Blum, "The Rise of Second Serfdom in Eastern Europe."

340 Makkai, "Neo-Serfdom: Its Origin and Nature in East Central Europe."

341 Ernst Wangermann, *The Austrian Achievement, 1700-1800* (New York: Harcourt Brace Jovanovich, 1973), 71.

342 Dickson, *Finance and Government under Maria Theresa, 1740-1780*, 126.

charging the peasants unnecessary official fees for levying tax and even failing to pay them for fire and weather damage.[343]

The newly created bureaucratic apparatus played a crucial role in implementing the regulations. In Bohemia, Moravia, and the hereditary lands, the decrees were implemented by local state officials who oversaw conducting new land surveys and enforcing new regulations. The only notable exception was Hungary, where the noble-controlled counties were left in charge of implementing the orders of the crown.[344]

The reduction of weekly labor dues and other regulations of labor practices brought about by the royal decrees constituted "the most serious challenge that any sovereign had yet dared to throw down to a socially powerful nobility."[345] The landlords were not inclined to surrender their long-established rights and actively resisted conceding to royal propositions. Yet the crown was also determined; in Bohemia and Styria, for instance, the changes were accepted even without the concurrence of the estates.

Moreover, the crown actively sought new ways to circumvent the opposition of the estates. One particularly illustrative example is a pilot project known as Raab's land reform. In 1775, Franz Anton Raab undertook a project on two crown-owned estates in Bohemia under instructions from Maria Theresia and Joseph II. The project probed to replace the *robot* system with one based on cash returns. The scheme proved quite successful and was expanded in 1777 to additional crown-owned estates. The success of the project showed to the estates as well as the crown that the existing privileges and practices could be replaced by an alternative.[346]

The next critical step in revolutionizing agrarian relations and undermining the economic power of the nobility was abolishing serfdom. In 1781, Joseph II unilaterally abolished personal serfdom in Bohemian Lands through two consecutive Emancipation Patents.[347] The patents were then extended to Inner Austria and Galicia in 1782 and Hungary in 1785.[348] The new decrees gave the peasants the right to buy hereditary tenure and commute *robot* through cash

343 Ibid.

344 Beller, *A Concise History of Austria*, 93; Fichtner, *The Habsburg Monarchy, 1490-1848: Attributes of Empire*, 77.

345 Wangermann, *The Austrian Achievement, 1700-1800*, 71-72.

346 Beller, *A Concise History of Austria*, 93.

347 The phrase abolition of serfdom was used in the November Patent.

348 Ingrao, *The Habsburg Monarchy, 1618-1815*, 201.

payments. In addition, landowners were forbidden to fine or physically punish the peasants, and they lost control over matters of peasant marriage, movement, and choice of occupation.[349]

Some historians contend that the actual consequences of the abolition of serfdom were less dramatic than they appeared.[350] The opposition of the nobility, particularly vehement in Hungary, limited the applicability of the new regulations. Despite the limitations, however, the abolition of serfdom in 1781 marked a key step in realizing Maria Theresia's goal of replacing the *robot* system with the division of landed estates among rent-paying peasants. In addition to paving the way for the establishment of capitalistic agrarian production, the abolition of serfdom significantly contributed to the development of industry in the imperial lands throughout the nineteenth century.[351] The peasants that obtained the freedom of mobility and employment constituted the labor pool that the growing textile, glass, iron, and paper industries would draw upon in the late eighteenth and early nineteenth centuries.

Two additional developments in agrarian relations were the institution of a uniform land tax and the regulation of feudal dues. In 1789, Joseph II ordered a comprehensive land registers survey to be used in implementing direct taxation. The new bureaucracy played a key role in this enterprise: the compilation of the new register and the estimation of average yields from estates were entirely completed by the lower (i.e., of exclusively non-noble origin) ranks of the new bureaucracy.[352] The Josephinian survey revealed a great deal of land, which had previously not been taxed and thereby "deprived the privileged orders of the last de facto remnants of the immunity from direct taxation."[353]

As noted, in addition to being exempt from direct taxation, the nobles were traditionally in charge of estimating and collecting any taxes they were subject to. Josephinian reformers considered manorial tax collectors "unqualified and unsuitable" for collecting the new taxes. Joseph appointed state-employed tax

---

349 Okey, *The Habsburg Monarchy: From Enlightenment to Eclipse*, 42-43.

350 Ibid.; Blum, *Noble Landowners and Agriculture in Austria 1815-1848: A Study in the Origins of the Peasant Emancipation of 1848*.

351 For a full English translation of the patent, see C. A. Macartney, *The Habsburg and Hohenzollern Dynasties in the Seventeenth and Eighteenth Centuries*, The Documentary History of Western
(New York: Harper & Row, 1970), 115-16; Josef Karniel, *Die Toleranzpolitik Kaiser Josephs II* (Gerlingen: 1986).

352 Wangermann, *The Austrian Achievement, 1700-1800*, 92.

353 Ibid., 93.

collectors throughout the monarchy. The preparation of the land registers and the collection of taxes by state officials "deprived the estates of one of their last surviving practical functions."[354]

An even bigger dent to the nobility was the regulation of feudal fees. To prevent the landlords from exploiting the complicated rules regulating the fees on agricultural income and thereby squeezing extra revenue from the peasants, Joseph II declared via the February Patent of 1780 that the peasants must be allowed to retain at least 50 percent of their gross income for sustenance. Given the approximately 12 percent land tax and 20 percent for village contribution that landlords were subject to, the new arrangement practically capped the share of the landlords at roughly 18 percent of the gross yield. In some places, the net effect of the new regulations reached a 60 percent reduction in feudal fees of the landlords. Landlords protested but obtained only relatively minor concessions.[355]

To oversee the implementation of his major agrarian policies, Joseph II created several special court commissions (*Hofkomissionen*). The most important court commissions were the Domains and Robot Abolition Commission and the Tax and Urbarial Commission, which oversaw the implementation of the 1781 Emancipation Patents and the 1789 Tax and Urbarial Patents, respectively.[356]

To dismantle the organizational capacity of the noble estates to oppose the reforms, Joseph II also sought to make changes in the provincial administration. In 1782, he discontinued the feudal estates committees (*Ständische Auschüsse*) in the provinces, incorporating them into the previously created royal provincial office, *Gubernium*. Even in Hungary, where previous administrative reforms were much less effective, Joseph II undertook a major overhaul: following a comprehensive military census of the population, the Josephinian government decided to reduce the number of counties and grouped them into 10 new civil districts presided over by a state-appointed commissar. He also unilaterally suspended further meetings of the contentious county assemblies.[357]

---

354 Ibid.

355 One concession was that the peasants settled on seigniorial land and were excluded from the new maximum. Also, in Bohemia, Galicia, and some other places, the lords were allowed to exact labor services for two more years following the decree.

356 See Dickson, "Monarchy and Bureaucracy in Late Eighteenth Century Austria," 331, for a list of other special court commissions and their functions.

357 Ibid.: 329-30. These special court commissions were in turn linked to the United Offices (*Die Vereignigten Hofstellen*) created in 1783 by the union of the Bohemian-Austrian Chancellery, *Hofkammer* and Ministerial Bank Deputation.

In sum, Joseph II's reforms achieved considerable progress toward the goal of overriding traditional local institutions. As Beller notes, "for the first time, the Habsburg monarchy possessed a functioning bureaucracy," which was crucial in implementing the reforms.[358] Even though Joseph II was ultimately disappointed by his achievements, the administrative system that he and his mother, Maria Theresia, created was "far more efficient, honest and responsive than most other European governments." Relative to other European countries, the Habsburg state at the end of the eighteenth century was "neither weak, nor backward, nor in decline."[359]

Now we can turn to industry and trade, where the institutional changes pursued by the ruling elites were geared toward undermining the power of the nobility and effectively redistributing economic resources to urban capital holders.

Until the mid-eighteenth century, manufacturing in the Habsburg lands was essentially limited to two activities: manorial production based on serf labor and artisan production in cities under strict guild controls. Manorial production for the market was dominant in the western regions, most notably Bohemia and Moravia. Taking advantage of serf labor, entrepreneurial members of the landed nobility in the late seventeenth and early eighteenth centuries had set up cotton mills and textile workshops on their demesnes. In most cases, manorial production worked in conjunction with a putting-out system where landlords lent their serfs to putting-out firms.[360] even though manorial and putting-out manufacturing were oriented toward the market, the production itself still took place within feudal relations. The landlords benefited immensely, whereas the profits of trading firms remained low, not to mention that the workers were unpaid.[361]

The second main site of manufacturing before the mid-eighteenth century, artisan production under guild control, was not capitalistic either. Craft guilds limited the import and export of raw materials and manufactured goods, dictated prices, and kept the workforce on a tight leash. Artisan manufacturing was open to guild members only. Moreover, guild membership was limited to Catholics, creating an insurmountable barrier of entry for foreign workers, Protestants, and

358 His epitaph read, "[H]ere lies a prince whose intentions were pure, but who had the misfortune to see all his plans collapse." Beller, *A Concise History of Austria*, 103.

359 Ingrao, *The Habsburg Monarchy, 1618-1815*, 219.

360 Arnost Klima, "The Role of Rural Domestic Industry in Bohemia in the 18th Century," *Economic History Review* 27 (1974).

361 Klima, "Industrial Development in Bohemia, 1648-1781."

Jews. Guild privileges and practices were traditionally maintained by the ruling elites, which had aligned themselves with the nobility.

As noted earlier, the "unnatural barriers" to manufacturing and trade embodied in manorial and guild-controlled production lay at the core of the objections raised by urban capital holders. Cameralists like Schröder, Morgenthaler, and Becher were critical of guild regulations, which they contended stunted independent manufacturing and trade by limiting the dissemination of know-how and expertise, controlling most skilled labor, and distorting prices.

The elimination of guild privileges was a key objective of the eighteenth-century reforms. As early as 1749, the Viennese government began to loosen such privileges by granting permissions to entrepreneurs seeking to establish stores and warehouses in the major cities. Considerable progress in marginalizing the guild regulations in manufacturing was achieved under Joseph II, who "chipped away at such regulations industry by industry."[362]

As an extra incentive, enterprises that were established outside guilds were designated exempt from taxation for extended periods. Manufacturers, who previously had trouble obtaining raw materials,[363] now obtained preferential customs on the import of raw materials.[364] In addition to tax exemptions, the state made considerable loans and subsidies to new enterprises.[365] The total of annual subsidies to manufacturing reached one million florins in 1770.[366]

A specialized department, the General Commercial Directorate, played a crucial role in supporting manufacturing enterprises. Through subsidiary offices in the provinces, the Directorate supervised such enterprises by providing technology, information, and know-how. Where workers and employers would not replace old production techniques, "the government forced change upon them."[367] The Commercial Directorate, staffed by civil servants, was charged with collecting and evaluating trade and industry information and making

362 Fichtner, *The Habsburg Monarchy, 1490-1848: Attributes of Empire*, 83.

363 Under feudal guild regulations, town merchants and craftsmen were not able to buy raw materials directly from the producers but had to go through country middlemen, who were able to dictate prices, thanks to their close ties with the landowners.

364 Klima, "Industrial Development in Bohemia, 1648-1781," 94.

365 Ivan Berend, *History Derailed: Central and Eastern Europe in the Long Nineteenth Century* (Berkeley: University of California Press, 2003), 144.

366 Ingrao, *The Habsburg Monarchy, 1618-1815*, 212; Richard L. Rudolph, *Banking and Industrialization in Austria-Hungary* (Cambridge: Cambridge University Press, 1976).

367 Fichtner, *The Habsburg Monarchy, 1490-1848: Attributes of Empire*, 71.

policy recommendations based on their analyses.[368] In the 1760s, the Directorate prepared, for the first time, the so-called *Operationspläne*. These documents were akin to modern national development plans; they identified industries to be supported and which geographical areas were to specialize in particular industries.[369]

The state not only allowed but also actively encouraged importing foreign experts and skilled labor to come and work in manufacturing enterprises.[370] Non-Catholic artisans and skilled workers were given state protection and monetary incentives. As a result, large groups of skilled labor, particularly textile workers from Britain and German territories, came to the monarchy. Foreign skilled labor was increasingly employed in Bohemian and Austrian lands and Hungary.[371]

Combined with the sizeable unskilled workforce released by the relaxation of the noble control over peasants, the influx of foreign labor into the Habsburg lands led to the rapid growth of the total workforce available to bourgeois manufacturers. Klima shows that in 1780 there were 231,164 textile workers in Bohemia alone. The number of textile workers doubled in less than 20 years; in 1798, over 528,870 workers were employed in Bohemian textile manufactures.[372] These numbers are in line with the estimations of Okey, who reports that the number of textile workers in Bohemia increased from 237,000 in 1780 to 590,000 in 1798.[373] The industrial workforce grew in other imperial lands as well. Ingrao estimates that the number of workers in Lower Austria quintupled between 1765 and 1785, reaching over 100,000.[374]

In addition to supporting the burgeoning private sector, the Habsburg state owned several enterprises. An early example was the Brno Fine Cloth Factory, directly funded by the government in the 1760s and 1770s. Even though it went bankrupt in 1789, it significantly contributed to the development of the textile

---

368 John Komlos, "Institutional Change under Pressure: Enlightened Government Policy in the Eighteenth-Century Habsburg Monarchy," *Journal of European Economic History* 15 (1986): 432.

369 Freudenberger, "An Industrial Momentum in the Habsburg Monarchy," 343.

370 Good, *The Economic Rise of the Hapsburg Empire, 1750-1914.*

371 Berend, *History Derailed: Central and Eastern Europe in the Long Nineteenth Century*, 136.

372 Klima, "Industrial Development in Bohemia, 1648-1781," 82.

373 Okey, *The Habsburg Monarchy: From Enlightenment to Eclipse*, 61.

374 Ingrao, *The Habsburg Monarchy, 1618-1815*, 212-13; Wangermann, *The Austrian Achievement, 1700-1800*, 109.

industry in the region.[375] Yet another state-owned enterprise was the woolen fabrics factory in Linz, reportedly the largest in Europe at the time. Founded privately in 1672, the factory was partly taken over by the state-supported Oriental Company in 1719 and then made an entirely state-owned enterprise in 1754. In addition to producing goods for the Western European markets, the factory "carried out numerous government functions in helping out other industrial units, both private and public."[376]

In addition to removing guild privileges and other labor restrictions and providing permissions, tax exemptions, loans, and subsidies to the newly established industrial enterprises, the state played an active role in creating an imperial market for domestically produced goods. The critical step toward that goal was the elimination of internal tolls and customs duties—artifacts of feudal trade originally intended to protect individual counties and regions.

After 1763, Maria Theresia passed several legislations to reduce such tolls and customs duties among the various lands of the empire.[377] In 1775, she eliminated all internal tolls within the hereditary lands, except Tyrol. In addition, a much closer commercial union was established with the Austrian Netherlands in 1777. By the end of the eighteenth century, an imperial common market was created where goods were traded freely, unhindered by internal tolls.[378] Domestic manufacturers were protected from foreign competition through high tariffs (in general one-third of the value of imported goods[379]) and import quotas.[380] The imperial government also tried to strengthen the infrastructure of trade throughout the empire. Under Maria Theresia and Joseph II, the transportation network was constantly improved by dredging rivers and constructing new roads.[381]

---

375 In fact, the main reason why it went bankrupt was its inability to compete with the new enterprises founded by its previous employees. Herman Freudenberger, *The Industrialization of a Central European City: Brno and the Fine Woolen Industry in the Eighteenth Century* (Edington, Willts: Pasold, 1977).

376 Freudenberger, "An Industrial Momentum in the Habsburg Monarchy," 344.

377 Gross and Komlos, "Austria-Hungary in World Economy."

378 Andrea Komlosy, "State, Regions, and Borders: Single Market Formation and Labor Migration in the Habsburg Monarchy, 1750-1918," *Review* XXVII (2004).

379 Berend, *History Derailed: Central and Eastern Europe in the Long Nineteenth Century*, 143.

380 Helen Liebek, "Free Trade and Protectionism under Maria Theresa and Joseph II," *Canadian Journal of History* 14 (1979).

381 Jerome Blum, "Transportation and Industry in Austria," *Journal of Modern History* 15 (1943).

Lastly, the crown made a sustained effort to provide a legal framework for the free market. In 1775, Maria Theresia issued an imperial decree that marked a sharp departure from the feudal conception of justice in labor relations. The decree stipulated that no one should force a person to work against his will for an entrepreneur under conditions disadvantageous to the employee.[382] By stipulating a contractual relationship between the employer and employee, the state laid the legal groundwork for market exchange.

The social relations of production underwent significant changes in this period as well. First, in sharp contrast to the dominant modes of production before 1770, the entire process of production was now taking place in factories.[383] Second, manorial lords engaged in production for the market were increasingly crowded out by entrepreneurs of urban origin, such as bankers, merchants, and even some wealthier craftsmen.[384]

Some of the earliest "industrialists" were landowning nobles.[385] Yet they were not capitalists, as they were well protected from market competition and employed many serfs.[386] Bourgeois manufacturing, which initially existed alongside noble enterprises, became dominant in the late eighteenth century. The number of large bourgeois manufacturing enterprises rose drastically; almost all cotton mills by the end of the century were bourgeois enterprises.[387]

The importance of nobility in manufacturing and industry declined steadily throughout the nineteenth century. Noble-owned enterprises were primarily restricted to sectors where production remained closely linked with land, such as coal and iron-ore mining, where there was little technical development. Therefore, the inability to upgrade was relatively less of an obstacle. In contrast to Bohemia, Moravia, and Austria, where the embourgeoisement of industry was most profound, Hungarian nobility retained their role in the industry for longer. Relatively more market-oriented ones among Hungarian estates were

382 Klima, "Industrial Development in Bohemia, 1648-1781," 97.

383 Wangermann, *The Austrian Achievement, 1700-1800*, 107.

384 Rudolph and Komlos, "Social Structure and the Beginning of Austrian Economic Growth"; Milan Myska, Sheilagh C. Ogilvie, and Cerman Markus, "Proto-Industrialization in Bohemia, Moravia and Silesia," in *European Proto-Industrialization* (Cambridge: Cambridge University Press, 1996).

385 Herman Freudenberger, *The Waldstein Woolen Mill: Noble Enterpreneurship in Eighteenth-Century Bohemia* (Massachusetts: Cambridge University Press, 1963).

386 Berend, *History Derailed: Central and Eastern Europe in the Long Nineteenth Century*, 144; Fichtner, *The Habsburg Monarchy, 1490-1848: Attributes of Empire*, 72.

387 Klima, "Industrial Development in Bohemia, 1648-1781."

engaged in the new economic activities (e.g., flour milling and sugar-beet processing).[388] Nonetheless, the noble manufacturers who proved competitive in the long run were the ones who forged partnerships with middle-class bankers and entrepreneurs.[389]

4. The Legacy of State Formation

The process of centralization reached its peak during the last few years of Joseph II's reign. So did the noble opposition to the reforms. The opposition of the Hungarian magnates was particularly threatening as they were prepared to mount an armed resistance against the crown, whom they accused of trespassing on their traditional rights and privileges. Chief among the trespassed privileges of Hungarian magnates was exemption from taxation, which even Maria Theresia was unwilling to take away.[390] Facing vehement opposition, Joseph II slowed the pace of reforms during his last few years on the throne and even rescinded some of his orders on his deathbed.

It is a matter of historical controversy to what extent the accomplishments of the Theresian and Josephinian eras were lost after 1790. In this section, I argue that even though some of the policies were reversed by the conservative leaders of the first half of the nineteenth century, the legacy of the 1740-1790 reforms was essentially intact. The rulers of the reactionary period, Leopold II (1790-1792) and Francis II (1792-1804, and 1804-1836 as Francis I)[391] not only preserved the institutional core of the fiscal state but also helped bring the reforms to a culmination with the establishment of the neo-absolutist state in 1848. I also show that the centralized state apparatus created in the 1740-1790 period directly affected the industrialization of the Habsburg lands throughout the nineteenth century.

On the surface, the brief reign of Leopold II (1790-2) was a period of stagnation and relapse.[392] One of his first acts after being unexpectedly enthroned

---

388 Okey, *The Habsburg Monarchy: From Enlightenment to Eclipse*, 83.

389 Freudenberger relates the case of the fine woolen factory established in Namest (in Moravia in 1795), among others, as an example of this phenomenon. Freudenberger, "An Industrial Momentum in the Habsburg Monarchy."

390 Fichtner, *The Habsburg Monarchy, 1490-1848: Attributes of Empire*, 85-86.

391 The confusion pertaining to the name of the emperor stems from a technicality regarding the official title of the monarchy. In 1804, Francis II legally dissolved the Holy Roman Empire and declared himself the first emperor of the Austrian Empire, Francis I.

392 For an account of Leopold II's reign, see Adam Wandruszka, *Leopold II* (Wien: Verlag Herold, 1963).

following the death of Joseph II was to reduce state control over taxation and revenue disbursement.[393] However, a closer look at Leopold II's motivations for reversing the fiscal policy reveals that the imminent threat posed by the nobility to the survival of the monarchy played a decisive role in the rollback. Given the strong opposition of the nobility, Leopold II had little choice but to give in to some of their demands. Yet by doing so, he ultimately saved the monarchy from the turmoil that could have permanently undone the achievements of 1740-1790. Ingrao credits Leopold II for preserving "the greater part of Joseph II's legacy while averting the very real prospect of internal rebellion."[394]

Leopold II's successor, Francis I, followed an even more cautious policy. The primary factor driving Francis I's conservatism was the looming influence of the French Revolution and the Napoleonic Wars. As the head of the most powerful dynastic monarchy on the continent, Emperor Francis I was understandably timid about the very tangible international threat to the monarchy.[395] Antagonizing the nobility through further reforms would have only exacerbated the danger. The fear of revolution dominated the policies of the Habsburg governments up until 1848. Political conservatism reached its climax during the so-called *Vormärz* (pre-March) period, the last 13 years before the outbreak of the 1848 revolutions when the emperor kept the growing Austrian civil society under close surveillance.

Nonetheless, beneath the political conservatism of this period was the resilience of the major legacies of the reform era. First, even though the government was not cautious about enacting anti-noble policies, it nevertheless "distanced itself politically from the landed class" and "was correspondingly disliked by it."[396] Second, the coalition that the ruling elites had formed with urban capital holders after 1660 was intact and thriving.

During Metternich's term as prime minister under Francis I, the Viennese government followed the very capital-friendly policies that Maria Theresia and Joseph II had promoted. For instance, the commercial colleges were expanded under Metternich and continued to support native industries and entrepreneurs.

393 Fichtner, *The Hab sburg Monarchy, 1490-1848: Attributes of Empire*, 90.

394 Ingrao, *The Habsburg Monarchy, 1618-1815*, 202. Other historians also agree that Leopold II retained much of Joseph II's reforms. Okey, *The Habsburg Monarchy: From Enlightenment to Eclipse*; Steven Beller, *Francis Joseph* (London; New York: Longman, 1996).

395 Gross and Komlos, "Austria-Hungary in World Economy"; Fichtner, *The Habsburg Monarchy, 1490-1848: Attributes of Empire*.

396 Okey, *The Habsburg Monarchy: From Enlightenment to Eclipse*.

The National Bank was formed in 1816 to alleviate credit scarcity and reliance on foreign capital. The state continued to improve the infrastructure and transportation network of the monarchy. It financed several railway-building programs and continued road-building projects initiated under Maria Theresia. By carrying out these policies, Francis I and Metternich were "tacitly confessing their need for both the energies of an entrepreneurial middle class and the revenues its activities generated."[397]

Capital holders also had reasons to continue supporting the Habsburg government: it provided incentives and subsidies to investors and protected the townsmen's rights. The two most important legal reforms in Habsburg history took place under Francis: The Criminal Code of 1803 and the General Law Code of 1811. The latter was particularly important as it established the principle of equal citizenship, which was instrumental in establishing a capital-friendly property rights regime.[398]

Capital holders pursued their interests more actively in the first half of the nineteenth century. The first industrial associations were formed in Prague and Graz in 1837 and Vienna in 1838. The stated purpose of the associations, which found high membership among industrialists, merchants, and even artisans, was "to focus the imperial regime on the needs of the business."[399] Industrial associations proved an effective vessel for articulating capital's interests.

The state's continuing involvement was a decisive factor in the steady growth of the Habsburg economy throughout the nineteenth century. The nature and extent of the Habsburg economic development during this period, however, has only recently been appreciated by economic historians. Earlier accounts were inclined to describe the economic development of the Habsburg Empire in the nineteenth century in negative terms. Most notably, Alexander Gerschenkron's seminal *An Economic Spurt That Failed* popularized the notion that Habsburg economic growth in the nineteenth century never amounted to full-blown industrialization and was ultimately a failed attempt.[400]

Gerschenkron's analysis of Habsburg economic development was later challenged by a revisionist school of Habsburg economic history that questioned not only the conclusion that Habsburg industrialization failed but also the very

---

397 Fichtner, *The Habsburg Monarchy, 1490-1848: Attributes of Empire*, 114.

398 Beller, *A Concise History of Austria*, 104-05.

399 Fichtner, *The Habsburg Monarchy, 1490-1848: Attributes of Empire*, 119.

400 Gerschenkron, *An Economic Spurt That Failed: Four Lectures in Austrian History*.

paradigm of "economic spurt."[401]Instead of emphasizing periodization and attempting to ascertain at what point industrialization did or did not break out, the revisionists underlined the "wider prevalence of slow and protracted industrialization, which was neither economic stagnation nor spurt-like growth."[402] The revisionist economic historians traced the origins of Habsburg industrialization to the eighteenth century.[403] They asserted that the Theresian and Josephinian reforms "laid the basis of Habsburg agriculture,"[404] "laid the groundwork for capitalist transformation along the western lines,"[405] and "provided [the monarchy] with an economic and even a political basis with which it was able to operate fairly successfully for about another 140 years."[406]

Econometric analyses indicate that the monarchy had achieved sustained growth by 1850 as an outgrowth of the changes in the eighteenth century.[407] The annual economic growth rate from 1820 to 1850 is estimated at 2.5 percent[408] and for the 1830-1845 period 3.3 percent.[409] Berend and Ranki calculate the overall rate of the monarchy's industrial development at 3.5 percent in the first half of the nineteenth century.[410]

---

401 N. T. Gross and Carlo M. Cipolla, "The Habsburg Monarchy," in *The Emergence of Industrial Societies, Part One* (Fontana, 1973); Gross and Komlos, "Austria-Hungary in World Economy"; Rudolph and Komlos, "Social Structure and the Beginning of Austrian Economic Growth"; Good, *The Economic Rise of the Hapsburg Empire, 1750-1914.*

402 Gross and Komlos, "Austria-Hungary in World Economy," 39.

403 Rudolph and Komlos, "Social Structure and the Beginning of Austrian Economic Growth"; Rudolph, "The Pattern of Austrian Industrial Growth from the Eighteenth to the Early Twentieth Century"; Komlos and Heintel, "The Threat of a Malthusian Crisis in the Habsburg Monarchy."

404 Good, *The Economic Rise of the Hapsburg Empire, 1750-1914*, 34.

405 Berend, *History Derailed: Central and Eastern Europe in the Long Nineteenth Century.*

406 Freudenberger, "An Industrial Momentum in the Habsburg Monarchy," 339.

407 David F. Good, "Austria-Hungary," in *Patterns of European Industrialization: The Nineteenth Century*, ed. Richard Sylla and Gianni Toniolo (London and New York: Routledge, 1991), 224.

408 John Komlos, *The Habsburg Monarchy as a Customs Union: Economic Development in Austria-Hungary in the Nineteenth Century* (Princeton, NJ: Princeton University Press, 1983).

409 Rudolph and Komlos, "Social Structure and the Beginning of Austrian Economic Growth."

410 Gyogy Ranki and Ivan Berend, "On the Economic Development of Austro-Hungarian Monarchy," in *Underdevelopment and Economic Growth: Studies in Hungarian Social and Economic History* (Budapest: Akademiai Kiado, 1979), 100.

Perhaps even more impressive than the steady rates of growth (which was skewed toward the bottom given that growth is distributed unevenly among regions) is the development of certain sectors, most notably the textile industry. The early decades of the nineteenth century, especially the 1820s and 1830s, were a period of textile boom in the Habsburg Empire. Komlos calculates that the textile industry grew 3.7 percent annually between 1784 and 1803, 11 percent annually between 1826 and 1835, and 8.5 percent between 1835 and 1847.[411] As a leading producer of textiles on the continent, the monarchy's raw-cotton import grew as well: the average annual raw-cotton import was 8,484,944 pounds in 1821-1830, which almost tripled to 23,565,406 in 1831-40, which once again doubled to 45,608,674 in 1841-1847.[412] By the mid-nineteenth century, textiles constituted 41 percent of the monarchy's industrial output; food processing came in second with 21 percent.[413] Foodstuffs production, particularly sugar-beet processing, grew at an annual rate of 4.8 percent between 1830 and 1848.[414]

The textile boom was generating economic dynamism in other sectors as well. More than two-thirds of textile production was done in factories, which replaced the putting-out system as the primary mode of production. The proliferation of textile and food-processing factories supported the machine-building industry, which continued to grow into the second half of the nineteenth century.[415] Austrian and Bohemian machine builders exported large quantities of specialized equipment for cotton production and sugar industry to other parts of the monarchy as well as Russia, France, Sweden, and Italy.[416]

Other macroeconomic indicators also point to sound industrialization in the Habsburg Empire. The share of agricultural labor in economically active population continued to decline throughout the nineteenth century. In 1850, approximately 75 percent of the labor force in Austria was employed in agriculture. In 1890, roughly 55 percent were agricultural workers. In Bohemia, the share of agricultural labor at the end of the century was as low as 35 percent. The only

---

411 Komlos, *The Habsburg Monarchy as a Customs Union: Economic Development in Austria-Hungary in the Nineteenth Century*, 99.

412 Gross and Komlos, "Austria-Hungary in World Economy," table 2.

413 Berend, *History Derailed: Central and Eastern Europe in the Long Nineteenth Century*, 147.

414 Good, *The Economic Rise of the Hapsburg Empire, 1750-1914*, 49.

415 Arnost Klima, "The Beginning of the Machine-Building Industry in the Czech Lands in the First Half of the 19th Century," *Journal of European Economic History* (1975).

416 Rudolph, *Banking and Industrialization in Austria-Hungary*, 31.

notable exception was Hungary, where about 69 percent of the active population was employed in agriculture at the turn of the century.[417]

Yet another proxy of industrialization, steam power capacity, indicates strong industrial development. Steam power capacity grew over 15-fold from 1840 to 1860. In 1860, Austria ranked fourth (after Britain, France, and Germany) with 330,000 horsepower capacity. Over half of this capacity was used in the textile industry, whereas mining and iron industries came in distant second and third.[418]

The *Vormärz* government (1835-1848), despite its political conservatism, followed the policy of supporting merchants, entrepreneurs, and industrialists. In addition to providing incentives, loans, and subsidies through specialized state agencies, the Habsburg state in the first half of the nineteenth century was involved in the economy in two additional ways: planning and financing railroads and spearheading the establishment of the domestic banking sector.

The Viennese governments, since Theresia, were heavily investing in the transportation network of the empire, which was crucial to the intra-imperial trade. Several new major road projects were completed during the *Vormärz* period, most notably the Vienna-Trieste road, the Alpine road connecting Tyrol and Lombard, and the Ampessaner road between Conegliano and Toblach. In the *Vormärz* period alone, over 2,240 km of primary roads were constructed, and the length of secondary roads was doubled.[419]

The investment in railroads was equally impressive. Under Francis I, the state began to finance several railroad projects throughout the monarchy. The 1841 imperial decree provided the government with wide-ranging powers to undertake large construction.[420] The total length of steam railroads in the monarchy rose from 144 km in 1840 to 1,357 km in 1850, a rate of growth which was relatively higher even than that of Britain in the same period (from 1,349 km to 10,660 km).[421] By the end of the century, the railroad density of the monarchy would reach 805 km per million population, which compared favorably to Britain's 925 km and Germany's 870 and was much higher than Russia's 395 km.[422]

Historians concur that state-sponsored development projects played a key role in Habsburg industrialization. Klima argues that railroad construction was

---

417 Good, *The Economic Rise of the Hapsburg Empire, 1750-1914*, 47.
418 Ibid., 60.
419 Ibid., 65.
420 Blum, "Transportation and Industry in Austria."
421 Gross and Komlos, "Austria-Hungary in World Economy," table 5.
422 Ibid., table 12.

of "major consequence for both industry and transport."[423] Similarly, Matis notes that in the 1840s the railroads "gave the entire economy a stimulus…The industrial centers of northern Bohemia and Moravia became bound with those of Lower Austria and Styria."[424] Good,[425] Blum,[426] and others[427] agree that the pre-1848 railroad development created the ideal conditions for the further industrial growth in the latter half of the nineteenth century.

The expansion of industrial production and the proliferation of costly railroad projects in the nineteenth century rendered the provision of credit a priority. To supplement direct loans and subsidies, the state took the initiative in creating several private banks to meet the credit needs of the industry. With the support of the government, major banks like *Niederösterreichische Escompte-Gesellschaft, Banca Commerciale Triestina,* and, most importantly, *Creditanstalt für Handel und Gewerbe* were established.[428] In addition to providing short-term credit, these banks were specifically assigned the role of "initiators of development." All banks established in this period had provisions in their statutes for the promotion of industrial enterprises.[429] Even though the banks never replaced the state as the leading provider of loans and credit to industrial enterprises, they proved effective in mobilizing capital. They succeeded, particularly after 1880, in amassing large sums of loanable funds and facilitated economic growth by reducing the transference of the funds from low- to high-demand areas.[430]

I argued above that the political conservatism of post-1790 governments, motivated by the backlash of the nobility and fueled by the fear of popular revolution, had slowed down institutional changes but did not undo the coalition between the urban middle classes and the ruling elites, as evidenced by the continuation of the capital-friendly policies. The period of slow institutional change

423 Klima and Komlos, "Industrial Growth and Entrepreneurship in the Early Stages of Industrialization in the Czech Lands," 560.
424 Herbert Matis, "Technik Und Industriealisierung Im Österreichischen Vormarz," *Technikgeschichte* 36 (1969): 18-19. Quoted in Good, *The Economic Rise of the Hapsburg Empire, 1750-1914*, 66.
425 Good, *The Economic Rise of the Hapsburg Empire, 1750-1914*, 66.
426 Blum, "Transportation and Industry in Austria."
427 Gyorgy Ranki and John Komlos, "On the Economic Development of Austro-Hungarian Monarchy," in *Economic Development in the Habsburg Monarchy* (New York: Columbia University Press, 1983).
428 Rudolph, *Banking and Industrialization in Austria-Hungary.*
429 Rudolph, *Banking and Industrialization in Austria-Hungary*, 69.
430 Ibid., 189-90.

ended abruptly with the 1848 Revolution, which reintroduced absolutism in the Habsburg monarchy. During the neo-absolutist era, ushered in with the enthronement of Franz Joseph (1848-1916), centralization again accelerated.[431]

Franz Joseph, very much like Maria Theresia and Joseph II, ruled the monarchy "disregarding the power of noble estates and relying solely on the power of his bureaucracy."[432] The key to the re-centralization of the state apparatus was the administrative reforms implemented in the early 1850s, known as the *Bach reforms*, after Joseph Alexander Baron von Bach.[433] These reforms, which are usually compared to those of Joseph II in their radicalism and scope,[434] aimed at subordinating all imperial territories to a centralized state apparatus. All crown lands were again subdivided into consistent administrative units (*Gemeinde, Bezirk, Kreiz, and Staathalterei*). The state took over all administrative and judicial powers of the landowning nobles.[435]

The bureaucratization of the central state apparatus reached its climax in this period as all levels of officialdom were staffed by professionals chosen based on merit and education rather than social status and rank. The new bureaucracy was hierarchically ordered down to the district level, extending the infrastructural power of the central government to all domains of the monarchy. Beller notes, "[F]or the first time, all of the monarchy was ruled from Vienna by a German-speaking officialdom."[436]

Armed with the new bureaucratic apparatus, the ruling elites of the monarchy proceeded to complete the key reforms initiated in the latter half of the eighteenth century. Noble tax privileges and feudal dues were abolished. All labor servitudes and personal bondages were eliminated, bringing the emancipation of the peasantry to its culmination.[437] The *Gewerbeordnung* (industrial code) of

431 Heinrich Benedikt, *Die Wirtschaftliche Entwicklung in Der Franz-Joseph-Zeit* (Wien: Verlag Herold, 1958); Beller, *Francis Joseph*, Katrin Unterreiner, *Emperor Franz Joseph, 1830-1916: Myth and Truth*, 1st ed. (Wien: C. Brandstätter, 2006).

432 It is said that Francis Joseph ruled with four armies: one that marched (the military), one that sat (the bureaucracy), one that knelt (the clergy), and one that crawled (the informers). Beller, *A Concise History of Austria*, 31.

433 Christoph Stoelzl, *Die Aera Bach in Boehmen: Sozialgeschichte Studien Zum Neoabsolutismus, 1849-59* (Munich: 1971).

434 Beller, *A Concise History of Austria*, 132.

435 Heindl, "Bureaucracy, Officials and the State in the Austrian Monarchy: Stages of Change since the Eighteenth Century," 44.

436 Beller, *A Concise History of Austria*, 133.

437 Blum, *Noble Landowners and Agriculture in Austria 1815-1848: A Study in the Origins of the Peasant Emancipation of 1848*.

1859 abolished craft guilds. In short, the post-1848 neo-absolutist state successfully removed all the remaining barriers to industrial production and trade.

The Habsburg economy continued its steady growth in the second half of the nineteenth century. Despite the continued, yet narrowing, developmental gaps across regions, the entire Habsburg economy grew in this period at an annual rate of 1.5 percent (Austria 1.58 percent, Hungary 1.39 percent), which was the third highest annual growth rate in Europe in this period, after the rapidly growing smaller economies of Sweden (2 percent) and Denmark (1.6 percent).[438]

The last aspect of the economic growth in the Habsburg lands in the nineteenth century is the spread of economic growth toward the east. Even before the eighteenth century, there was a significant developmental gap between the western and eastern regions, which in turn reflected, as many historians noted, the broader developmental gradient in Europe.[439] The eighteenth-century reformers were very much aware of the economic backwardness of the eastern provinces. The resilience of pre-capitalist land tenure patterns and the dominance of Hungarian magnates posed higher barriers to change than anywhere else in the empire.

Some historians argue that Theresian mercantilism was based on a division of labor between the western and eastern Habsburg holdings, a kind of "inner-European colonial empire."[440] The western parts, Bohemia, Moravia, and Austria, housed the industrial base of the empire, while the eastern parts served as an agricultural hinterland. Barkey argues that the Theresian policies while promoting economic growth created two modes of development, "a more economic industrial model in the western lands" and "a more ideological revolutionary model in the eastern lands."[441]

---

438 For comparison, the annual growth rates of other European countries: Great Britain 0.9 percent, Belgium 1 percent, Germany 1.3 percent, France 1.1 percent, Norway 1.2 percent, Russia 1.3 percent, Italy 0.4 percent. Good, "Austria-Hungary," 228.

439 Alexander Gerschenkron, *Economic Backwardness in Historical Perspective, a Book of Essays* (New York: F. Praeger, 1965); Jászi, *The Dissolution of the Habsburg Monarchy*; Ivan Berend and Gyorgy Ranki, *East Central Europe in the 19th and 20th Centuries* (Budapest: Akademiai Kiado, 1977); Andrew Janos, "The Politics of Backwardness in Continental Europe, 1780-1945," *Comparative Politics* 41, no. 3 (1989).

440 Fichtner, *The Habsburg Monarchy, 1490-1848: Attributes of Empire*, 71.

441 Barkey, Escherik Joseph W., and Young Eric, "Changing Modalities of Empire: A Comparative Study of Ottoman and Habsburg Decline." The duality in the developmental trajectories facilitated the rise of Magyar nationalism in the nineteenth century, paving the way for the Dual Settlement of 1867.

Despite the historical gap between Hungary and the rest of the empire, evidence indicates that the sustained growth in the west throughout the nineteenth century significantly contributed to economic development in eastern lands. [442] Berend finds that the west-east division of labor ultimately proved desirable for both parties, at least in the nineteenth century: "The rising industry in the western provinces and the agricultural prosperity in the eastern parts of the monarchy were closely interrelated. The division of labor in the empire positively affected the parts of the monarchy."[443]

As the Bohemian and Austrian regions had the early lead in textile production, Hungarian manufacturers, which were integrated with their western counterparts within the Austro-Hungarian customs union, specialized in agricultural industries, food processing in particular.[444] Aside from food processing, mining and metallurgy were also growing.[445] Lastly, Hungarian entrepreneurs—including large landowners who had little choice but to switch to capitalistic production methods at this time—invested in machine building. An active machine-building industry in Hungary existed in the late 1880s.[446]

In short, the initial developmental gap between the two halves of the empire, a combined product of the historical west-east gradient in Europe and the mercantilist policies of the eighteenth century, never fully disappeared. However, the sustained economic growth of the western regions since the mid-eighteenth century ultimately affected the eastern regions, which highlights the far-reaching effects of the institutional reforms of the 1740-1790 period.

5. Conclusion

This chapter offered a causal narrative of the transformation of the Habsburg monarchy from a highly decentralized imperial state dependent on local intermediaries to a centralized fiscal state with much higher infrastructural capacity. More specifically, I demonstrated the following:

---

442 Good, *The Economic Rise of the Hapsburg Empire, 1750-1914*, ch.5.

443 Berend, *History Derailed: Central and Eastern Europe in the Long Nineteenth Century*, 148.

444 The leading foodstuffs sectors were flour milling and sugar-beet production.

445 Good, *The Economic Rise of the Hapsburg Empire, 1750-1914*, 140-7.

446 On the economic development of Hungary in the nineteenth century, see Laszlo Katus and E. Pamlenyi, "Economic Growth in Hungary During the Age of Dualism 1867-1913: A Quantitative Analysis," in *Social and Economic Researches on the History of East-Central Europe* (Budapest: Akademiai Kiado, 1970).

(1) A realignment took place in the structure of intra-elite conflict as early as 1660. The ruling elites, responding to the decay in the state's fiscal strength, broke their long-standing coalition with the rural elites, who had become a significant threat to the revenue-extracting capacity of the central elites. To balance the threat posed by the rising power of the nobility, the ruling elites formed a political coalition with the urban capital holders.
(2) The ruling elites in the eighteenth century, now allied with the urban capital holders, undertook a series of administrative and fiscal reforms. The reforms were aimed not only at dealing with the fiscal crisis by broadening the state's tax base but also at undermining the power of the landed nobility by redistributing their economic resources to capital holders. The outcome was a substantial increase in the infrastructural capacity of the state. Centralization of administrative and resource extraction mechanisms (previously dominated by the noble estates) and forming a legal-rational bureaucracy loyal to the crown provided the central elites with an enhanced fiscal capacity.
(3) The ruling elite then redeployed this newfound infrastructural and fiscal capacity to mobilize market forces and promote economic development. Through a series of reforms in agrarian relations, manufacturing, and trade, the ruling elites gradually removed the barriers to economic growth and promoted economic development by providing incentives and benefits to capital holders. As a result, Habsburg lands, initially the western provinces to be followed by Hungary later in the nineteenth century, industrialized, as evidenced by steady annual growth rates, development of competitive manufacturing sectors, expansion of the non-agricultural workforce, development of a railroads network, and establishment of a domestic banking sec tor.

Chapter 5 Intra-Elite Conflict in the Ottoman Empire, 1299-1600

The previous chapter argued that the Habsburg elites, responding to the seventeenth-century fiscal crisis, reconstructed the fiscal structures of the state through a series of bureaucratic and institutional reforms that centralized revenue extraction. The current chapter asks: why did the Ottoman elites, facing a similar set of incentives emanating from an equally devastating fiscal crisis in the seventeenth century, not follow the path that their Habsburg counterparts did and pursue a centralized fiscal state?

The question is even more puzzling when one considers the fact that the Ottoman rulers had a much more bureaucratized and centralized state apparatus to begin with. As discussed in Chapter 3, the Habsburg state had low infrastructural reach and consequently relied heavily on local intermediaries to govern the provinces. Yet, the reforms in the seventeenth and eighteenth centuries generated a higher infrastructural and fiscal capacity. In contrast, the Ottoman state started with a more centralized administrative structure and suffered fewer constraints on infrastructural power. However, the elites ultimately ended up with a much shorter infrastructural reach and reduced fiscal capacity. What explains this reversal of fortunes?

The answer to this puzzle lies in the different structures of intra-elite conflict (independent variable) in the two cases, particularly in the incentives that the elites in these two cases were facing at the post-crisis juncture. In the previous chapter, I demonstrated that the incorporation of urban capital holders (intervening variable) by the ruling elites into the political coalition was essential for the formation of a centralized fiscal state in the Habsburg case. More specifically, I showed that to balance the rising power of the landed nobility (the first causal mechanism), the central elites of the Habsburg Empire forged a coalition with the urban capital holders. To transfer economic resources from their rivals to their new allies (the second causal mechanism), the elites undertook a series of reforms, which ultimately centralized the process of revenue extraction (dependent variable).

I claim that in the Ottoman case, the structure of the intra-elite conflict, particularly the absence of a strong nobility to threaten the ruling elite, provided disincentives for the elite to incorporate the capital holders. I further argue that within the political and economic formation of the empire, the merchants constituted a major challenge to the resource extraction capacity of the ruling elites.

The exclusion of the capital holders at the post-crisis critical juncture, in turn, put the Ottoman elites on a different path ending with fiscal decentralization.

In this chapter, I explain the first part of the causal chain: the origins and dynamics of the intra-elite relations in the Ottoman Empire and the incentives provided by the structure for the exclusion of capital holders from the ruling coalition even at the time of crisis. The second part of the chain, i.e., the process of post-crisis elite realignment and the subsequent institutional reforms, is covered in Chapter 6.

The chapter is organized in three parts. In the first part, I discuss the expansion of the Ottoman state in Anatolia and the Balkans in the fourteenth and fifteenth centuries. I argue that the neutralization of the local elites in this period of empire formation produced a vertically integrated imperial structure where peripheral areas were connected to the imperial core through direct rule. I show that this mode of imperial organization was coupled with a unified elite structure in the Ottoman Empire.

In the second part, I take a closer look at the structure of the Ottoman elites. After analyzing the distinction between the elites (*askeriyye*) and non-elites (*reaya*), and the functional differentiation among the elites (*kalemiyye*, *seyfiyye*, *ulema*), I show that the elites were ultimately united in their shared interest in perpetuating their rule over the *reaya*. I discuss in detail why the merchants posed a threat to the monopoly of the central elites over the economic resources.

In the third and last section of this chapter, I discuss the seventeenth-century crisis and its effects on the Ottoman state. After briefly analyzing the sources of the crisis, I move on to show that the most important consequence was the aggravation of the conflict between the central elites and the urban capital holders, which paved the way for the further exclusion of the latter from the ruling political coalition.

1. The Origins of Intra-Elite Relations in the Ottoman Empire

1.1 Vertical Empire

The Ottoman state, like the Habsburg monarchy, was established at the turn of the fourteenth century. The greater region of Eastern Europe would be the primary area of imperial expansion for both states, the Great Alföld (Hungarian Plane) demarcating the boundary between the two. However, beyond these commonalities in timing and geography, the conditions of the formation of the Ottoman state differed significantly from those of the Habsburg state.

The founder of the Habsburg dynasty, Rudolph von Habsburg, and his successors faced formidable external adversaries in the territories that they managed to add to their empire, particularly in Bohemia, Moravia, Inner Austria, and Hungary. Given the very limited military and political means at the disposal of these early Habsburg rulers, they had little choice but to concede a great deal of economic and political autonomy to the local elites. This mode of expansion produced a horizontal imperial organization.

In contrast, the Ottoman state rose to ascendency in a power vacuum left by two declining powers in the region: Seljuk Sultanate in Anatolia and Byzantium in the Balkans. In addition, the historical patterns of land distribution in the Balkans and Anatolia heavily favored independent peasantry at the expense of landowning families. Thus, the early Ottoman rulers, who had presided over an effective military apparatus in the fourteenth and fifteenth centuries, were able to naturalize/co-opt local native elites in the conquered areas, who were much weaker to begin with in comparison to those in the Habsburg Empire. As a result, the provinces were linked to the imperial center through relatively unmediated channels, constituting a vertical mode of imperial formation.

The key significance of empire building is that it directly shaped the structure of intra-elite relations in the subsequent periods. In the horizontally organized Habsburg Empire, the ruling elite remained divided between central ruling elites and local nobility. The central and rural elites competed over the distribution of economic resources. In contrast, in the vertically integrated Ottoman Empire, the ruling elite was a unified elite marked by relatively lower levels of conflict among different branches. Unhindered by a strong local nobility, the ruling Ottoman elites in the center were able to keep the productive sectors of the society under tight control.

The Ottoman state originated from the *beylik* (principality) founded by Ertuğrul in Western Anatolia in the late thirteenth century. Ertuğrul's *beylik* was one of many nomadic Turkic principalities established in Asia Minor. The main function of these principalities was to defend the western border of the Seljuk Sultanate by providing a buffer zone between the Seljuks and the Byzantium. Ertuğrul's principality was located at the westernmost part of this zone and served as an outpost.[447]

---

447 For the early history of the Ottoman Empire, see Halil İnalcık, *The Ottoman Empire; the Classical Age, 1300-1600*, History of Civilisation (London: Weidenfeld & Nicolson, 1973), 5-17; Mehmet Fuat Köprülü, *The Origins of the Ottoman Empire*, Suny Series in the Social and Economic History of the Middle East (Albany, NY: State University

Traditional accounts of the early Ottoman history, most notably Paul Wittek's[448] and Fuat Köprülü's,[449] underlined the role of the holy war and the presence of *ghazis* (religious warlords) as the primary factor fueling the rapid expansion of the Ottoman principality in the early fourteenth century. Though Wittek's thesis was severely criticized,[450] the strategic positioning of the Ottoman principality in the westernmost regions of Asia Minor and the resulting "frontier culture" did play a key role in motivating and sustaining the expansionary policy of the early Ottoman rulers.[451]

Ottoman expansion was greatly facilitated by the decline of the Byzantine Empire, which after the thirteenth century was unable to defend its borders.[452] The most critical Ottoman territorial gains at the turn of the fourteenth century were the poorly defended Byzantine cities in Western Anatolia, starting as early as 1265 with the conquest of Söğüt by Ertuğrul. After Ertuğrul died in 1281, his son Osman became the ruler of the tribe. In a short period, Osman emerged as the leader of *ghazis* and in 1299 declared himself sultan, marking the official establishment of the House of Osman.

Osman I's soldiers waged a series of wars against Byzantine forces in Anatolia and Thrace. The victory against the Byzantine outside the historically important city of Nicaea (Iznik) allowed the Ottomans to settle in large numbers in the outer rims of the remnants of the Byzantine Empire. Osman I laid siege to Bursa but died before his son and successor Orhan (1326-1359) captured the city in 1326. Ottoman expansion in Western Anatolia in the fourteenth century continued with the conquest of Nicaea in 1331, Nicomedia in 1337, and Edirne (later the second capital city of the Ottoman state) in 1361.

---

of New York Press, 1991); Jason Goodwin, *Lords of the Horizons: A History of the Ottoman Empire* (London: Chatto & Windus, 1998).

448 Paul Wittek, *The Rise of the Ottoman Empire*, Royal Asiatic Society Monographs (London: The Royal Asiatic Society of Great Britain and Ireland, and sold by its agents Luzac and co., ltd., 1958).

449 Köprülü, *The Origins of the Ottoman Empire*.

450 Lowry, *The Nature of the Early Ottoman State*.

451 On the role of "frontier" in the rise of empires, see Peter Turchin, *War and Peace and War: The Life Cycles of Imperial Nations* (New York London: Pearson Education, 2005).

452 Halil İnalcık, "The Rise of the Ottoman Empire," in *A History of the Ottoman Empire to 1730*, ed. M. Cook (Cambridge, London, New York, Melbourne: Cambridge University Press, 1976); Doukas and Magoulias, *Decline and Fall of Byzantium to the Ottoman Turks*; John Julius Norwich, *Byzantium: The Decline and Fall* (New York: Knopf, 1996).

The conquest of the Byzantine strongholds provided the Ottoman rulers with a resource base to expand further. Not only did the Ottomans gain access to the riches of the acquired territories, but also the prospect of conquest helped lure large numbers of soldiers from other nomadic tribes to join Ottoman forces. Under Murad I (1359-1389), the Ottoman state grew in two separate directions. In Anatolia, Murad I fought wars against the remaining Turcoman principalities that were resisting Ottoman expansion. The opposition of the particularly strong dynasty of Karaman was put down in 1387. The remaining principalities (Aydın, Sarukhan, Menteşe, Hamid, Germiyan, and others) were neutralized by Bayezid I.[453]

While dealing with the resistance of the Anatolian principalities, the Ottoman rulers of the fourteenth century also managed to make further inroads by capturing territories in the Balkans through a series of wars against Bulgarian, Hungarian, and particularly Serbian forces. The most important gain was the Ottoman victory at the Battle of Kosovo, which reduced Serbia to a tribute-paying vassal state. By the beginning of the fifteenth century, the Ottoman state had consolidated its rule in Anatolia and expanded its territories into the Balkans, encircling the last remaining stronghold of the Byzantine Empire, Constantinople.

How did the Ottomans govern the territories they conquered in Anatolia and the Balkans? İnalcık argues that the Ottoman expansion strategy consisted of two systematically applied stages: the Ottomans first established a form of suzerainty over the target state by forcing them to recognize Ottoman supremacy and pay annual tributes. Then in the second stage, they sought "direct control over these countries by the elimination of the native dynasties."[454]

The two-staged Ottoman method of conquest thus contrasts with the strategy of expansion followed by the Habsburg rulers who expanded the boundaries of the state with a series of diplomatic and marriage alliances backed by the threat and occasional application of military force. The territorial gains in the fourteenth century (Carinthia, Carniola, Tyrol) and the major additions to the empire in the early sixteenth century (Bohemia and Moravia) were outcomes of this expansionary strategy. When the Habsburgs acquired sovereignty over the smaller states in Central and Eastern Europe, they faced a class of politically and economically well-entrenched native elites, a product of the post-Roman landholding patterns.

453 İnalcık, "The Rise of the Ottoman Empire," 24.
454 İnalcık, "Ottoman Methods of Conquest," 104.

In contrast, in the primary area of Ottoman expansion in Europe, the Balkans, states were controlled by a relatively weaker landed nobility[455] (with the exception of Romanian boyars[456]) whose political power was constrained by their limited hold over the independent peasantry. Similarly, Anatolia had been dominated by small peasant households since the times of the Roman Empire.[457] Like the Byzantine Empire, the Ottoman state essentially took over this particular social structure.

The Ottomans not only faced weaker local elites but also were more successful in eliminating/co-opting any local elements that could potentially impede the imposition of direct rule. The first, yet not the main, instrument at the disposal of the Ottoman rulers to neutralize the native elites was the large, well-trained, and highly motivated military machinery. At the core of the Ottoman military were the cavalrymen known as *sipahi.* These highly mobile units were located in and provisioned by the provinces through the *tımar* system.[458]

In the conquest of the Balkans, the superior Ottoman army played a key role in the neutralization of the local elements. For instance, it was a common practice for the Ottomans to place garrisons in several fortresses of strategic importance for the conquered city and then demolish all the remaining fortresses in the area, which in turn helped prevent the "reemergence of centers of resistance under local lords."[459] The soldiers stationed in these garrisons were not subordinate to the local governor or any local authority; they took their orders directly from the capital.[460] Once again, this particular military practice contrasts with

---

455 Berend and Ranki, *East Central Europe in the 19th and 20th Centuries*, 9-10.

456 Stokes, "Social Origins of East European Politics," 227-30.

457 Çağlar Keyder, "Small Peasant Ownership in Turkey: Historical Formation and Present Structure," *Review* VII, no. 1 (1983).

458 For an overview of the evolution of the Ottoman army, see Virginia Aksan, "Review Article: Ottoman Military Matters," *Journal of Economic Literature* 6, no. 1 (2002); Virginia Aksan and Eric Zürcher, "Ottoman Military Recruitment Strategies in the Late Eighteenth Century," in *Arming the State: Military Conscription in the Middle East and Central Asia, 1775-1925* (New York: I.B. Tauris, 1999); Stanford J. Shaw, "The Origins of Ottoman Military Reform: The Nizam-ı Cedid Army of Sultan Selim III," *The Journal of Modern History* 37, no. 3 (1965). For comparisons of Ottoman and Habsburg military powers see, Agoston, "Habsburgs and Ottomans: Defense, Military Change and Shifts in Power"; Fodor and David, *Ottomans, Hungarians, and Habsburgs in Central Europe: The Military Confines in the Era of Ottoman Conquest.*

459 İnalcık, "Ottoman Methods of Conquest," 107.

460 İnalcık, "The Rise of the Ottoman Empire," 47.

Habsburg methods of conquest. Lacking a standing army well into the seventeenth century, the Habsburg rulers had little choice but to leave the armies of the local nobility in place, whom they had to rely on during peacetime to maintain law and order in the provinces.

The Ottoman army possessed an extensive communication network for the transmission of directives from the imperial center to the provinces. Specialized units in the army, known as *ulaks*, *çavuşes,* and particularly well-trained Tatar regiments, traveling on "excellent imperial highways and caravan routes," rapidly carried the directives and decisions from the central administration to *sancaks* and garrisons.[461] By the reign of Mehmed II (1451-1481), the network linking the imperial center to the provinces had been perfected.

Even though the Ottoman army played a key role in the conquests and dispensing with the resistance of the remaining local elites, military force alone was not sufficient to rule. As discussed, "rule through army" is not a viable strategy in the long run, especially when the ruling state seeks continued territorial expansion, as the Ottoman state did well into the seventeenth century. Conquest through an army requires concentrating forces, whereas ruling such distant localities necessitates dispersing them.[462] While not impervious to the logistical constraints on infrastructural power, the Ottoman state was nevertheless able to maintain, from the fourteenth to the seventeenth century, a relatively centralized administrative apparatus, which allowed the central elites to rule the provinces without having to rely extensively on local intermediaries.

The key feature of the Ottoman central administration was that it allowed the ruling elites to integrate the remaining elements in the provinces into the central state apparatus as *tımariots* (*tımar*-holders), thereby keeping centrifugal tendencies under control. In the next section, I discuss the *tımar* system and other main tenets of the Ottoman central administration.

---

461 J. E. Mautz, "Transmission of Directives from Center to Periphery in the Ottoman State until the Seventeenth Century," in *Decision Making and Change in the Ottoman Empire*, ed. F. Farah Ceaser (Kirksville, Missouri: The Thomas Jefferson University Press, 1993).

462 Mann's discussion of infrastructural power and imperial rule draws on a large body of scholarship on the historical sociology of empires, most notably Eisenstadt, Kautsky, and, of course, Weber's discussion of the role of honoratories under patrimonial rule.

1.2 Central Administration

Ottoman provinces were organized into administrative units called *sancaks*. The boundaries of *sancaks* frequently mirrored those of the pre-Ottoman administrative units in that area,[463] which helped reduce transition costs. Ottoman *sancaks* were thus functionally similar to the *Kreise* (circuits) in the Habsburg Empire. However, unlike the circuits where representatives of the local nobility were responsible for maintaining law and order, collecting taxes, and organizing the military levy, the officials in *sancaks* were directly appointed by and accountable to the Ottoman sultan.

The sultan had two main representatives in each *sancak*: the *bey*, the military governor responsible for administration, and the *kadı,* who oversaw legal matters. The curious aspect of this dual arrangement was that the *kadı* was independent of the *bey* in his rulings, yet it was the *bey* that could execute the sentences. Similarly, the *bey* was not allowed to dispense any justice without the approval of *kadı,* who received his commands directly from the sultan.[464] The differentiation of administrative from legal matters and the division of labor between the *bey* and the *kadı* increased the central elites' capacity to monitor their agents' compliance.

As the empire grew, the administrative structure became more complicated. The territorial gains under Murad I and Bayezid I necessitated reforming the administrative structure based on individual *sancaks*, each directly tied to the sultan. After 1361, a new administrative unit of *beylerbeylik* was created. Each *beylerbeylik* had jurisdiction over several *sancaks* and served as an intermediary link between the *beys* in each *sancak* and the central government. When Bayezid I crossed into Rumeli (the territories west of Bosphorus), he created a separate *beylerbeylik* of Anatolia. The number of new *sancak*s and *beylerbeylik*s increased steadily throughout the fifteenth and sixteenth centuries.

Tımar was the primary vehicle of tax collection and military organization in the provinces of Anatolia and the Balkans.[465] At the core of the *tımar* system was the assignment of agricultural revenues to the troops stationed in the provinces. These soldiers, known as *tımarlı sipahis,* resided in villages and collected taxes directly from the peasantry, mostly paid in kind. *Sancakbeyi*, the military governor of the *sancak,* was the commander of *tımarlı sipahis.* He was responsible

463 İnalcık, "Ottoman Methods of Conquest," 108.

464 İnalcık, *The Ottoman Empire; the Classical Age, 1300-1600*, 104.

465 For a comprehensive account of the *tımar* system, Howard, *The Ottoman Tımar System and Its Transformation, 1563-1656.*

for maintaining public order and executing justice in addition to preparing and leading the soldiers to war. It is estimated that the total number of *tımarlı sipahis* mobilized at the time of war reached 80,000 in the early sixteenth century, which was about twice as large as the number of *kapıkulu* soldiers, who were paid directly by the palace.[466]

The assignment of tax revenues directly to troops was an established practice in Western Asia even before Ottoman rule. Military fiefs existed in the Byzantine Empire under the name of *pronoia*. When the Ottomans conquered the Balkans, they built upon the existing *pronoia* system and converted them to *tımars*.[467] For the Ottomans, *tımar* was ultimately more than a tax collection mechanism. As a "political-administrative institution" and a method of agricultural production based on small peasantry, *tımar* helped incorporate the peasant household into the imperial state and prevented the emergence of landowning nobility in the countryside.[468] The *tımar* system also allowed the central state elites to neutralize the local elites in the conquered territories by incorporating them into the state apparatus as *tımar*-holders.[469] The Ottoman record books indicate that many Ottoman *tımar*-holders in the fifteenth century were direct descendants of the pre-Ottoman local nobility.[470]

The process of incorporating the native elites into the Ottoman administrative machinery was facilitated by the two stages of Ottoman expansion. In most cases, the local nobles in the Balkans initially served as auxiliary forces in the Ottoman army during the vassalage of their countries. At this stage, the Ottoman administration essentially guaranteed that the positions of these nobles would not be infringed upon as long as they remained loyal to the sultan. In the second stage, the administration added the vassal territories to the empire, eliminating the most rebellious local elements. The remaining families in Bosnia, Serbia, Macedonia, Thessaly, and Albania usually retained the greater part of their patrimonies, but their existing land-holding rights were converted into *tımars*. The *tımar*-holders who adopted Islam could even become eligible to attain the highest administrative positions, including the post of *bey*.[471]

---

466 Pamuk, *Osmanlı-Türkiye Iktisadi Tarihi, 1500-1914*, 42.

467 İnalcık, *The Ottoman Empire; the Classical Age, 1300-1600*, 108-9.

468 Sunar and İslamoğlu-İnan, "State and Economy in the Ottoman Empire," 66; Pamuk, *Osmanlı-Türkiye Iktisadi Tarihi, 1500-1914*, 43-44.

469 Lowry, *The Nature of the Early Ottoman State*.

470 İnalcık, "Ottoman Methods of Conquest," 113.

471 Ibid., 114-15.

The Ottoman policy of strategically distributing *tımar*s to neutralize local elements with potentially centrifugal tendencies was not restricted to the Balkans. The same policy was applied to the Turkic principalities in Anatolia. After the conquest of Karaman, which had strongly resisted Ottoman rule in Anatolia, most of the remaining native Turkic nobility were given large *tımar*s and the title of *beys*. In most cases, the children of the pre-existing nobles were also granted the right to hold *tımar*s. Such positions, however, never attained an automatically hereditary status that would have provided the *tımar*-holders with an independent economic basis. İnalcık notes that "time worked in favor of the Ottomans" as "the new generations lost their local connections and were assimilated into the vast army of *tımariots*."[472]

The Ottoman administrative and fiscal policy, like that of the Habsburg state, was very much driven by and adaptable to the local conditions in conquered areas. The key difference in terms of the local conditions was the relative weakness of the local nobility in the Ottoman territories. The Ottomans' use of *tımar*s to incorporate local elites initially built upon and ultimately reinforced these local conditions.

Nevertheless, Ottoman rule was still subject to principal-agent problems that often trouble imperial states. Additional features of the Ottoman rule prevented the local intermediaries from escaping the hold of the central administration and transforming themselves into rural political elites with independent economic bases. The first feature was the state's "absolute control of the land, unimpeded by any private property rights."[473] Under the Ottoman regime, most agricultural land was *miri,* crown-land. The peasants who worked the land were of the status of "hereditary tenant," possessing only *usufruct* rights. In practice, the right to toil the land frequently passed from father to son but selling or transferring property was not possible except with the permission of the state. Similarly, the *tımar*-holding soldiers in the provinces did not possess the land but only the authority to collect revenue from the people in a clearly defined territory. The *tımar*, like individual peasant's land, was indivisible, unalterable, and untransferable.[474]

The only notable exception to state-owned agricultural lands was the *mülk* (literally, property) lands and *vakıfs* (religious organizations). Yet even such

---

472 Ibid., 120.

473 İnalcık, *The Ottoman Empire; the Classical Age, 1300-1600*, 109.

474 For the legal origins of the *miri* property and a documentary history of the Ottoman land regime, see Halil İnalcık, "Köy, Köylü Ve Imparatorluk," in *Osmanlı Imparatorluğu: Toplum ve Ekonomi*, ed. Halil İnalcık (Istanbul: Eren, 1996).

theoretically private properties were subject to strict state control and even confiscation, as exemplified by the transfer of ownership of more than 20,000 villages and farms to the state by order of Mehmed II in 1470.[475]

Another aspect of the Ottoman administration that prevented the *tımar* system from degenerating into a feudal land regime was the extended reach of the state bureaucracy. The *kul* system constituted the backbone of the Ottoman bureaucratic apparatus. The *kul*s (slaves) were recruited to the sultan's palace by means of *devşirme* (child levy). The practice of *devşirme* was based on Islamic law that held that one-fifth of all prisoners of war belonged to the ruler. As early as the fourteenth century, the Ottomans began to recruit male children from the Christian villages (every 3–7 years). These children, usually between the ages of 8 and 20, were then converted to Islam and trained in the palace.[476]

Two different career paths were open to the converted servants. Based on their performance in early education, they were either selected to be trained as soldiers, particularly *Janissaries* who served as the personal army of the sultan and were instrumental in imposing the central authority on the provinces or could continue to serve as public servants as high-ranking officials in the palace and the provinces. The *kul* system was first introduced under Murad I, but it was Mehmed II who developed it to the point that all the key positions in the administration (including military commanders, viziers, and grand viziers as well as taxation officers) came from the mechanism.[477]

Thus, like the *tımar* system, which facilitated the pacification of the nobles in the Balkans and Anatolia by incorporating them into the administration, the *kul* system helped neutralize the remaining members of nobility by turning them into members of the Ottoman elite. In fact, in the fifteenth century, the great majority of the grand viziers (the second highest position in the state) came from noble Christian origins.

The presence of a group of well-trained officials who were irrevocably severed from any preexisting social loyalties allowed the ruling elites to ensure that the *tımar*-holders in the provinces would not systematically exploit their authority.

475 İnalcık, *The Ottoman Empire; the Classical Age, 1300-1600*, 109. For other types of private and semi-private property in the Ottoman state, see Pamuk, *Osmanlı-Türkiye Iktisadi Tarihi, 1500-1914*, 49-52.

476 For the definitions and brief histories of the kul and devşirme systems, see Selçuk Akşin Somel, *Historical Dictionary of the Ottoman Empire*, Ancient Civilizations and Historical Eras (Lanham, MD: Scarecrow Press, 2003), 159.

477 İnalcık, "The Rise of the Ottoman Empire," 47.

Indeed, the entire process of tax collection by *tımar*-holders was conducted under the direct supervision of the central bureaucracy.

The *tımar* regime necessitated careful bookkeeping. State-appointed bureaucrats recorded the distribution of population as well as the sources of revenue in each province in official registers (*tahrir defterleri*). Immediately following the conquest of a region, a government official (*il yazıcısı*) was sent to that region to compile these registers, which were then updated at regular intervals. The commissioner recorded every family in every village and the amount of land that the household owned. Based on the distribution of land, the *il yazıcısı* would then determine the expected revenue from each village, on which the direct taxes would be based. A certain portion of the total revenue from each village would be cast aside for state treasury (i.e., for the viziers, *beys*, and, of course, the sultan). The remainder would then be distributed among the *tımar*-holding cavalrymen.

The registers of *cizye* (capitation paid only by non-Muslims) and *avarız* (an emergency tax) were to be drawn up separately by the kadıs and submitted to the sultan.[478] *Il yazıcısı* would later prepare a second register summarizing the distribution of various taxes and detailing the rates and conditions according to which the *sipahis* of the *sancak* would collect them. The monitoring and enforcement of such conditions would be solely in the hands of the *bey* and *kadıs* of the *sancak*. For purposes of accountability and possible dispute resolution, copies of the tax registers would be sent to the central government and the *beylerbeylik*.

In short, the administration of the *tımar*-lands was entirely in the hands of the government-appointed officials. The central government used its considerable administrative capacity to protect the independent peasantry and prevent the emergence of feudal lords. The *corvée* system was historically not as widespread in the Balkans and Anatolia as it was in Central Europe. Nevertheless, the Ottomans made sure to dismantle any pre-existing obligations involving forced labor and replace them with various fixed taxes of the *tımar* system.

2. The Changes in the Structure of Intra-Elite Relations

2.1 Unified Elites

I defined elites as those sections of society that were organizationally capable of appropriating surplus from non-elites.[479] The Ottoman social structure was

478 İnalcık, "Ottoman Methods of Conquest," 111.

479 This definition is based on Lachmann, *Capitalists in Spite of Themselves: Elite Conflict and Economic Transitions in Early Modern Europe*.

marked by a clear-cut distinction between the elites and non-elites. The ruling group, *askeriyye*, was headed formally by the sultan and included not only the members of the army but also all high-ranking state officials. Members of *askeriyye* were not involved in the production and did not pay taxes.[480] The productive and tax-paying sectors of Ottoman society, i.e., the peasants, artisans, and merchants, constituted the non-elites and were called *reaya*.

In this section, I show that during the classical era of Ottoman history (1300-1600), the members of Ottoman *askeriyye* acted as an essentially *unified* elite in extracting agricultural surplus from the productive sectors of the society. While the Ottoman elite was unified in this period, there was still conflict over the distribution of economic resources. The main axis of this conflict was between the elites and merchants. I show in this section that the main source of threat to the power of *askeriyye* was the commercial sectors of *reaya*. The commercial sectors, the manufacturers, and merchants, who had the potential to divert resources away from the imperial center, were considered a hazard to the capacity of the ruling elites.

At the top of the Ottoman society's ruling elites was the sultan's office and his close circle, including the viziers and the grand vizier. Beneath the top elite, the *askeriyye* branched into three subcategories: *kalemiyye* (bureaucracy), *seyfiyye* (military), and *ulema* (religious/legal officials). The majority of personnel in the bureaucracy and military came from within the *kul* order. Often misconstrued as a system of slavery, the *kul* system functioned as a cost-efficient recruitment method and even a quintessentially meritocratic system of bureaucratic advancement for Christian converts. Thus, the crucial aspect of the Ottoman regime was that the bureaucratic and military apparatus were staffed by persons with undivided allegiance to the ruler. Indeed, within the three-partied differentiation of the *askeriyye*, the high-ranking bureaucrats were considered, politically and legally, members of the ruling elite.

While the *kalemiyye* and *seyfiyye* branches of central government allowed the central administration to project its coercive and infrastructural power into the provinces, the third branch of *askeriyye*, *ulema*, added an ideological dimension to the vertical integration between the imperial core and periphery. The religious and legal officials of the Ottoman state (from the *Şeyhülislam*, the highest religious authority, to the local *kadıs* and *imams*) had a monopoly on religious/legal matters, which they used to legitimize the very division between the elites

480 Halil İnalcık, "Capital Formation in the Ottoman Empire," *Journal of Economic History* 29, no. 1 (1969).

and non-elites. The *ulema* acted as "an intermediary between the state and the society," preventing the emergence of "alternatively organized ideological power networks"[481] that could challenge the elites.

It is well established in Ottoman historiography that "the *askeriyye* were not an aristocratic class with historically established rights."[482] The nominal ownership of all lands within the Ottoman realm by the sultan and the *tımar*-system based on independent peasantry practically rendered the formation of a social group with inherited rights and privileges impossible. While the *askeriyye* was a privileged group that exercised authority over the society, their authority was directly derived from and contingent upon the sultan's delegation. Unlike the provincial elites in the Habsburg Empire, the Ottoman elites under the traditional regime did not possess an independent economic basis, which they could rely upon to project political and military power.

However, an idealized image of the Ottoman regime where the "sultan was the state itself" is incomplete and misleading. While the Ottoman monarchs possessed a greater degree of autonomy when compared to their Western European counterparts, their power was subject to, both in legality and in practice, a myriad of restraints. By the practice known as *meşveret*, the sultan was expected to consult with leading members of the central government. The council of the *divan*, akin to the Privy Council in the Western European monarchies, was the primary venue for such institutionalized consultation. İnalcık notes that the "success of a sultan depended on the ways in which he used his authority to maintain balance and harmony between the bearers of delegated power."[483] This system was "designed to prevent any members of the government from acquiring complete control."[484]

Ottoman history is full of instances where one section of the ruling elite, such as a grand vizier or the *janissary* corps, grew disproportionately strong and sought to dethrone the sultan. Yet, in the last instance, these were "characteristically patrimonial conflicts that tended to upset political authority…rather than revolutions intended to transform the overall structure of society."[485] In

481 Tim Jacoby, *Social Power and the Turkish State* (London; Portland, OR: Frank Cass, 2004), 32.

482 İnalcık, "Ottoman Methods of Conquest," 112.

483 Halil İnalcık, "Decision Making in the Ottoman State," in *Decision Making and Change in the Ottoman Empire*, ed. Halil İnalcık and Ceaser E. Farah (The Thomas Jefferson University Press, 1993), 11.

484 Ibid., 12.

485 Sunar and İslamoğlu-İnan, "State and Economy in the Ottoman Empire," 64.

the Ottoman social formation, only the members of the *askeriyye* had a claim on surplus. The principal division within the *askeriyye* was essentially a *functional* differentiation corresponding to the functions each branch served in the extraction of resources embodied in the *tımar* system.[486]

The unity of the ruling elites reached a climax around the mid-fifteenth century when Sultan Mehmed II centralized the Ottoman administration through a series of reforms. Abou-el-Haj argues that throughout the fifteenth and sixteenth centuries, "the Ottoman ruling class was unified enough and mustered sufficient coercive power to assert its will and discourage local resistance" and set up "institutional structures …to facilitate a regulated and legitimized exploitation of material and human resources."[487]

The common thread that unified the elite of the Ottoman Empire was their interest in controlling the production, distribution, and consumption of commodities, thereby preventing the emergence of political actors that could threaten the elite's capacity to extract surplus. The peasantry, organized into small and independent households in Anatolia and the Balkans, was the easiest to control among the productive sectors. The state ownership of all *miri* lands and agricultural production based on the institution of *tımar* provided a direct economic and political linkage between the peasantry and the imperial center. The urban productive sectors, in contrast, posed a greater challenge to the ruling elites.

2.2 Central Elite and Urban Capital Holders

Anatolia was a major trade center well before its conquest by the Ottomans. Anatolia became the highway of intra-regional trade between Europe and Asia with the establishment of Mongol rule in the thirteenth century. Caravans carrying commodities from the east (raw material for manufacture and luxury goods like silk, spices, etc.) met with the European merchants, most notably Italian maritime states, in the port cities along southern and northern Anatolia.[488] These ports were linked to Constantinople through land and sea. In addition to the prominent east-west trade, there was a secondary north-south trade route in

486 Huri İslamoğlu-İnan and Çağlar Keyder, "Agenda for Ottoman History," in *The Ottoman Empire and the World Economy* (CUP, 1987).

487 Abu-el-Haj, *Formation of the Modern State: The Ottoman Empire, Sixteenth to Eighteenth Centuries*, 12-13.

488 Mehmet Bulut, "The Role of the Ottomans and Dutch in the Commercial Integration between the Levant and the Atlantic in the Seventeenth Century," *Journal of Economic and Social History of the Orient* 45, no. 9 (2002).

the thirteenth century that ran between Eastern Europe (the Khanate of Golden Horde and other regions along the coast of the Black Sea) and Arab lands.[489]

The Ottomans gained control of the historical trade routes in Anatolia and the Balkans by conquering major cities in the fourteenth and fifteenth centuries. Following its capture in 1326, Bursa became not only the political center of the Ottoman Empire but also the "most important trading city and an entrepot for the east-west trade."[490] Antalya and Alanya on the Mediterranean coast were captured by Sultan Bayezid in 1399. They were the main ports of entry to Anatolia for goods imported from the Arabian Peninsula and India. With the conquest of the remaining Turkic principalities in Central and Western Anatolia, the Ottomans secured control over the overland trade routes in Anatolia and, indirectly, the sea routes over the Mediterranean.[491]

Ottoman conquests in the Balkans brought about the integration of the major trade centers in the region, including Belgrade, Plovdiv, Sofia, Skopje, Monastir, and Salonica. Balkan towns were connected to the major commercial centers of Anatolia, Edirne, Bursa, and Istanbul via three important highways: the historical *Via Egnatia* road through Albania, Monastir, and Salonica; the military road through Belgrade, Sofia, and Plovdiv; and the road stretching from lower Danube region to Edirne.[492]

Ottoman governments followed a policy geared toward the rapid development of trade centers in the Balkans and Anatolia.[493] The local governments, under the direction of the central administration, built *caravanserais* and *bedestans* (covered marketplaces) in all big cities. Historical roads were kept in good repair and were supplemented with additional tracks. The government even encouraged local villages to build and maintain new roads by providing them with tax exemptions and other incentives. In addition, the state took measures to maintain the security of merchants by posting special guardians (*derbendci*) in key locations such as mountain passes, fords, and bridges.

489 For Anatolian trade routes before Ottoman conquest, see İnalcık, *The Ottoman Empire; the Classical Age, 1300-1600*, ch.14, Albert Howe Lybyer, *The Influence of the Rise of the Ottoman Turks upon the Routes of Oriental Trade* (Washington: 1916).

490 İnalcık, *The Ottoman Empire; the Classical Age, 1300-1600*, 121.

491 Ibid., 122-23.

492 Ibid., 146.

493 Genç, "The Principle of Ottoman's Economical World View."

The protective policies of the government contributed to the growth of intra-empire trade throughout the fifteenth and sixteenth centuries.[494] The growth of intra-regional trade and the expansion of towns were mutually reinforcing processes: trade spurred the growth in major towns throughout the empire; the demand for agricultural goods in these towns, in turn, increased the volume of traded goods.

The capital, Istanbul, led the trend of urban growth throughout the empire. After the conquest in 1453, which partially destroyed the infrastructure of the city as well as its populace despite Sultan Mehmed II's explicit orders,[495] Istanbul was reconstructed and repopulated in the latter half of the fifteenth century. Largely because of the Ottoman administration's population policies, the total number of inhabitants, around 80,000 in 1475, climbed to 400,000 in the first half of the sixteenth century—then doubled to 800,000 by the end of the century.[496] Istanbul became the largest urban center of the eastern Mediterranean and possibly of Europe by the seventeenth century.[497]

The growing population of major cities in Anatolia and the Balkans meant a great deal of demand for a wide range of commodities that could not be supplied locally: grain, rice, salt, meat, oil, fish, and luxury goods for the consumption of the public as well as the palace and the army. The raw materials used by artisans in urban guilds had to be imported. Istanbul was dependent on imports from various regions. While some of the grain and other agricultural commodities consumed in Istanbul were supplied from Balkan and Aegean port cities,[498] international trade continued to provide most luxury goods and other food and raw materials. "If the trade slowed down or stopped, the results for the city would be disastrous."[499]

Supplying grain and other crucial commodities to the cities was also important to the bureaucratic elite for additional reasons. In the Ottoman Empire, as in

---

494 Mehmet Genç, "15. Ve 16. Yüzyıllarda Osmanlı Ekonomisinde İç ve Dış Ticaret," in *Osmanlı İmparatorluğunda Devlet Ve Ekonomi*, ed. Mehmet Genç (İstanbul: Ötüken, 2003).

495 Crowley, *1453: The Holy War for Constantinople and the Clash of Islam and the West.*

496 İnalcık, *The Ottoman Empire; the Classical Age, 1300-1600*, 144.

497 Quataert, *Manufacturing in the Ottoman Empire and Turkey, 1500-1950*, 52-3.

498 Pamuk, *Osmanlı-Türkiye Iktisadi Tarihi, 1500-1914*, 37-8; Tevfik Güran, "The State Role in the Grain Supply of Istanbul: The Grain Administration, 1793-1839," *International Journal of Turkish Studies* (1984); Eyup Özveren, "Black Sea & the Grain Provisioning of Istanbul: Imperial Legacies in Retrospect," (2002).

499 İnalcık, "Capital Formation in the Ottoman Empire," 103.

European societies of the period, the ability to purchase luxury goods was a critical part of the lifestyle of elites and, ultimately, a marker of social status that separated them from non-elites.[500] The growing urban demand for agricultural and luxury goods closely shaped the government's economic policy of "providing cheap, good, and abundant supply of goods to the state and its urban populations."[501] The principle of *provisionism* (*iaşe*) was the main tenet of the Ottoman elites' economic view.[502] The need to maintain a constant flow of foodstuffs, raw materials, and luxury goods pushed the ruling elites of the empire to strictly regulate "everything from the distant producer to the retailer in Istanbul"[503] to ensure "the flow of raw and finished materials."[504]

In the countryside, the central elites of the empire closely supervised agricultural production by the independent peasantry. The *tımar* system allowed the elites to extract the portion of the agricultural surplus required to maintain the army. The remaining agricultural produce was then allocated for domestic consumption. The export of agricultural commodities was curtailed by prohibitions, quotas, and taxes until the demand of the domestic market was met.[505] In contrast, imports were encouraged and facilitated. As a result, exports remained "a marginal sector that the state taxed and, most of the time, actively hindered."[506] Seen in this light, provisionism was the mirror image of mercantilism in terms of the relative importance of imports and exports.[507]

The artisanal guilds were the main instrument in the hands of the Ottoman elites to control the production and distribution of goods. State-supported guilds

---

500 Max Weber, *The Theory of Social and Economic Organization* (New York: Free Press, 1997).

501 Quataert, *Manufacturing in the Ottoman Empire and Turkey, 1500-1950*, 6.

502 Genç, "The Principle of Ottoman's Economical World View"; Mehmet Genç and Donald Quataert, "Ottoman Industry in the Eighteenth Century: General Framework, Characteristics and Main Trends," in *Manufacturing in the Ottoman Empire and Turkey (1500-1950)* (New York: State University of New York Press, 1994); Pamuk, "The Evolution of Fiscal Institutions in the Ottoman Empire, 1500-1914."

503 İnalcık, *The Ottoman Empire; the Classical Age, 1300-1600*, 145.

504 Quataert, *Manufacturing in the Ottoman Empire and Turkey, 1500-1950*, 6.

505 Mehmet Genç, "Osmanlı Iktisadi Dünya Görüşünün İlkeleri," in *Osmanlı İmparatorluğunda Devlet Ve Ekonomi*, ed. Mehmet Genç (İstanbul: Otuken, 2003), 47.

506 Genç and Quataert, "Ottoman Industry in the Eighteenth Century: General Framework, Characteristics and Main Trends," 60.

507 Şevket Pamuk, "Osmanlı Ekonomisinde Devlet Müdahaleciliğine Yeniden Bakış," in *Osmanlı Ekonomisi ve Kurumları* (İstanbul: Türkiye Is Bankası Kültür Yayınları, 2007).

held monopolies in the big cities throughout the empire (Istanbul, Bursa, Salonica, Aleppo) and smaller towns. Like many other imperial institutions, the Ottoman state inherited the overall structure of the guild system from the states that had reigned in Anatolia before the thirteenth century, the Byzantine and Seljuk Empires specifically, and adapted them to their own needs. İnalcık argues that before the Ottoman Empire, the "guilds were much freer and much stronger."[508] With the centralization of administration in the fifteenth century, the Ottoman ruling elites tightened their control over the guilds and used them to effectively control prices and collect taxes from urban manufacturers.

Guilds controlled every aspect of production and exchange in cities. Raw materials were transported by merchants, entered the city through particular gates, and were carried through certain streets to predetermined markets or caravanserais, where they were sold under the close supervision of guild officials. Valuable goods—particularly susceptible to contraband—had to be sold through brokers under direct government control. Guild representatives weighed the goods to assess taxes. Only then were the goods distributed to guild masters who oversaw manufacturing. Guild masters were subject to property taxes for each shop and sales taxes for the goods sold in the marketplace. Tax rates were determined by the central administration for each province. Only state-authorized merchants could buy goods in the marketplaces, and the delivery of the purchased goods to consumers was also strictly controlled to prevent smuggling.[509]

Merchants[510] played a vital role in the guild-based manufacturing system and the Ottoman economy in general. However, the government's attitude toward the merchants was "profoundly ambiguous."[511] On the one hand, intra-regional trade was indispensable for supplying consumer goods to urban populations and raw materials to artisan guilds. Merchants, Muslim and non-Muslim alike,[512] were strongly encouraged to import commodities. Neither in Islamic law nor the Ottoman *kanun*s were any specific limitations on the accumulation of capital by merchants. However, merchants were only supported as long as their activities

508 İnalcık, *The Ottoman Empire; the Classical Age, 1300-1600*, 155.

509 Ibid., 144-55.

510 İnalcık defines merchants (tüccar) as "big businessman who engaged in international and intra-regional trade or in the sale of goods imported from afar." İnalcık, "Capital Formation in the Ottoman Empire," 98.

511 Pamuk, "The Evolution of Fiscal Institutions in the Ottoman Empire, 1500-1914," 12.

512 İnalcık, *The Ottoman Empire; the Classical Age, 1300-1600*, 151.

"facilitated the reproduction of the social order at the top of which the central bureaucracy was placed."[513]

The strict control over the division of labor among various economic sectors was the key to reproducing the Ottoman political order. As rational actors responding to market incentives, merchants were bound to expand the scope of their activity "into areas formerly closed to production."[514] The elites were concerned that the merchants could transform into "a new and powerful social actor" that could potentially undermine "not only the existing economic system but the very socio-political order and hierarchy."[515] The contradiction between the economic rationality of merchant capital and the political rationality of the Ottoman social formation pushed the ruling elites to make every effort to "limit the degree of functioning of merchant capital" and to ensure it remained "within politically desirable bounds."[516] Consequently, the central administration's economic policies were geared toward the control of merchants, not their protection.[517]

The bureaucratic elite was very apprehensive of any manufacturing activity outside strict guild regulations. Genç notes that the restrictive state policies particularly targeted "the activities that likely were to supply the long-distance trade, i.e., those with proto-industrial potential." He adds that the "state not only acted policies that worked against the development of manufacturing, but it also created certain obstacles for capital accumulation that might have prepared the grounds for these developments."[518]

Various mechanisms were in place to control merchants and prevent the diversion of commodities to export markets and other sorts of profiteering. For instance, the central administration often imposed caps on profits. The state determined the legitimate profit in all industrial and commercial transactions between 5 and 15 percent. Higher profits were subject to severe punishment, and the average rate of profit remained below 10 percent.[519] The interaction between profit caps and interest rates provided disincentives for investment.

---

513 Pamuk, "Osmanlı Ekonomisinde Devlet Mudaheleciligine Yeniden Bakis," 21.

514 İslamoğlu-İnan and Keyder, "Agenda for Ottoman History."

515 Genç, "Osmanlı Iktisadi Dünya Görüşünün Ilkeleri," 51.

516 İslamoğlu-İnan and Keyder, "Agenda for Ottoman History," 55.

517 Pamuk, "The Evolution of Fiscal Institutions in the Ottoman Empire, 1500-1914."

518 Genç and Quataert, "Ottoman Industry in the Eighteenth Century: General Framework, Characteristics and Main Trends," 66.

519 Genç, "Osmanlı Iktisadi Dünya Görüşünün Ilkeleri."

Although problematic in Islamic law, interest was common in the Ottoman Empire. Interest rates were almost always well above the legitimate rates of profit, usually between 15 and 25 percent. The difference between the maximum profit that can be attained through investment in manufacturing and trade and the interest that can be earned on capital limited the credit flow into industry and commerce and provided strong disincentives for the holders of urban capital to expand their economic activity into these realms.[520]

Once again, there is a sharp contrast between the Habsburg and the Ottoman states in terms of the position of the urban capital holders and the central elite's perception of this social class. In the Habsburg case, where the main axis of conflict was between the central and rural elites, towns and merchants were of lesser significance until the seventeenth century. Habsburg rulers intervened in the affairs of towns only to the extent that it was demanded by the landed nobility, who had a stake in keeping the towns under a tight leash. The importance of urban capital holders as political actors rose significantly after 1660 when the conflict between the central and rural elites escalated. As a result, the ruling elites of the Habsburg state began to adopt capital-friendly policies, which limited imports, encouraged exports, and supported urban capital holders vis-à-vis landed nobility.

Before moving into the seventeenth-century economic crisis, which heightened the sensibilities of the Ottoman elites and exacerbated the conflict they had with the urban capital holders, two brief points regarding the non-existence of mercantilist policies in the Ottoman Empire should be noted.

First, the problem of supplying goods and services to urban centers was by no means peculiar to the Ottoman Empire. Rulers of the agrarian states of early modern Europe faced similar difficulties with supplying major cities.[521] Nonetheless, the provisioning of cities played a much more critical role in the Ottoman Empire. Any disruption in the flow of goods into Istanbul could produce irrevocable consequences for the central bureaucracy and the sultan. As a result, the provisionist policies remained in force through the mid-nineteenth century.

---

520 Genç and Quataert, "Ottoman Industry in the Eighteenth Century: General Framework, Characteristics and Main Trends," 64.

521 Steven Laurence Kaplan, *Provisioning Paris: Merchants and Millers in the Grain and Flour Trade During the Eighteenth Century* (Ithaca, New York: Cornell University Press, 1984).

As Genç notes, "among the contemporaries of the Ottoman Empire there is no other state where provisionist policies were so long-lasting and ubiquitous."[522]

Second, there are solid reasons suggesting that the predatory policies of the Ottoman elites were *not* grounded in ideational factors. To begin with, Islamic law was not particularly restrictive of trade. Interestingly, when compared to the practices of the contemporaneous Islamic states, the Ottomans intervened much more frequently in the economy. Neither were the Ottoman elites unaware of the mercantilist ideas that swayed European states, including the Habsburg Empire, at this time. Early eighteenth-century Ottoman historian and thinker Naima, for instance, publicized a set of ideas, which were inspired by European mercantilist thinking: the necessity to limit imports and support domestic producers.[523] However, such mercantilist ideas were not adopted by the Ottoman elites precisely because the elites were concerned that supporting manufacturers and merchants beyond what was needed for the provision of the urban centers would undermine the elite's monopoly.

2.3 Effects of the Seventeenth-Century Crisis on the Elite Conflict

The long seventeenth century was a period of economic decline and political turmoil for large agrarian monarchies. The Ottoman Empire, like the Habsburg Empire, was caught in the fallout caused by the general crisis of the seventeenth century. The total expenditure for the first time exceeded state revenue in the late sixteenth century, and the budget deficit continued to rise throughout the seventeenth century.[524] The fiscal problems of the Ottoman state in the seventeenth and eighteenth centuries had two sources: the cyclical changes of the emerging world-economy and the increasing financial burden of geopolitical competition and warfare. Let me start with the former.

The Ottoman state from its foundation in the fourteenth century sought to establish control over international trade routes. By the sixteenth century, the

522 Mehmet Genç, "Osmanlı Iktisadi Dünya Görüşünün Klasik Prensipleri Ve Temel Değerleri," in *Osmanlı İmparatorluğunda Devlet Ve Ekonomi*, ed. Mehmet Genç (İstanbul: Ötuken, 2003), 81.

523 Pamuk, "The Evolution of Fiscal Institutions in the Ottoman Empire, 1500-1914"; Naima, "Tarih-i Naima."

524 Barkan, "The Price Revolution in the Sixteenth Century"; Barkan and Cook, "Research on the Ottoman Fiscal Surveys"; Agoston, David, and Fodor, "The Costs of the Ottoman Fortress-System in Hungary in the Sixteenth and Seventeenth Centuries."

Ottomans had practically monopolized eastern silk and spice trades. Anatolian towns had become key entrepôts and transit points of the east-west trade. The discovery of the trade route around the Cape, and the following shift of the major trade routes from overland to sea routes, adversely affected the revenues of the Ottoman state.[525] Contrary to common conception, the shift in trade routes was slow and gradual. Its negative effects on the Ottoman state were quite delayed as well, partly due to the deliberate efforts of the Ottomans to resist the Portuguese, and later British and Dutch expansion in the Indian Ocean. Moreover, the overland caravan trade continued to function largely unaffected at least for another century after the discovery of sea routes.[526]

The negative effects of the discovery of trade routes were delayed but, for the most part, irreversible. Among the most fundamental consequences was the interruption of cash flow into the treasury. With the marginalization of overland trade routes, the Ottomans incurred significant losses from customs dues, which were one of the main sources of direct revenue in addition to the direct taxes on agricultural production.[527] The contraction of the transit trade indirectly affected native manufacturing sectors articulated into the intra-regional commodity flows. Cities like Bursa (a major silk-processing center) and Aleppo, which had emerged as centers of manufacturing and trade in the previous century, declined.[528]

Even more critical in the long run for the Ottoman economy than the decline of the overland transit trade was the expansion of the Western European economy. Before the latter half of the sixteenth century, imports from Europe to the Ottoman Empire were limited to luxury and specialty items. These imports did not constitute a threat to the local Ottoman industry; they were encouraged by the state as they generated customs revenue and met urban demand. Ottoman exports to Europe were limited due to the provisionist policies.

This favorable picture, however, changed dramatically in the latter half of the sixteenth century. With the expansion of the European economy, European

525 Halil İnalcık and Donald Quataert, *An Economic and Social History of the Ottoman Empire, 1300-1914* (New York, NY: Cambridge University Press, 1994); İnalcık, "Impact of the Annales School on Ottoman Studies and New Findings"; İslamoğlu-İnan and Keyder, "Agenda for Ottoman History."

526 Lane, "The Mediterranean Spice Trade"; Pach, "The Shifting of International Trade Routes in the 15th-17th Centuries."

527 İslamoğlu-İnan and Keyder, "Agenda for Ottoman History," 51.

528 Murat Çizakça, "Price History and the Bursa Silk Industry: A Study in Ottoman Industrial Decline, 1550-1650," *The Journal of Economic History* 40, no. 3 (1980).

imports began to threaten Ottoman domestic production. European manufacturers and merchants sought to sell greater quantities of goods in the Ottoman Empire. European states with their newly adopted mercantilist policies also limited the imports from the Ottoman Empire of raw materials and foodstuffs (which were higher in demand, as I discuss below) while sealing off their domestic markets to finished goods.[529]

Another development that negatively affected the Ottoman economy was the injection of large amounts of American silver and gold into the European economy. The increase in money supply led to, among other things, inflation of the prices of basic commodities.[530] Price movements in the European economy were mirrored closely in the Ottoman Empire as in other parts of the emerging world economy. Pamuk calculates that consumer prices in Istanbul increased six-fold from the late fifteenth until the end of the seventeenth century.[531]

Barkan documents the increase in the prices of foodstuffs based on a longitudinal analysis of the *imaret* records and *narh* registries. According to his calculations, the composite index of foodstuffs rose steadily throughout the latter half of the sixteenth century, reaching its climax in the early seventeenth century. After a short period of decline in the early seventeenth century, prices continued to rise into the latter half of the seventeenth century.[532] The price inflation put considerable strain on the Ottoman treasury and forced the ruling elite to take some immediate measures. Among these measures was the debasement of the Ottoman currency, *akçe*. Throughout the seventeenth century, the Ottoman treasury constantly had to decrease the silver content of currency.[533]

While such debasement temporarily relieved the pressure on credit, it caused political as well as economic problems. Most notably, *janissary* troops, who were

529 Klima, "Mercantilism in the Habsburg Monarchy- with Special Reference to the Bohemian Lands."

530 F. P. Braudel and F. Spooner, "Prices in Europe from 1450 to 1750," in *The Cambridge Economic History of Europe, Vol IV.*

531 Şevket Pamuk, "Fiyat Devrimi'nin Osmanlı İmparatorluğundaki Yansımalarına Yeniden Bakış," in *Osmanlı Ekonomisi ve Kurumları*, ed. Şevket Pamuk (İstanbul: Türkiye Is Bankası Kültür Yayınları, 2007).

532 Barkan, "The Price Revolution in the Sixteenth Century."

533 Ibid.; Şevket Pamuk, "The Price Revolution in the Ottoman Empire Reconsidered," *International Journal of Middle East Studies* 33 (2001). Also, Pamuk, "A Monetary History of the Ottoman Empire," in *Cambridge Studies in Islamic Civilization* (New York: Cambridge University Press, 2000); Pamuk, "Prices in the Ottoman Empire, 1469-1914," *International Journal of Middle East Studies* 36 (2004).

stationed in Istanbul and paid directly from the treasury, revolted on several occasions in objection to being paid by debased currency. Other measures to counter the fiscal problems included changes in the taxation scheme. The *avarız* tax (an irregular tax used only for special cases of military emergency) became an annual levy and was progressively made heavier. Similarly, the capitation tax that the Christian subjects were subject to was increased severalfold starting in the latter half of the sixteenth century.[534]

The costs of geopolitical competition and warfare in the seventeenth century further exacerbated the pressure caused by external economic factors. Throughout the seventeenth century, Ottoman Empire was engaged in prolonged military conflicts on three major fronts: the wars with the Safavid Empire in the East, the rivalry with the European maritime powers in the Mediterranean, and the enduring conflict with the Habsburg Empire in Eastern Europe. I previously discussed the costs of Ottoman-Habsburg rivalry for the Habsburgs. The conflict was equally, if not more, costly for the Ottomans, who were usually the attacking party and thus incurred higher costs during wartime.

After the conquest of Constantinople in 1453, the subsequent conquest of Serbia in 1459, and southern parts of Bosnia in 1464, Ottomans turned their attention to Hungary. Throughout the second half of the fifteenth century, the well-organized Hungarian defense along the border resisted Ottoman expansion. However, with the introduction of new weaponry, the Ottoman Empire gained a definite advantage vis-à-vis the Hungarian defense.[535] After a series of territorial gains in the early sixteenth century, Ottomans won a decisive victory over the Hungarians in 1526 at the Battle of Mohacs, which brought northern and western Hungary under Ottoman rule.

The Habsburgs, as the heir to the Holy Roman Empire, were naturally alarmed by the Ottoman westward expansion that could eventually threaten Vienna and the entire continent.[536] After the initial period of low-intensity military conflict in Hungary (1528-1533), the tension between the two empires escalated in 1540 with the death of John Zapolya, the Transylvanian monarch, who had been appointed as king by Ottoman Sultan Suleiman in return for accepting vassal status. Following the crisis in the Hungarian crown, Ferdinand I of Habsburg attacked

534 See Mehmet Genç, "Osmanlı Ekonomisi Ve Savaş," Yapıt IV-V, 1984.

535 Pál Fodor and Géza Dávid, *Ottomans, Hungarians, and Habsburgs in Central Europe: The Military Confines in the Era of Ottoman Conquest*, Vol. 20 (Leiden; Boston: Brill, 2000), XIV.

536 Jean Berenger, *A History of the Habsburg Empire* (London; New York: Longman, 1994).

Buda,[537] starting the prolonged and costly tug-of-war between Ottoman and Habsburg Empires.[538]

After 1541, Ottomans created garrisons in Buda and Pest and stationed a large number of troops in them. Fodor observes that in the seventeenth century, "the Ottoman Empire was required to spend a significant amount of its Balkan tax revenues on maintaining its military positions in Hungary."[539] For instance, the annual payment made to the 10,328 soldiers stationed in the fortresses in Buda *sancak* alone amounted to 23,046,862 akce in 1558-9. This expenditure was well beyond the tax revenue extracted from Buda, 6,434,585, which covered only 28 percent of the expenses.[540]

The frequency of warfare and the changes in military technology in the seventeenth century also brought about an expansion of the Ottoman army. The number of *janissaries* (infantry) as well as the *sipahis* (cavalry) increased considerably, which put an additional fiscal strain on the treasury.[541] While the numbers of *janissaries* and *sipahis* both increased, the rate of growth was higher for *janissaries* than for *sipahis*. The *janissary* troops, which until then had a relatively limited role in the Ottoman military as the guardians of the Porte, began to be deployed in the provinces in lieu of traditional cavalry.

The widening of the franchise closely reflected the changes in warfare due to the military revolution in the sixteenth century. The relative significance of the cavalry class declined and armies throughout Europe began to rely more

---

537 Caroline Finkel, *The Administration of Warfare: The Ottoman Military Campaigns in Hungary, 1593-1606*, Beihefte Zur Wiener Zeitschrift Für Die Kunde Des Morgenlandes (Wien: 1988).

538 Hauszmann, *Ungarn*, 93-113.

539 Pal Fodor, *In Quest of the Golden Apple: Imperial Ideology, Politics, and Military Administration in the Ottoman Empire*, Analecta Isisiana (Istanbul: Isis Press, 2000). It should also be noted that this situation is by no means peculiar to the Hungarian campaigns. Kütükoğlu's study of the 1578-90 Persian campaigns demonstrate that the resources required for warfare had to be drawn from Moldavia, Wallachia, and Danube, as well as Egypt and Cyprus. Cited in Finkel, *The Administration of Warfare: The Ottoman Military Campaigns in Hungary, 1593-1606*.

540 Calculated in golden florins, for the sake of easier comparison with European figures, the deficit in 1558-9 was 225,506. Agoston, David, and Fodor, "The Costs of the Ottoman Fortress-System in Hungary in the Sixteenth and Seventeenth Centuries."

541 Aksan, "Review Article: Ottoman Military Matters"; Virginia H. Aksan, *Ottoman Wars 1700-1870: An Empire Besieged*, Modern Wars in Perspective (Harlow, England: Longman/Pearson, 2007).

on infantries, which were relatively cheaper to maintain.[542] The importance of musket-wielding janissaries rose vis-à-vis the traditional mounted cavalry. The competitive pressures resulted in changes in the size and composition of the Ottoman army and the subsequent increase in the costs of warfare.[543] The increase in the relative weight of infantry vis-à-vis cavalry had an additional economic effect due to the special role played by the cavalry within the *tımar* regime.[544] With the decline of the cavalry, this highly effective mechanism of resource extraction was severely undermined.

The *tımar* system was adversely affected not only by the changing realities of warfare but also, indirectly, by the volatility in agricultural prices. As a mechanism that extracted agricultural surplus in kind and transformed the revenue directly into military power, the *tımar* system was not quite adaptive to an economic environment of volatile prices. "Squeezed between the millstone of the set stipends and rising prices," the *tımariots* found it increasingly difficult to find the cash to properly equip themselves for campaigning.[545] Since the assignment of *tımars* by the state officials was contingent on uninterrupted service, many *tımariots* lost their lands, the revenue of which was reassigned to the palace to pay for the growing military expenditure.

Lastly, the Ottoman state was suffering the consequences of "imperial overstretch"[546] in this period. With the vast territorial gains in the sixteenth century in the Middle East as well as in Eastern Europe, the Ottoman state had passed the "optimum" territorial limit.[547] With the slowing down of territorial expansion

542 Parker, *The Military Revolution: Military Innovation and the Rise of the West, 1500-1800*, 265. Also, see Tilly, Ardant, and Social Science Research Council. Committee on Comparative, *The Formation of National States in Western Europe*, Tilly, *Coercion, Capital, and European States, AD 990-1992.*

543 Finkel, *The Administration of Warfare: The Ottoman Military Campaigns in Hungary, 1593-1606*, 123.

544 İnalcık, *The Ottoman Empire; the Classical Age, 1300-1600*; İnalcık, "Land Problems in Turkish History"; Halil Berktay, "The Search for Peasant in Western and Turkish History," *Journal of Peasant Studies* 183-4 (1992); Keyder, "Small Peasant Ownership in Turkey: Historical Formation and Present Structure"; Keyder, *State and Class in Turkey: A Study in Capitalist Development.*

545 Goldstone, "East and West in the Seventeenth Century: Political Crisis in Stuart England, Ottoman Turkey, and Ming China," 111.

546 Paul Kennedy, *The Rise and the Fall of Great Powers: Economic Change and Military Conflict from 1500-2000* (New York: Vintage, 1987).

547 Barkan, "The Price Revolution in the Sixteenth Century," 18.

and the revenue generated by such conquests, the defense of the previously conquered lands began to draw larger shares of the ordinary revenue, as in the Ottoman holdings along the Hungarian border.

Provinces in other regions of the empire were exhausting their revenues and demanding from the central government substantial subsidies, mostly in the form of gold and silver. To pay for the administrative costs of Iran, for instance, the Ottoman administration was forced to spend, in excess of the revenues of these territories, a large part of the tax income of adjacent provinces such as Aleppo, Diyarbakır, and Erzurum, which had previously supplied part of the budget of the central government. "Forced to do without this income, the imperial treasury became exhausted."[548]

I demonstrated so far that the sources and basic dynamics of the fiscal crisis in the Ottoman and Habsburg Empires were strikingly similar. In both cases, the fiscal decay was precipitated by two sets of factors: the cycles of the world economy and the rising costs of warfare. Furthermore, in both empires, the crisis brought about not only a contraction in the state revenues (and an increase in expenses) but more importantly a relative decline in the capacity of the state to extract resources, as exemplified by the crisis of *tımar* system in the Ottoman Empire and the difficulties the Habsburg rulers experienced after 1620 in collecting taxes.

The crisis of the seventeenth century altered the preferences of both the merchants and the ruling elites in the Ottoman Empire. The booming demand from Western Europe and the increase in agricultural prices incentivized the merchants to escape the tight state control and divert their economic activity away from the imperial center. The central elites began to perceive them as a factor undermining the existing social and political order. The intensity of the conflict between the two increased, ultimately resulting in the further exclusion of the merchants from the ruling political coalition.

As early as the late sixteenth century, the merchants in the Ottoman Empire, Muslim and non-Muslim alike, were beginning to respond positively to the market signals emerging from Europe. The increase in European commodity prices started a process by which "commodities were sucked out of Ottoman markets."[549] As a result, by the seventeenth century, agricultural commodities like grain and wheat as well as critical raw materials for manufacturing such as copper and wool came in short supply in major Ottoman cities, which in turn

548 Ibid., 19.
549 Ibid.

exacerbated the inflationary pressures initially created by the injection of precious metals. Since the Ottoman economic policy based on the principle of provisionism severely restricted the export of basic commodities, the lure of high prices outside the boundaries of the empire led Ottoman merchants to increasingly engage in smuggling and contraband trade.

In an effort to prevent the diversion of basic commodities away from the major urban centers, the Ottoman elites tightened the restrictive policies: controls on the export of strategic commodities augmented, contraband goods seized in transit were expropriated, and all violators faced severe criminal punishment.[550] However, the new measures on exports only ended up providing additional incentives for contraband.[551] As Barkan notes, "the profits to be gained from illicit smuggling of grains to the European markets were so enormous that this traffic continued to attract participants" and "contraband commerce became for many persons in the empire a normal trade and for some social classes a source of far more riches than they had ever been able to amass before."[552]

The contraband trade set in motion by the price revolution and the growth of the Atlantic economy in the late sixteenth century remained relatively vibrant during the slowing down of the prices in the seventeenth century. When the period of stagnation ended in 1660, the growing European economy once again provided a strong pull for the Ottoman merchants. In addition to the growing European markets, the "almost uninterrupted succession of wars and revolutions" in this period "created immense opportunities for profiteering."[553]

Once cracked by the expanding mercantile capital the rigid economic system of the empire became much more difficult to control for the bureaucratic elite. The availability of export markets in Europe constituted a new impetus for commodity production and accelerated the monetization of small producers.[554] With the advent of commercial agriculture, merchants became conduits between Ottoman producers and European markets by exporting raw materials to Europe and importing back manufactured European products. In the eighteenth century, the merchants began to export commercial crops (cotton, tobacco, maize,

550 Karpat, "The Transformation of the Ottoman Empire, 1789-1908."
551 İslamoğlu-İnan and Keyder, "Agenda for Ottoman History," 51.
552 Barkan, "The Price Revolution in the Sixteenth Century," 6.
553 Karpat, "The Transformation of the Ottoman Empire, 1789-1908," 816-17.
554 Keyder, "Small Peasant Ownership in Turkey: Historical Formation and Present Structure," 60.

etc.), livestock, and commercial fibers to Europe in addition to the contraband trade in grains and other basic commodities.

France was the leading customer of Ottoman exports. In the eighteenth century, 83 percent of the total imports in France were coming from the Levant; cotton exports constituting 70 percent of the total.[555] Largely because of the industrial growth following the mid-eighteenth-century reforms of Maria Theresia and her successors, Austria was importing large quantities of raw materials from the Ottoman Empire as well. In parallel with the growing demand from Western Europe, new commerce networks emerged in the Balkans. These networks were "detrimental to the imperial system, not only because they mediated the diversion of goods away from the imperial centers, but also because they effectively blocked the transmission of cash revenues from these wealthiest provinces to the capital."[556]

As the ruling elites tightened state controls over production and commerce, the productive sectors of the *reaya* resisted the state.[557] Throughout, the seventeenth-century manufacturing and trading guilds frequently petitioned the Porte complaining about the price limitations and heavy taxes. Ottoman merchants fought "prolonged battles" in this period to reduce or eliminate taxes and tariffs on exports.[558]

One of the most frequent and effective means of resistance available to the artisans and manufacturers was to close shops and suspend production. A major artisan uprising took place in Istanbul in 1651. When the government attempted to force the artisans to buy some confiscated commodities at high prices, the artisans collectively resisted. They went to the imperial council and demanded that the grand vizier be punished. Initially driven away by force, the artisans re-grouped the next day. Approximately 150,000 men—many of them armed—marched to the palace and forced the sultan to dismiss the grand vizier.[559]

Perhaps surprisingly, non-Muslim artisans and merchants were even better positioned to articulate their interests than their Muslim counterparts. Starting in the seventeenth century, non-Muslim capital holders frequently sought the protection of foreign states.[560] In the eighteenth and nineteenth centuries, when

555 Karpat, "The Transformation of the Ottoman Empire, 1789-1908," 818.
556 Ibid., 821.
557 Faroqhi and Veinstein, *Merchants in the Ottoman Empire.*
558 Quataert, *Manufacturing in the Ottoman Empire and Turkey, 1500-1950.*
559 İnalcık, *The Ottoman Empire; the Classical Age, 1300-1600*, 161.
560 Faroqhi and Veinstein, *Merchants in the Ottoman Empire.*

the Ottoman state was politically much more vulnerable to foreign interference, the non-Muslim merchants in the Ottoman Empire essentially would opt out of the Ottoman legal system where the transaction costs were higher.[561]

3. Conclusion

This chapter accomplished three objectives:

(1) It described the origins and dynamics of the vertically organized Ottoman Empire. It showed that Ottoman rulers in the fourteenth and fifteenth centuries, capitalizing on the power vacuum left by the declining Byzantine Empire in the Balkans and the Seljuk Empire in Anatolia, expanded the boundaries of the Ottoman principality. Combined with the key features of the social structure in the conquered areas—the historically weak landed nobility and strong independent peasantry—the rapid expansion allowed the Ottoman elites to establish direct mechanisms of rule that connected provinces to the imperial center. Ottoman institutions like tımar and kul systems constituted the backbone of the vertically organized administrative structure.

(2) The most important implication of the vertical imperial organization was that it sustained the unified state elite. The incorporation of the relatively weaker native elites into the Ottoman administrative structure made sure that the potential distributive conflicts between the central elites and their local representatives remained less intense, particularly in comparison to the Habsburg Empire, where the horizontal state structure was accompanied by high-intensity conflict. I also showed that the most important threat to the unified Ottoman elite was urban capital holders. Within the closed economic system of the Ottoman Empire, where the state elite had the sole claim to agricultural surplus, merchants posed the most immediate threat to the capacity of the elite to appropriate revenue from the non-elites. While a key part of the provisioning of major cities, the merchants were kept under strict control by the ruling elite.

(3) It explained the origins and consequences of the seventeenth-century crisis. The sources of the crisis were essentially the same in the Ottoman Empire as in the Habsburg Empire: the cyclical changes in the emerging world-economy and the rising costs of warfare. I showed that while these factors

561 Timur Kuran, "Islamic Commercial Crisis: The Institutional Root of Economic Underdevelopment in the Middle East," *Journal of Economic History* 63, no. 3 (2003).

put considerable strain on the imperial budgets both by increasing expenses (e.g., military expenditures) and decreasing revenues (e.g., loss of customs fees), their most important consequence was the undermining of the capacity of the state to extract revenue. The booming demand for agricultural goods in Western Europe and the increasing prices incentivized Ottoman merchants to reorient their activities beyond the boundaries of the empire. Thus, the immediate impact of the cyclical changes in the world economy on the Ottoman Empire was the intensification of the conflict between ruling elites and urban capital holders. The intensification of the ruler-capital conflict, in turn, proved instrumental in precluding the possibility of incorporating the capital into the ruling coalition.

Chapter 6 Elite Realignment and Institutional Change in the Ottoman Empire, 1600-1881

Having described the critical antecedents of institutional change in the previous chapter, I now move on to the post-crisis period. I demonstrate how the intra-elite conflict—both the demand- and supply-side dynamics—produced the coalitional (exclusion of capital) and institutional (fiscal decentralization) outcomes.

The chapter is divided into four sections. Section 1 discusses the fiscal strategies of the bureaucratic elite in the aftermath of the crisis, including the expansion of the scope of tax farming. Section 2 argues that the changes in taxation were accompanied by the formation of a political coalition between the bureaucratic elites and the tax farmers, the *ayan*. Section 3 examines the commercialization of Ottoman agriculture and the establishment of large commercial estates, which directly threatened the capacity of the ruling elites to extract revenue, paving the way for the intensification of the conflict between the central and provincial elites.

Section 4 analyzes the changes in the supply side of the conflict: the bureaucratic elite, now threatened by the provincial landholding elites, partially undermined the latter's power through institutional reforms throughout the 1820s and 1830s. Moreover, to balance the *ayan* threat, the bureaucratic elite acted strategically and attempted to forge an alliance with the merchants. However, this attempt at realignment (1839-1856) failed primarily because the merchants opted out of a partnership with the central elite.

I explain capital's strategy as a function of (1) the type and nature of trade they engaged in and (2) their expectation that the costs of seeking state protection would outweigh its benefits. In conclusion, I demonstrate that the failed attempt to re-centralize the state in the first half of the nineteenth century directly contributed to the economic decline of the Ottoman state.

1. Elite Response to the Fiscal Crisis

Ottoman central administration reacted quickly to the declining state finances in the early seventeenth century and made several changes in the taxation scheme. One of these changes was the conversion of some extraordinary taxes and fees into regular sources of state revenue. Wartime taxes like *avarız-ı divaniyye* and *tekalif* began to be collected during peacetime and at increasingly higher rates.

The administration instituted several extraordinary new taxes called *imdadiyye* (emergency).[562]

Even though *avarız, tekalif, imdadiyye,* and other taxes brought temporary relief to the treasury, in the long term they caused tension between the state and taxpayers. Increasing tax rates and the arbitrariness of the new taxation scheme became a source of civil strife later in the seventeenth century, particularly in Anatolia and the Balkans. Members of the *reaya*, unable to afford to pay heavy taxes, began to flee their land. The peasant exodus and the corresponding decline in agricultural production adversely affected tax revenue.

Still under fiscal strain, the bureaucratic elite could not afford further destabilization of agriculture. Starting in the first half of the seventeenth century, the central government began to rely on local notables in the provinces for the fulfillment of administrative tasks and the provision of social order, empowering these notables. Thus, the initial changes that could have fostered the extractive capacity of the state inadvertently paved the way for greater reliance on local intermediaries in the provinces.

The second main change in Ottoman fiscal policy was converting state-owned *miri* land to *mukataa*, i.e., lands to be farmed out to private tax collectors. This is a fundamental departure from the traditional *tımar* system, where most of the agricultural land was directly under the control of the central administration. The Ottoman tax farming system (*iltizam*) entailed selling a source of revenue (usually the tax revenue of a region) by government auctions to a private person (or a group of persons) for a specific period.[563] The highest bidder in the auction, *mültezim*, was required to make a cash down payment (*muaccele*), followed by monthly, quarterly, or semi-quarterly installments.[564] In the earlier stages of the move toward the tax farming system, auctions and contracts were directly supervised by the state. An appointed official (*emin*) was responsible for the fulfillment of the conditions of the auction. The tax farmers who fell behind in their payments to the treasury immediately lost their contracts.

562 Pamuk, *Osmanlı-Türkiye Iktisadi Tarihi, 1500-1914*, 147; Halil İnalcık, "Military and Fiscal Transformation in the Ottoman Empire, 1600-1700," *Archivum Ottomanicum* VI (1980): 313.

563 Pamuk, "The Evolution of Fiscal Institutions in the Ottoman Empire, 1500-1914"; İnalcık, "Military and Fiscal Transformation in the Ottoman Empire, 1600-1700."

564 Pamuk, *Osmanlı-Türkiye Iktisadi Tarihi, 1500-1914*, 147.

Tax farming as a relatively inexpensive method of tax collection was commonplace in the Islamic world from the Mediterranean to the Indian Ocean[565] as well as in the agrarian states of feudal Europe.[566] Indeed, pre-Ottoman rulers of Anatolia—Anatolian Seljuk Empire and the Byzantine Empire—had both used variants of tax farming.[567] When they conquered these regions in the early fourteenth century, the Ottomans adopted some of the existing institutions.[568] However, under Ottoman rule, the application of tax farming remained limited to certain geographic areas and within those areas to certain sources of revenue. Before the early seventeenth century, Ottoman elites relied on tax farming almost exclusively to collect urban taxes. Agricultural taxes, which constituted the bulk of the tax revenue of the state, were collected mostly in kind through the *tımar* system.[569]

At the core of the Ottoman elite's response to the fiscal crisis of the seventeenth century was the expansion of the *iltizam* system to include new revenue sources (e.g., agricultural taxes) as well as new geographic regions that were previously dominated by the *tımar* system. The conversion of agricultural land into *mukataa* continued throughout the eighteenth century. Moreover, tax farming contracts were extended from 1-3 to 5 years and ultimately became indefinitely renewable.

The immediate fiscal effects of the expansion of tax farming in the seventeenth century were positive. Kasaba argues, "[I]n the short run, tax farming did fulfill the expectations that were placed in it."[570] The revenues generated by the large down payments of the auctioned-out properties boosted the cash receipts in the treasury. The initial success of tax farming as a source of much-needed liquidity, however, paved the way for auctioning out the tax revenues of a region for increasingly longer periods and demanding higher percentages of the value of the contract as a down payment. The long-term consequence was the

565 Şevket Pamuk, "Institutional Change and the Longevity of the Ottoman Empire, 1500-1800," *Journal of Interdisciplinary History* 35 (2004).

566 Bonney, *The Rise of the Fiscal State in Europe, C. 1200-1815*; Carolyn Webber and Aaron Wildawsky, *A History of Taxation and Expenditure in the Western World* (New York: Simon & Schulster, 1986).

567 Tax farming in the Seljuk Empire was known as *iqta*, in the Byzantine as *pronoia*.

568 Pamuk, *Osmanlı-Türkiye Iktisadi Tarihi, 1500-1914*, 147; İslamoğlu-İnan and Keyder, "Agenda for Ottoman History," 58.

569 Pamuk, "The Evolution of Fiscal Institutions in the Ottoman Empire, 1500-1914," 18.

570 Reşat Kasaba, "Incorporation of the Ottoman Empire, 1750-1820," *Review* X, no. 5/6 (1987).

emergence of a powerful tax farming elite, the *ayan*, and the consequent erosion of the tax base of the Ottoman state and its fiscal capacity.

Who were the tax farmers? Many contract holders came from within the bureaucratic elite: high government officials in the imperial center, *kapıkulu* commanders and provincial governors, and religious administrators. These sectors were typically exempt from taxation[571] and, therefore, possessed the capital to invest in tax farming contracts. High-ranking state officials (including viziers and grand viziers) and military commanders typically acquired contracts by pledging their salaries toward the fulfillment of payments. This particular practice of paying high bureaucrats with *iltizam*s instead of salary was favored by the state since it lowered the cash burden.[572] In addition to the members of the bureaucratic elite, sections of money-changers (*sarraf*) and traders residing in the provincial cities were among contract holders.

The turning point in the fiscal transformation of the Ottoman state was the introduction of the *malikane* (private estate) system at the end of the seventeenth century. The positive effects of the initial wave of the tax farming contracts (particularly the down payments) proved short-lived. Due to the rising defense costs and other state expenditures, the budgetary crisis proved persistent. In 1693, the Ottoman state had the highest recorded budget deficit in its history: the difference between the revenues and expenditures increased from -12,333,543 *akçe* in the 1660/61 state budget to -44,644,388 in 1669/70, to -262,217,191 in 1692/93—approximately 21-fold increase in 33 years.[573]

Shortly after, in early 1695, Ottoman Sultan Ahmed II issued an imperial decree permitting various revenue sources to be farmed out on a life-time basis. Under the new arrangement, the *malikane* system, the highest bidders in auctions were given the right to unilaterally renew their limited term contracts. The new arrangement also guaranteed preferential treatment to the legal successors of contract holders. Properties were still to be auctioned out after the death of

---

571 Jacoby, *Social Power and the Turkish State*. Also, see Halil İnalcık and Rustow, "The Nature of Traditional Society," in *Political Modernization in Japan and Turkey* (New Brunswick, NJ: Princeton University Press, 1964); Linda Darling, *Revenue-Raising and Legitimacy: Tax Collection and Finance Administration in the Ottoman Empire, 1560-1660* (Leiden: 1996); Huri İslamoğlu-İnan, *State and Peasant in the Ottoman Empire: Agrarian Power Relations and Regional Economic Development in Ottoman Anatolia During the Sixteenth Century*, The Ottoman Empire and Its Heritage (Leiden; New York: E.J. Brill, 1994).

572 Genç, "Osmanlı Maliyesinde Malikane Sistemi," 112-13.

573 Ibid, 104.

the original contract holder; however, the sons (or other male relatives of the deceased) were granted the right to continue possessing their estates as long as they agreed to match the highest bid in the auction.[574]

In practice, preferential treatment of the heirs of life-term tax farmers signaled a major departure from the traditional Ottoman property regime and the *de facto* establishment of private property rights over extended territories. The institution of the *malikane* system in 1695 inadvertently made "a major contribution to the rise of a new landlord class with the rights, as free holders, over large tracts of state-owned land."[575]

According to the bureaucratic elite, the rationale behind the move from limited tax farming contracts toward life-term arrangements was to give additional incentives to tax farmers to "take better care" of the tax source. The bureaucrats argued that under the limited-term tax farming arrangement, contract holders were prone to pursue short-term profit maximization, abuse the sources of revenue assigned to them, and exploit the peasants through heavier taxes without paying any consideration to the long-term economic effects of such exploitation.[576]

However, economic historians hold that the primary rationale behind the move was to borrow larger sums of money from domestic creditors using future tax revenues as collateral. With the 1695 decree, the central administration not only increased the length of contracts but also began to demand from the auction winners larger sums as down payments. Pamuk argues that in comparison to the original tax farming system, the *malikane* order "represented an important shift toward longer-term borrowing by the state."[577] Similarly, Barkan notes that the tax farmers "by paying in advance a large part of their debts to the state… acted as a kind of 'credit agency' in a country where the lack of a public credit institution was severely felt."[578]

Most importantly, the new taxation scheme marked an implicit alliance and co-dependency between the state elites and tax farmers. While life-term

574 Pamuk, *Osmanlı-Türkiye Iktisadi Tarihi, 1500-1914*, 149.

575 İnalcık, "Military and Fiscal Transformation in the Ottoman Empire, 1600-1700."

576 İslamoğlu-İnan and Keyder, "Agenda for Ottoman History," 58; Genç, "Osmanlı Maliyesinde Malikane Sistemi," 105; Şevket Pamuk, *Osmanlı Ekonomisi Ve Kurumları* (İstanbul: Türkiye Is Bankası, 2007), 138.

577 Pamuk, "The Evolution of Fiscal Institutions in the Ottoman Empire, 1500-1914," 19.

578 Barkan, "The Price Revolution in the Sixteenth Century," 25.

contracts with larger down payments provided short-term fiscal relief, they also caused the bureaucratic elites to grow dependent on local intermediaries.

The new system substantially increased the capital requirements of long-term tax farming for contract holders, which in turn paved the way for the development of new social networks outside the control of the state. Initially, the major players in government auctions typically were members of the state elite, high-ranking bureaucrats, and military commanders, in particular.[579] Even though they possessed the capital required to bid in auctions, longer contract terms and higher down payments after 1695 forced the contract-holders to seek new sources of capital. They turned to private financiers.

As a result of the changes in the capital requirements of tax farming after 1695, private financiers began to play an important role in the tax collection process. Non-Muslim capital holders (particularly Greeks, Armenians, and Jews) who were formally prohibited from holding *malikane* contracts began to insert themselves into the *malikane* system as financiers, brokers, and accountants.[580] By loaning large amounts of money to the tax farmers to be used as down payments in auctions, the private financiers made usury a central aspect of the process.[581]

A second implication of the greater capital requirements of tax farming after 1695 was the extension of *malikane* subcontracting. Tax farmers, particularly the strongest buyers who monopolized government auctions for *malikane* revenues, began to have trouble efficiently collecting taxes from their growing estates. Given their higher financial obligations, the contract holders needed more efficient ways to collect revenue. Particularly in the second half of the seventeenth century, they started dividing the *malikane*s into smaller units and selling them to secondary *mültezim*s. The size of the subcontracted revenue sources would range from 1/2 of the original *malikane* to 1/150.[582] The private financiers who loaned capital to contract holders were instrumental; they mobilized their connections in the provincial towns, brokered the subcontracting agreements, and in many cases helped organize the actual collection of taxes.[583]

The key aspect of the subcontracting system is that while the original owners of *malikane*s who bid on the government auctions typically belonged to the state elite, the secondary *mültezim*s came from the ranks of local notables in

579 Pamuk, *Osmanlı-Türkiye Iktisadi Tarihi, 1500-1914*, 149.
580 Pamuk, "The Evolution of Fiscal Institutions in the Ottoman Empire, 1500-1914," 25.
581 İslamoğlu-İnan and Keyder, "Agenda for Ottoman History," 58.
582 Genç, "Osmanlı Maliyesinde Malikane Sistemi," 114.
583 Pamuk, *Osmanlı-Türkiye Iktisadi Tarihi, 1500-1914*, 150.

the provinces.[584] Though these local notables lacked an independent economic basis, they could still use their social ties to assist in the estimation and collection of taxes in the name of the contract holder in absentia.

By the mid-eighteenth century, subcontracting had become a common practice within the *malikane* system. As the number and the value of subcontracted estates increased, the largest subcontractors in the provinces also began to divide and distribute their shares to *sub*-sub-contractors. The result was "a chain of interdependent *mültezims* along the vertical line, extending from imperial capital town to small provincial *kadıs*."[585]

Subcontracting inadvertently contributed to the coherence of tax farmers as an interest group. The *malikane* contracts typically stipulated that the contract holder not only lay down all his private property as a guarantee but also show reliable third-party securities. Consequently, even the wealthiest tax farmers had to form mutually beneficial partnerships with others. Thus, the strict security stipulations that were initially intended as a failsafe protecting the state vis-à-vis private parties ended up facilitating the "emergence of a closely-knit group of wealthy people with growing influence on local and state affairs."[586]

2. The Coalition of the Bureaucratic Elite and the Tax Farmers

In this section, I take a closer look at the rise of this new class of provincial elites, known as *ayan* as a political and economic power. The main argument is that by assuming critical roles in daily administration, military organization, and tax collection in the Anatolian and Balkan provinces, the new local gentry became part of the ruling coalition in the eighteenth century. In contrast to the Habsburg Empire, where the post-crisis realignment produced a coalition between the ruling elites and the merchants, realignment led to the opposite outcome in

584 Yücel Özkaya, *Osmanlı İmparatorluğunda Ayanlık* (Ankara: AUDTCF Yayınları, 1977); Huri İslamoğlu-İnan, *State and Peasant in the Ottoman Empire: Agrarian Power Relations and Regional Economic Development in Ottoman Anatolia During the Sixteenth Century.*

585 İnalcık, "Military and Fiscal Transformation in the Ottoman Empire, 1600-1700," 328. For an overview of business partnerships in the Ottoman Empire, see Murat Çizakça, *A Comparative Evolution of Business Partnerships: The Islamic World and Europe, with Specific Reference to the Ottoman Archives* (Leiden: Brill, 1996).

586 İnalcık, "Military and Fiscal Transformation in the Ottoman Empire, 1600-1700," 327-28.

the Ottoman case: a hitherto weak, practically non-existing social actor attained economic and political power through allying with the ruling elites. Since the bureaucratic elite needed the cooperation of the provincial elites to collect taxes, they continued to distribute side payments to their partners.

From the seventeenth century onward, the local notables in the provinces actively organized and managed the collection of regular taxes from farmed-out revenue units. The *ayan* began to assume a crucial role in the preparation of registers (*tevzi defterleri*) of town expenses and the collection of additional taxes for the treasury, including the emergency military tax *imdadiyye*[587]—a role well beyond the scope of tax farming as originally intended. By the end of the eighteenth century, the *ayan* was solely in charge of "determining and compiling local expenses and apportioning them among the people."[588]

As the fiscal and administrative responsibilities of the provincial elites increased, the bureaucratic elite gradually relinquished control over tax farming. Initially, the contracts contained stipulations that allowed the state to unilaterally annul the agreement if the *mukataa* (revenue unit) was being farmed out below its effective market value. A state official was assigned to each tax farming contract to supervise the account. Yet, as the power of the tax farmers rose, the state lost its capacity to monitor and enforce contracts, as evidenced by the fact that most contracts remained in the hands of their original holders and under their original, below-market value.[589]

The bureaucratic elite provided selective benefits to tax farmers throughout the eighteenth century. For instance, to facilitate the collection of taxes in the provinces, provincial administrators were required to assist the tax collectors by providing them with troops and other personnel if needed. As the local notables assumed new responsibilities in tax collection, they allied themselves with the *kethüda-yeri*s (local commanders of *kapıkulu sıpahi*s) and *emin*s (state-appointed supervisors).

Consequently, the state's infrastructural capacity to monitor the relationship between tax farmers and peasants declined. As discussed earlier, traditionally, the Ottoman bureaucratic elite was highly concerned with the protection of the peasantry from any infringements on their rights, and the *tımar* system allowed the elite to effectively intervene in agricultural relations in favor of the peasantry.

587 Halil İnalcık, "Centralization and Decentralization in the Ottoman Empire, 1600-1700," *Archivum Ottomanicum* 6 (1980): 29-31.
588 İnalcık, "Military and Fiscal Transformation in the Ottoman Empire, 1600-1700," 322.
589 Pamuk, *Osmanlı-Türkiye Iktisadi Tarihi, 1500-1914*, 151.

After the seventeenth century, the tax farmer was at "a total liberty to use a multitude of means to realize his objective," and "against these, the peasants no longer had any way of acquiring real protection."[590] By allowing the tax farmers to establish direct and reciprocal economic links with the peasantry, the central state lost its capacity "to intercede on behalf of the *reaya* and control economic exchange," resulting in "a process of feudalization and a rise in the strength of the local gentry."[591]

Capitalizing on their role as local enforcers of tax farming contracts and encouraged by the declining capacity of the state to monitor them, the *ayan* began to "intercept most of the state revenues,"[592] resulting in "less and less of the revenue base reaching the capital."[593] Indeed, after fees and other transaction costs, only one-third of the net tax revenue ended up in the treasury, while the remaining two-thirds was "divided among the members of the 'grand coalition' consisting of high bureaucracy, *malikane*-holders, and tax-collecting provincial elites."[594] In the eighteenth century, it is estimated that 1,000 to 2,000 individuals in the capital city of Istanbul, together with 5,000 to 10,000 individuals based in the provinces, controlled the majority of state assets.[595]

The *ayan* had also assumed additional responsibilities and authority in provincial administration. Ottoman provincial government was divided into administrative units called *sancaks*. Each *sancak* was governed by a military governor (*sancakbeyi*) appointed directly by the sultan. While the *sancakbeyi* oversaw military and administrative matters, legal and social issues were under the jurisdiction of *kadı* (highest legal official), which was independent of the former and directly accountable to the central administration. This mechanism of checks and balances functioned reasonably well before the seventeenth century in keeping potential centrifugal forces at bay.[596]

From the seventeenth century onward, the central administration began to have trouble with rebellious governors in the Balkans and Anatolia. These

590 Wallerstein et al., "The Incorporation of the Ottoman Empire into the World-Economy," 809.

591 Jacoby, *Social Power and the Turkish State*, 39.

592 İnalcık, "Military and Fiscal Transformation in the Ottoman Empire, 1600-1700," 331.

593 Aksan, *Ottoman Wars 1700-1870: An Empire Besieged*, 122.

594 Pamuk, *Osmanlı-Türkiye Iktisadi Tarihi, 1500-1914*, 151-2.

595 Ariel Salzman, "An Ancien Regime Revisited: "Privatization" And Political Economy in the Eighteenth-Century Ottoman Empire," *Politics and Society* 21 (1993). Also see, Jacoby, *Social Power and the Turkish State*, 39-40.

596 İnalcık, *The Ottoman Empire; the Classical Age, 1300-1600.*, particularly Chs 12-13.

governors were initially encouraged by the government to recruit large militia units from within the peasantry (*sekban* forces) in times of war. While the policy of allowing provincial governors to recruit troops helped alleviate the costs of defense, it ultimately backfired when some governors exploited their newfound military capabilities to resist the central administration. In the early eighteenth century, "[t]he sultan was compelled to create countervailing forces to limit the governor's growing authority."[597] The *kadıs*, originally intended to balance the administrative and military power of the governors, enlisted the help of the provincial notables.

The governors and *beys* "either chose to appoint or were forced to select" their deputies from the local *ayan*.[598] Having attained official political posts as deputy governors, local notables became, in the long run, even more powerful than the *sancakbeyis* primarily because while the *sancakbeyis* were frequently replaced by the central administration through the policy of rotation, the deputies typically remained in their posts. Government officials were becoming "less secure in their tenure," and "in order to make the most of their brief appointments, they resorted to venality and nepotism."[599]

İnalcık observed that "while steadily making themselves indispensable to the government…, the *ayan*-deputies at the same time used and abused their state-delegated authority to reinforce their influence in the provinces."[600] In addition to enhancing their control over the assessment, collection, and distribution of tax revenues in the provinces, the *ayan* exploited their political capital and economic wealth to maintain *sekban* troops, presumably to protect local populations against bandits.[601]

Through this process of political delegation and military empowerment, the *ayan* found themselves in control of the political and coercive instruments of the state in the provinces. As İnalcık notes, the *ayan* came to be "considered quasi-representatives of the state."[602] In the eighteenth century, as their relative wealth and influence grew, local notables began to displace the high bureaucracy and other members of the state elite at the critical nodes of tax farming. Ultimately,

597 Halil İnalcık, "Centralization and Decentralization in Ottoman Administration," in *Studies in Eighteenth Century Islamic History*, ed. Thomas Naff and Roger Owen (Carbondale, 1977), 28.

598 Ibid., 31.

599 Kasaba, "Incorporation of the Ottoman Empire, 1750-1820," 812.

600 İnalcık, "Centralization and Decentralization in Ottoman Administration," 31.

601 Barkey, *Bandits and Bureaucrats: The Ottoman Route to State Centralization.*

602 İnalcık, "Military and Fiscal Transformation in the Ottoman Empire, 1600-1700," 328.

the *ayan* supplanted the governors and central bureaucracy in deciding who would be appointed as tax farmers.

As *ayan* continued to play a critical role in maintaining law and order in the countryside, they gained the support and confidence of the local population. They became representatives of the peasants and townspeople in their dealings with the government. In the early eighteenth century, the local notables in the Anatolian and Balkan provinces started to elect a single *ayan* as their official leader. The *reis-i ayan* (chief among notables) was issued a certificate by the state-appointed governor, officially recognizing his role in the government and local population relations.[603] By the mid-eighteenth century, many *kaza*s (smaller administrative units) had their own recognized *ayan* in administrative matters. By the end of the eighteenth century, the notables had "effectively interposed themselves between the people and the central bureaucracy."[604] Election of an *ayan* as the representative of a *kaza* from among other local notables and his recognition by the state marked the "most significant stage in the development of the [institution of *ayan*]."[605]

Another new local institution created by the local notables was the so-called *councils of ayan*. This local council—similar (in function if not size) to noble councils in Bohemia, Hungary, and Slovene lands of the Habsburg Empire—consisted of the local *kadı*, a representative of the *janissaries* stationed in the area, and six members of the *ayan*. This council performed several public and municipal services, such as looking after the economic welfare of the city and the surrounding villages, safeguarding guild regulations, maintaining public buildings, and appointing public officials. According to the contemporary foreign observers of Rumelian towns, the council of *ayan* "acted as a kind of oligarchy that directly controlled the administration and thereby reducing the governors to total ineffectiveness."[606]

As the local notables occupied key offices, they used their influence to monopolize tax farming contracts by ensuring that the contracts remained in the hands of their original owners. These local *ayan* who maintained their tax farming rights over long periods emerged as semi-dynastic families in the Balkans and

---

603 İnalcık, "Centralization and Decentralization in Ottoman Administration," 46. Pamuk, *Osmanlı-Türkiye Iktisadi Tarihi, 1500-1914*, 143.

604 Kasaba, "Incorporation of the Ottoman Empire, 1750-1820," 812.

605 İnalcık, "Centralization and Decentralization in the Ottoman Empire, 1600-1700," 46.

606 İnalcık, "Centralization and Decentralization in Ottoman Administration," 43.

Anatolia.[607] By the end of the eighteenth century, these families had become "de facto rulers of Anatolia and the Balkans."[608]

The earlier generation of historians interpreted the rise of the *ayan* as the feudalization of the Ottoman Empire. Contemporary historians, however, criticized the argument that the emergence of new social actors in the provinces necessarily represented decentralization and decline.[609] Most notably, Salzman argued that the privatization of taxation did not contribute to economic and political disaffection with the state but facilitated a distinct form of integration. Since the provincial elites' material well-being depended on their ties to the central administration, these notables had no incentive to break away from the empire and thus did not constitute a centrifugal force. Salzman thus asserts that tax farming is not "the solvent of imperial structure" but simply an instance of state formation by other means.[610]

My argument that the expansion of tax farming in the eighteenth century was coupled with the formation of a grand coalition between the bureaucratic elite and the provincial notables is essentially parallel to Salzman's assertion that both the "Ottoman aristocracy of service" and tax farmers benefited from this arrangement. In other words, both perspectives agree that the two parties were mutually dependent on each other. Yet, Salzman neglects two important points. First, her assertion that the material well-being of the provincial elites was entirely contingent on their linkage to the central administration fails to differentiate between smaller and larger tax farmers. Salzman's argument captures the incentives of the smaller tax farmers much more accurately than the incentives of the larger, wealthier tax farming elite. Lesser tax farmers could not accomplish more than cutting into the resource flow from the countryside to the center.

---

607 İnalcık, "Military and Fiscal Transformation in the Ottoman Empire, 1600-1700"; Linda T. Darling, *Revenue-Raising and Legitimacy: Tax Collection and Finance Administration in the Ottoman Empire, 1560-1660*, The Ottoman Empire and Its Heritage (Leiden; New York: E.J. Brill, 1996).

608 Kasaba, "Incorporation of the Ottoman Empire, 1750-1820," 812. Also see, Özkaya, *Osmanlı İmparatorluğunda Ayanlık.*

609 Ariel Salzmann, *Tocqueville in the Ottoman Empire: Rival Paths to the Modern State*, Ottoman Empire and Its Heritage (Leiden; Boston: Brill, 2004); Salzman, "An Ancien Regime Revisited: "Privatization" And Political Economy in the Eighteenth-Century Ottoman Empire"; Linda Darling, "Ottoman Fiscal Administration: Decline and Adaptation," *Journal of European Economic History* 26 (1977).

610 Salzman, "An Ancien Regime Revisited: "Privatization" And Political Economy in the Eighteenth-Century Ottoman Empire."

However, it is not evident that wealthier tax farmers depended on the central authority to the same extent.

Second, and even more importantly, Salzman's account does not address the critical development in intra-elite relations in the late eighteenth century: the emergence of commercial estates (*çiftlik*). When the privatization of tax farming coincided with the commercialization of agriculture in the latter half of the eighteenth century, the interests of the provincial elites significantly diverged from those of the bureaucratic elite. The emergence of export-oriented landlords in the provinces resulted in the intensification of the intra-elite conflict by the nineteenth century, which paved the way for another period of elite realignment in the early nineteenth century. In the next section, I look closely at the commercialization of Ottoman agriculture.

3. Commercialization of Agriculture and the Rise of Export-Oriented Landlords

Ottoman agricultural production underwent a fundamental transformation after 1750, marked by the emergence of large-scale commercial estates (*çiftlik*), particularly in the Balkans, Thrace, and Anatolia.[611] The emergence of the *çiftliks* paved the way for the transition of the provincial tax farmers to export-oriented landlords and thus had a fundamental impact on the structure of intra-elite conflict.

The origin of *çiftliks* is directly related to the rise of the tax farming elites. After the institution of the *malikane* system in 1695, the tax farmers attained unprecedented control over agricultural production. Taking advantage of the long leash given to them by the central administration, tax farmers squeezed the peasantry to maximize revenue. The state's rationale for establishing life-term tax farming—to lengthen the time horizon of the tax farmers and incentivize them to treat the peasantry well—proved untenable. Tax farmers remained

611 For commercialization of Ottoman agriculture in the eighteenth and nineteenth centuries, see Mehmet Genç, "Ottoman Economy and War in the Eighteenth Century," *Yapıt, Toplumsal Araştırmalar Dergisi* 49-50 (1984); Şevket Pamuk and Huri İslamoğlu-İnan, "Commodity Production for World-Markets and Relations of Production in Ottoman Agriculture, 1840-1913," in *Ottoman Empire and the World Economy* (1987); Wallerstein et al., "The Incorporation of the Ottoman Empire into the World-Economy."

uninterested in the long-term productivity of their lands; "their concern with production was purely fiscal."[612]

Added to the pressure on the peasants by the tax farmers was the burden of "extraordinary" taxes the state collected. The peasants, adversely affected by the civil disorder caused by the widespread banditry, were unable to meet their tax obligations. They had two options: borrowing from private parties (mainly from the tax farmers) at high-interest rates or abandoning their lands for good.[613] In either scenario, the lands previously owned by independent peasantry fell under the control of notables.[614]

In addition to the lands appropriated from the peasantry, the local notables also began to attain control over large tracts of land opened to agricultural production by the central administration to increase the short-term cash flows to the treasury. Even though the Ottoman law, particularly the fifteenth-century *kanunnames* of Sultan Mehmed II, did not allow *de jure* private property in land, the local notables exploited the bureaucratic loopholes in the administration (e.g., founding *vakıfs* [pious foundations] that are exempt from such regulations[615]) and established *de facto* control over private property.[616] While the *ayan* did not operate in a preexisting legal infrastructure that secured property rights akin to feudal Europe, they managed to centralize agricultural production in their hands.[617] Thus, the extension of tax farming and the growing influence of tax farmers provided the groundwork for establishing large-commercial estates in the second half of the eighteenth century.

The second factor that directly contributed to the emergence of large-scale commercial estates in the eighteenth century was the shifts in international trade. The rapidly growing population of Western Europe, coupled with the expansion of manufacturing, increased the demand for agricultural commodities

612 Genç and Quataert, "Ottoman Industry in the Eighteenth Century: General Framework, Characteristics and Main Trends," 63.

613 Under Ottoman regulations, the lands of the peasants who fail to pay their taxes for several consecutive years (usually two) were automatically confiscated.

614 Pamuk, *Osmanlı-Türkiye Iktisadi Tarihi, 1500-1914*, 156-7.

615 For an overview of the pious institutions, vakifs, in Ottoman history, see İnalcık, *The Ottoman Empire; the Classical Age, 1300-1600*, 142-50.

616 For a comparison of private property regimes in the east and west, see Huri İslamoğlu-İnan, *Constituting Modernity: Private Property in the East and West*, Islamic Mediterranean (London; New York; New York: I.B. Tauris; Distributed by Palgrave Macmillan in the U.S., 2004).

617 Kasaba, "Incorporation of the Ottoman Empire, 1750-1820," 809.

first in Britain and then in other European countries. As Kasaba asserts, "[t]he relationship between the expanding world economy, the incorporation of the Ottoman Empire and the rise of *çiftlik* agriculture is clear: the most intense period of *çiftlik* formation corresponds to the late eighteenth century, which was a period of expansion in the world economy and was also one that offered enhanced marketing opportunities for the Ottoman products in the European markets."[618]

Ottoman tax farmers responded very positively to the change in the structure and volume of European agricultural markets. After 1750, the trade volume between the Ottoman Empire and Western Europe grew as some of the wealthiest Ottoman provinces started exporting most of their products to European traders.[619] The agricultural cash crops began to replace subsistence grains as the dominant agricultural commodity produced in provinces—wheat, maize, cotton, tobacco, and other cash crops that were in high demand by European traders. Given the provisionist policies of the state, which controlled domestic prices for these commodities, exporting them was much more profitable.[620]

The external market conditions not only closely shaped the crop patterns but also the locations of the commercial estates. Commodity production for the market became concentrated around the main arteries of transportation.[621] By the end of the eighteenth century, *çiftlik* agriculture had become the most prevalent form of production in much of Thessaly, Epirus, Macedonia, Thrace, Marcia Valley, Danube region, Kosovo, the coastal plains of Albania, parts of Bosnia, and in Western Anatolia (particularly contemporary Izmir and its hinterland).[622]

---

618 Ivan Berend and Gyorgy Ranki, *European Periphery and Industrialization: 1780-1914* (Cambridge, MA: Cambridge University Press, 1982); Bruce McGowan, *Economic Life in Ottoman Europe: Taxation, Trade, and the Struggle for Land, 1600-1800* (Cambridge; New York: Cambridge University Press, 1981); Alan S. Milward and S. B. Saul, *The Economic Development of Continental Europe, 1780-1870* (London: Allen&Unwin, 1973); Wallerstein, *The Modern World-System II: Mercantilism and the Consolidation of the European World-Economy, 1600-1750.*

619 Kasaba, "Incorporation of the Ottoman Empire, 1750-1820"; Wallerstein et al., "The Incorporation of the Ottoman Empire into the World-Economy"; Reşat Kasaba, *The Ottoman Empire and the World-Economy: The Nineteenth Century*, Suny Series in Middle Eastern Studies (Albany: State University of New York Press, 1988); Pamuk and İslamoğlu-İnan, "Commodity Production for World-Markets and Relations of Production in Ottoman Agriculture, 1840-1913."

620 İslamoğlu-İnan and Keyder, "Agenda for Ottoman History."

621 Reşat Kasaba, *Cities in the World-System*, Studies in the Political Economy of the World-System (New York: Greenwood Press, 1991).

622 Kasaba, "Incorporation of the Ottoman Empire, 1750-1820."

Given the close association between the cycles of the European economy and the changes in Ottoman agriculture, external economic factors played a key role in the decline of the classical prebendal system and its partial replacement by production in large commercial estates. However, as I argued in Chapter 2, systemic economic explanations cannot fully account for the variation in domestic outcomes unless they pay sufficient attention to micro-level processes.

The causal impact of the expansion of the European economy on Ottoman agriculture was mediated by the endogenous changes in the structure of intra-elite relations. The widespread commercialization of Ottoman agriculture in the late eighteenth and early nineteenth centuries could not have been possible without the rising prominence of the tax farming local notables in the previous century, which was, in turn, primarily a consequence of the elites' fiscal choices following the economic crisis of the seventeenth century. The *ayan*, acting in their capacity as tax farmers in the provinces, undermined the direct link between the Ottoman state and the peasantry, which in turn allowed the tax farmers-*cum*-landowners to respond to the structural changes in the European agricultural markets by establishing large-commercial estates producing export cash-crops.

The eighteenth century was not the first time Ottoman agricultural production expanded in response to a surge in external demand. Islamoğlu-Inan shows that in the sixteenth century, there was an increased market demand as well, but this did not replace the peasant household economy with large-commercial estates.[623] In explaining why the peasants did not lose their lands and why commercial farms were not formed, she underlines the role of the political-judicial structures of the state, which proved decisive in maintaining the integrity of peasant holdings. Similarly, Kasaba asserts that the formation of the *çiftliks* in the eighteenth century surpassed earlier periods of commercialization in terms of its geographical scope and long-term implications.[624] The effects of the commercialization of agriculture in the eighteenth century were unprecedented precisely because they acted in conjunction with the changes in the structure of intra-elite conflict.

---

623 İslamoğlu-İnan, *State and Peasant in the Ottoman Empire: Agrarian Power Relations and Regional Economic Development in Ottoman Anatolia During the Sixteenth Century*.

624 Kasaba, "Incorporation of the Ottoman Empire, 1750-1820," 825-27.

4. Intensification of Intra-Elite Conflict and Failed Capital Incorporation

The most important long-term consequence of the commercialization of Ottoman agriculture was undermining the bureaucratic elite's monopoly over the agricultural surplus. Responding to price differentials, export-oriented estate owners successfully diverted agricultural commodities away from the imperial center and the bureaucratic elite. By the beginning of the nineteenth century, the primary beneficiaries of the commercial relations between the Ottoman Empire were no longer the state elite but rather the agricultural exporters and traders.

In terms of the theoretical framework offered in Chapter 2, the increase in the relative power of the tax-farmer-*cum*-landowners marked a fundamental shift in the threat perception of the Ottoman state elite. The elites, who had relied on the local notables since the early seventeenth century for tax collection, started to perceive their partners as a direct threat to their elite status.

In line with the predictions of the intra-elite conflict framework and the proposed causal mechanisms of balancing and redistribution, the Ottoman bureaucratic elite took several institutional measures to undermine the political and economic power of the local notables. As noted earlier, by 1700, the *ayan* had inserted themselves into the local administrative institutions as intermediaries between the state and the population. Thus, it is not surprising that the initial steps taken by the bureaucratic elite to undermine the power of *ayan* were aimed at reducing their political influence.

The earliest attempt to curb *ayan*'s power was the imperial decree issued in 1765 under Sultan Mustafa III, which removed the power to elect the *ayan* from the governors and gave it to the grand vizier. The central administration aimed at regaining its control over the provincial governments using widespread bribery, corruption, and other malpractices in the selection and conferral of the official positions in the provincial administration as a pretext. The local notables could still nominate a candidate for a given post under the new arrangement, but the final appointment would be made by the grand vizier, who directly represented the sultan, after a thorough investigation of the candidate's qualifications and loyalty.

The new centralization initiative, however, was abandoned only after a few years following the breakout of the Ottoman-Russian war. The new procedure caused significant delays in the appointment of *ayan*, which disrupted the war effort since the local notables were responsible for fulfilling the government's wartime requisitions. The new decrees not only stated that the people of a *kaza* were to elect the *ayan* without any outside interference but also stressed that *ayan* were indeed the representatives of the local population. The centralization effort had backfired.

First in 1779 and then in 1784, the Ottoman central administration made new attempts to reinstate the reforms of 1765. However, the rebooted reforms did not significantly alter the relationship between the local notables and the central administration. Local popular elections were still to be held regularly, while the central administration could directly appoint *ayan* only under a specific set of extraordinary circumstances. The regulation of 1784 was largely ignored in the provinces, and most *ayan* acquired their posts under the established practices.[625]

Having failed to curtail the political power of local notables, the Ottoman bureaucratic elite took a radical step in April 1786 and unilaterally abolished *ayanship*. The imperial decree, prepared under grand vizier Koca Yusuf Paşa (1785-88), assigned all public and municipal functions previously performed by *ayan* to a new officer, *şehir-kethüdası,* to be elected by the local population. The decree also declared that persons "seeking *ayans*hip would be prosecuted for violating the law."[626] By outlawing the *ayan* and replacing them with the popularly elected *şehir-kethüdası*, the decree intended to curb the power of notables while preventing a possible backlash from local populations demanding representation.

While the abolition of *ayanship* in 1788 marked the intensification of the conflict between central and provincial elites of the empire, it did not significantly alter the balance of power between the two actors. The notables simply ignored the sultan's move. Indeed, the political, economic, and even military power of the local notables continued to grow under Sultan Abdülhamid I (1774-1789), which prompted Abdülhamid's successor Sultan Selim III (1789-1807), to initiate the most comprehensive set of centralization reforms in the history of the Ottoman Empire since Mehmed II (1451-1481).

Sultan Selim III, who ascended the throne shortly after the French Revolution in 1789, had a clear reformist agenda. He ordered his bureaucratic staff to prepare policy recommendations on possible areas of reform. He established a committee of reforms (1792-3) and, through that committee, promulgated a series of institutional changes, which came to be known as *Nizam-ı Cedid* (New Order).[627]

---

625 İnalcık, "Centralization and Decentralization in the Ottoman Empire, 1600-1700," 50.
626 Ibid.
627 The best historical account of this period is Stanford J. Shaw, *Between Old and New; the Ottoman Empire under Sultan Selim III, 1789-1807*, Harvard Middle Eastern Studies, (Cambridge, MA: Harvard University Press, 1971).

At the heart of his comprehensive reform policy was the formation of a stronger central army that could effectively compete against the modern European armies. The Janissary corps and the provincial cavalries had fallen behind their European counterparts in terms of equipment and training. Moreover, the overall discipline and unity of the janissary order had declined throughout the eighteenth century as the individual janissaries—who were traditionally prohibited from seeking any employment other than soldiering—began to start their own businesses. The Russian-Ottoman wars of 1768-1774 and 1787-1792, which ended in Ottoman defeat, had signaled to the central administration that the decline of Ottoman military power was approaching a critical point.[628]

Selim III's efforts to create a modern army and a new political order were indeed motivated by a desire to "assert the authority of the central government over the *ayan*" as a necessity to fight outside enemies.[629] As noted earlier, the *ayan* in the Anatolian and Balkan provinces had come to possess independent military forces. Recruited from within mercenaries, bandits, and disbanded *sipahis*, such provincial armies could rival Ottoman troops stationed in the provinces. The central administration was essentially trying to reassert itself vis-à-vis the provincial elites by restructuring the army and providing it with modern European weaponry, equipment, and training.

Besides the military reform, Selim III also launched a campaign to weaken the economic power of the *ayan*. To undermine the large commercial estates in Rumelia and Anatolia, Selim III reinforced its support of the peasantry, including Christian communities.[630] Additionally, he attempted to resuscitate the dormant—at least since the institution of the *malikane* system in 1695—*tımar* system by taking back the control of *tımar* lands left without proper administrators.

The largely unsuccessful policy of restoring the *tımar* system to its former efficiency reveals the limits of Selim III's reformism. In direct contrast to the label attached to the reform program, *Nizam-ı Cedid* (New Order), the basic

628 For the decline of the Ottoman military power, see Aksan, "Review Article: Ottoman Military Matters."; Shaw, "The Origins of Ottoman Military Reform: The Nizam-i Cedid Army of Sultan Selim III."

629 Karpat, "The Transformation of the Ottoman Empire, 1789-1908," 252.

630 An example of this policy can be found in the semi-official state support of Serbian minorities vis-à-vis the Muslim provincial elite. The state-appointed governor of Bosnia, Ebubekir pasa, allied himself with the Serbian rebels against the forces of the leading Pasbanoğlu family. The policy had more to do with indirectly supporting the Serbian drive for independence than undermining the *ayan*.

aim of the reforms was the revitalization of the *old* political order. By the turn of the nineteenth century, the bureaucratic elite of the Ottoman state had come to realize the unintended consequences of the devolution of the resource collection processes, and the reliance on tax farmers ultimately undermined the bureaucratic elite. They wanted to regain prominence by reversing the unintended consequences of their previous choices.

Sultan Selim III's efforts to restore the state to its former glory came to a halt in 1807 when the Janissaries stationed in the capital rebelled against the throne. Selim III's insistence on restructuring the Ottoman military along European lines had gone against the interests of the janissaries, who were accustomed to using their privileges for personal gain. The janissaries stationed in Rumelian provinces, Serbia, and Adrianople had already attempted an open rebellion earlier. In 1807, the rebellious soldiers managed to secure the support of disgruntled sectors of the high *ulema* (religious elite), including the *Sheikh-ul-Islam* (the highest religious authority), who issued a *fetva* (religious decree) condemning the reforms.[631] The rebels dethroned and imprisoned Selim III. Mustafa IV, put on the throne by the rebels even though he was considered by many unfit to rule, later had Selim III assassinated.

The most interesting aspect of the 1807 coup d'état was the role the *ayan* played in it. Selim III's efforts to strengthen the central administration through administrative reform, particularly his policy to revert the agricultural order to its traditional form based on the *tımar* system, were directly contradictory to the interests of the *ayan*. Nevertheless, the *ayan* did not adopt an openly hostile stance toward Selim III during his relatively brief reign but tried to manipulate his policy by articulating themselves into the policy-making process. The *ayan*'s cautionary policy of avoiding direct confrontation with the state and the bureaucratic elite could partially be explained by the fact that the new provincial elites, unlike the landowners in Central and Western Europe, lacked judicial autonomy. At least, in theory, the state could confiscate their estates and revoke their tax farming privileges.

The 1807 rebellion provided the *ayan* with an opportunity to influence policy directly. Upon receiving the news of the coup attempt, Alemdar Mustafa Paşa of

---

631 The religious bureaucracy was critical of Selim's reforms which they considered an imposition of western values on the Ottoman state. The decree stated that the sultan was guilty of "introducing among the Muslims the manners of infidels and showing an intention to suppress the janissaries." Patrick Balfour Kinross, *The Ottoman Centuries: The Rise and Fall of the Turkish Empire* (New York: Morrow, 1977), 433.

Ruscuk, "the most celebrated *ayan* of the period," rushed his personal army, several thousand troops in strength, to the capital to "save the throne." Even though the military intervention came too late to save Selim III, Alemdar Mustafa Pasha played a decisive role in the dethronement of Mustafa IV and his replacement by Mahmud II.

Mahmud II, who barely escaped being eliminated by Mustafa IV and found himself on the throne in 1808, began his reign "with the most humiliating concession to the *ayan*."[632] The *ayan* of Rumelia, capitalizing on their role in restoring Mahmud II to power, demanded a series of rights from the sultan. Mahmud II had little choice but to take their demands seriously, not only because the *ayan* had gathered over 7,000 troops in Istanbul but also because he had to continue to rely on these provincial elites to collect taxes.

Negotiations between the *ayan* and palace resulted in an imperial decree known as *Sened-i Ittifak* (Bill of Union) of 1808.[633] The decree formally delineated, for the first time in Ottoman history, respective domains of power and authority of the throne and the provincial elites. The signatory *ayan*, who claimed to also represent other *ayan* who could not attend the meeting in Istanbul, recognized the primacy of the throne and the authority of the sultan. Moreover, the *ayan* agreed, for themselves and their sons, to defend the monarchy by any means necessary against all internal and external foes. While on the surface, the *ayan*'s promise of military support in case of war and rebellion was a gain for the central administration, it also allowed the *ayan* to position themselves as the "protector of the throne."

Moreover, Article 5 of the 1808 decree explicitly stated that in return for the allegiance to the crown, *ayan* were officially granted property rights over their lands and the right to pass them on to their heirs. This clause is a major departure from the traditional Ottoman property rights regime. *Sened-i Ittifak* of 1808 transformed *ayan*'s *de facto* control over agricultural land into *de jure* property rights.[634]

---

632 Karpat, "The Transformation of the Ottoman Empire, 1789-1908."

633 Halil İnalcık, "Sened-I Ittifak ve Gulhane Hatt-I Humayunu," *Belleten* 28 (1964); 605-90; Stanford Shaw and Ezel Shaw, *History of the Ottoman Empire*, vol. Vol III (Cambridge: Cambridge University Press, 1977), 2.

634 Additional provisions of the negotiated agreement dealt with the role of the *ayan* and the central bureaucracy in matters of tax collection and treatment of peasants. The decree underlined the necessity of confining the authority of government officials to their designated offices and areas of jurisdiction. This clause, like many others, can be interpreted as a compromise between the central bureaucracy and the provincial

The negotiated settlement between the bureaucratic elite and the provincial elites represents both the high point of the process of devolution and decentralization *and* the peak of the conflict between the central and rural elites. The special rights granted to the *ayan* by the throne were akin to what Perry Anderson labeled the "parcelization of sovereignty."[635] However, unlike Western European feudalism, the parcelization in the Ottoman Empire was a "consequence of the vertical disassociation." Instead, the "horizontal integration of the estate system with the world market,"[636] lay at the root of Ottoman parcelization. As Sunar notes, "1808 marks the point in Ottoman history when the customary preoccupation of the state with immediate financial concerns caught up with it politically: the cumulative effects of revenue concerns gave rise to a constellation of social groups, which in time came to challenge the patrimonial power of the state."[637]

The events of 1808, particularly the demonstrated ability of the Rumelian *ayan* to transform their political and economic capital into military power, signaled the central elites in Istanbul that the provincial notables were no longer to be trusted. In terms of the explanatory framework employed here, the provincial elites in the early nineteenth century were now perceived as a threat to the revenue-extracting capacity of the central bureaucracy.

The post-1808 strategy of the central elite had two related goals—both in congruence with my argument: (1) undermining the power of the *ayan* by rechanneling access to economic resources *and* (2) forming an alliance with the merchants and other holders of urban capital. A partnership with the capital would allow the central elites to not only balance the threat posed by the provincial elites but also slow down, if not stop, the fiscal decay by bringing in new economic resources. This new strategy brought about a period of institutional reform that started right after the proclamation of the Bill of Union in 1808 and lasted until the end of Mahmud II's reign in 1839.

Like his predecessor Selim III, Mahmud II started his reform program by restructuring the military. The janissaries, who interrupted Selim III's reforms in 1807, were the first target of Mahmud II's agenda. In 1808, Mahmud II ordered the establishment of a new military unit. Experts and weapons were imported

elite. While the *ayan* was recognizing the authority of the central administration, the latter was also being forced to relinquish its control in the provinces.

635 Anderson, *Lineages of the Absolutist State*.

636 Sunar and İslamoğlu-İnan, "State and Economy in the Ottoman Empire," 72.

637 Ibid.

from various European countries for the new army.[638] In the face of the pressing external conflicts and domestic security threats, most notably the independent armies of the *ayan* in the provinces, Mahmud II made it a priority that the new army was trained and equipped according to modern standards.

The sultan and his bureaucracy also reformed the fiscal policies of the state. In the 1810s, the central administration started to reclaim existing *malikane* contracts from their original owners.[639] In their effort to diminish the fiscal authority of the *ayan*, the bureaucratic elite relied on various means, ranging from exploiting rivalries among provincial elites[640] to using brute military force. The efforts of the central administration to undermine the big tax farmers were also supported by the petty tax farmers who were adversely affected by the monopolistic practices of the former.

The critical turning point in the relations between the central and provincial elites came in 1826. After a decade of military reform, Mahmud II finally abolished the reactionary janissary order and replaced it with a modern army, *Asakir-i Mansure-i Muhammediyye* (Victorious Soldiers of Mohammed). Having a 75,000-strong army at his disposal, the sultan launched a full-fledged campaign against the *ayan*.

Equally importantly, a new government agency, the *Directorate of Vakıfs*, was established. As religious institutions, *vakıfs* had a privileged status, including exceptions from confiscation and taxes.[641] However, throughout the eighteenth century, the tax farmers and *çiftlik* owners in Anatolia and Rumelia established *vakıfs* to accumulate wealth beyond the central administration's reach. The new government directorate was to centralize the administration of *vakıfs* and other religious establishments and to rechannel their revenues toward the central administration.[642]

In 1831, the sultan also officially abolished the *tımar* order. Even though this method of tax collection had declined after the seventeenth century, the remaining *sipahis* (administrators of *tımars*) were now in close proximity to the

---

638 Aksan, "Review Article: Ottoman Military Matters."

639 Pamuk, "The Evolution of Fiscal Institutions in the Ottoman Empire, 1500-1914."

640 In 1813 the central administration tried to break the monopoly of the leading Karaosmanoğlu family in western Anatolia by assigning tax-collection duties to a member of the rival family. Pamuk, *Osmanlı-Türkiye Iktisadi Tarihi, 1500-1914*, 214.

641 Jon E. Mandaville, "Usurious Piety: The Cash Waqf Controversy in the Ottoman Empire," *International Journal of Middle East Studies* 10 (1979).

642 Ibid.

provincial *ayan*. With the abolition of *tımar*, the lands of the last *sipahi*s were confiscated by the state, their revenue to be used to finance the new army.

Despite all these changes, the reforms ultimately failed to produce a decisive shift in the balance of power between the central and provincial elites in favor of the former. There are two main reasons for the ineffectiveness of the centralization effort. First, the central elites did not possess the means to finance an expanded administrative and fiscal apparatus that would replace the existing order. As Sunar observes, "the successful attempts of Mahmud II were significant, but so was his failure…He was successful in eliminating the military power of the *ayan* and initiating military and administrative reforms. But he failed to provide an adequate tax basis for a sustained process of innovations, on the one hand, to pay simultaneously for wars and court and cultural life on the other."[643] Even in cases where the central administration successfully eliminated the fiscal and administrative posts filled by the provincial elites, "state functions had to rely on landholders and notables organized in their private capacities, or else on semi-bureaucratic organizations that were largely run by the very same local groups."[644]

Seen in this light, the institutional reforms in the first half of the nineteenth century were comparable (in terms of their limitations) *not* to the reforms of Habsburg ruler Maria Theresia and her successors in the second half of the eighteenth century but rather to the failed centralization efforts of Maximilian I (1459-1519) and Ferdinand I (1503-1564). These two Habsburg rulers undertook a series of institutional reforms in the early sixteenth century to impose a common legal, financial, and administrative system upon the imperial lands.[645] Even though such reforms produced the earliest forms of future centralized institutions, they were ultimately of very limited long-term consequence. The noble estates resisted centralization. Even more importantly, the reforms were eventually constrained by their reliance on the local elites for tax collection, administration, and military purposes, and lacked the resources to supplant them.

The second reason for the failure of the Ottoman institutional reforms concerns the diversification of the economic base of the provincial elites. Even though they started as tax farmers, during the commercialization of agriculture,

643 Sunar, "State and Economy in the Ottoman Empire."

644 Ibid.

645 Watzenig, "Die Finanz- Und Wirtschaftspolitik in Den Erblaendern Und Im Reich Unter Maximilian I in Den Jahren 1493 Bis 1507"; Fichtner, *Ferdinand I of Austria: The Politics of Dynasticism in the Age of Reformation*.

the provincial elites transformed themselves into owners/controllers of large commercial estates. Thus, while Mahmud II's reforms partially managed to reverse the development of *ayan* as tax farmers, the growth of commercial agriculture continued unabated.[646] On the contrary, commercialization sped up after 1820 when European demand for agricultural goods increased considerably with the onset of widespread industrialization.[647] The price differential between the domestic and external markets pushed the landowners to ramp up their production for European markets. About 90 percent of the Ottoman export to Europe consisted of agricultural commodities like tobacco, grapes, silk, nuts, olive oil, and grain.[648]

In the 1830s and 1840s, the central administration attempted to confiscate the largest estates in Anatolia and the Balkans.[649] In 1858, the policy of land redistribution produced a new Land Code, which formalized the rights over cultivated lands and distributed titles to peasant families.[650] The new legislation was geared toward reanimating the traditional (pre-1695) policy of the Ottoman state that protected the peasantry against landowners.

Even more important to the increasingly aggressive stance toward the landowners was the change in the attitude of the central elites toward the merchants. Displaying a radical departure from the unfavorable view of merchants, the bureaucratic elites of the 1830s sought to ally with them. The "reluctant but inevitable" alliance with the merchants "was designed to bypass the landholding class to provide increased revenue for the state."[651]

The development that marked the onset of the new policy was the issuing of the so-called *Gülhane Hatt-ı Şerifi* (aka *Tanzimat Fermanı*). Prepared and issued by order of the new sultan, Abdülmecid, who succeeded Mahmud II, this edict

646 İslamoğlu-İnan and Keyder, "Agenda for Ottoman History."

647 Berend and Ranki, *European Periphery and Industrialization: 1780-1914*; Tom Kemp, *Industrialization in Nineteenth Century Europe* (London: Longman Group, 1971). As noted earlier, even the western parts of the Habsburg Empire, Bohemia, and Moravia were industrializing and importing raw materials and foodstuff. For the industrialization of Central and Eastern Europe in the nineteenth century, see Berend, *History Derailed: Central and Eastern Europe in the Long Nineteenth Century*.

648 Pamuk, *Osmanlı-Türkiye Iktisadi Tarihi, 1500-1914*, 216. Also see, Quataert, *Manufacturing in the Ottoman Empire and Turkey, 1500-1950*.

649 Pamuk, *Osmanlı-Türkiye Iktisadi Tarihi, 1500-1914*, 199-200.

650 Keyder, "Small Peasant Ownership in Turkey: Historical Formation and Present Structure," 61.

651 Sunar and İslamoğlu-İnan, "State and Economy in the Ottoman Empire," 80.

proposed reorganization *(Tanzimat)* of the state "to bring the benefits of good administration" to the provinces of the empire through new institutions.[652] The document proposed several changes that would further undermine the provincial powers by redistributing economic resources from the landowners to the holders of merchant and financial capital.

Several key institutional reforms were accomplished in the decades following the *Tanzimat Fermanı*. The first Ottoman paper banknotes were introduced in 1840.[653] Throughout the 1840s, the Ottoman financial system was reorganized; a new Civil and Criminal Code, modeled after French law, was put together. The first steps toward phasing out the guild system were taken. In the administrative sphere, new agencies, including the Council of Public Instruction 1846, were established. To meet the personnel needs of the new agencies, the first modern universities were founded in 1848.[654] These developments were directly in the interests of the merchant and finance capital operating throughout the empire.

In the 1840s, life-term tax farming was systematically phased out. Along with the pulled-backed, long-term tax farming contracts, the *Tanzimat* policy also entailed the removal of *corvée* and other types of forced labor, which had permeated Ottoman agricultural production in the eighteenth century. However, as noted before, the central administration was not equipped to take away tax collection from the provincial elites entirely. The inefficiency of the state-appointed tax collectors forced the state to bring back, at least on an *ad hoc* basis, elements of tax farming. Indeed, tax farming on a smaller scale persisted until the end of the century.[655]

The nominal effect of centralization efforts on tax revenues is difficult to measure. The most reliable data available today indicate that at the end of the eighteenth century, the state could collect 3 percent of the GDP through taxes. After the reforms in the first half of the nineteenth century, the share of the GDP reaching the treasury rose to approximately 6 percent.[656]

The second wave of reforms came with the issuing of a new imperial edict in 1856, *Gülhane Hatt-ı Hümayunu* (aka *Islahat Fermanı*). On the surface, the

---

652 Şerif Mardin, *The Genesis of Young Ottoman Thought a Study in the Modernization of Turkish Political Ideas*, 1st Syracuse University Press ed. (Syracuse, NY: Syracuse University Press, 2000), 173.

653 Pamuk, "A Monetary History of the Ottoman Empire."

654 Ezel Shaw, "Tanzimat in the Ottoman Empire Age of Reform in Europe" (paper presented at the Tanzimat'in 150. Yıldönümü Uluslararası Sempozyumu, İstanbul, 1989).

655 Pamuk, *Osmanlı-Türkiye Iktisadi Tarihi, 1500-1914*, 200-01.

656 Pamuk, "The Evolution of Fiscal Institutions in the Ottoman Empire, 1500-1914," 20-21.

new charter was imposed by European powers pressuring the Ottoman state to protect the non-Muslim minorities in the empire. Indeed, the document opened with the following statement:

> The guarantees promised on our part by the Hatt-ı Hümayun of Gülhane, and in conformity with the Tanzimat, to all the subjects of my Empire, without distinction of classes or religion, for the security of their persons and property and the preservation of their honor, are today confirmed and consolidated, and efficacious measures shall be taken in order that they may have their full and entire effect. All the privileges and spiritual immunities granted by my ancestors *ab antiquo*, and at subsequent dates, to all Christian communities or other non-Muslim persuasions established in my empire under my protection shall be confirmed and maintained.

However, there were more to 1856 reforms than the recognition of the rights of religious minorities. Along with the civil clauses that reorganized the traditional *millet* system by guaranteeing the freedom of all religious communities, the decree of 1856 included several clauses geared toward enlisting the support of the merchants. In a frequently overlooked clause, the sultan announced that

> Steps shall also be taken for the formation of roads and canals to increase the facilities of communication and to increase the sources of the wealth of the country. Everything that can impede commerce and agriculture shall be abolished. To accomplish these objects means shall be sought to profit by the science, art, and the funds of Europe, and thus gradually to execute them.

The almost mercantilist tone of the decree and the promise to abolish everything that could impede commerce and agriculture are indicative of the strategy adopted by the bureaucratic elite after 1839. The strategy involved enlisting the support of the merchants in the escalated conflict against the provincial elites.

The parallel between the Ottoman elite's stance toward the capital in the 1850s and the Habsburg elite's mercantilist policy after 1660 is noteworthy. As discussed in Chapter 4, starting as early as 1660, the ruling elites of the Habsburg monarchy established capital-friendly institutions and policies. The main motivation underlying the Habsburg ruling elite's changing attitude toward the merchants and manufacturers was the high-intensity conflict between the ruling elite, and the landed nobility. Almost two centuries later, Ottoman ruling elites, reacting to the changes in the incentive structure, followed a similar strategy.

However, there are three important differences between the two cases. First, a shift in the elite strategy occurred almost two centuries late in the Ottoman case. Thus, the international economic environment, particularly the volume and composition of intra-regional trade, was different in the mid-nineteenth century, which shaped the interests of domestic actors, particularly the capital.

Second, while the Habsburg landed elites were a historically entrenched class of nobility, the *ayan*, which threatened the primacy of Ottoman elites, was essentially a product of the state policy in the early eighteenth century.

Third, and most importantly, while the Habsburg elite's effort to incorporate the capital into the ruling coalition succeeded, the Ottoman elite's strategy of enlisting the support of the merchants vis-à-vis the landlords *failed*. The deteriorating state finances left no choice but to borrow heavily from external financial markets, which resulted in the bankruptcy of the state and its loss of economic independence by the end of the nineteenth century. Before going into the growing debt and the ultimate economic demise of the Ottoman state in the latter half of the nineteenth century, let me explain why capital incorporation failed.

The bureaucratic elite's effort to enlist merchants' support failed because, for the merchants, the *costs* of incorporation outweighed expected *gains* from state protection. First, the nature of the economic activities that the merchants and other capital holders were engaged in at this time did not necessarily require the involvement of a centralized, hierarchical state to alleviate market imperfections.[657] On the contrary, as conduits in the export of raw materials to Europe and the import of manufactured goods back into the Ottoman domestic market, the institutional interests of the merchants were much more closely aligned with the export-oriented landlords; both sectors were in favor of rapid and direct integration to the world economy.[658]

Second, and equally important, the costs of seeking the protection of a centralized state would be unacceptably high for the merchants given the past provisionist economic policies of the state. In terms of the theoretical framework laid out in Chapter 2, the merchants preferred "independence" to "protection."

Throughout the nineteenth century, the conditions of the world economy were increasingly favorable to the Ottoman export-oriented sectors. The main factor was the increased demand generated by the new industries in Europe, particularly textiles. In addition, independent factors such as the trade policy of Britain, which was eager to purchase from the periphery to clear its accounts, and later the Crimean War and even the American Civil War, generated unprecedented

657 Spruyt, "Institutional Selection in International Relations: State Anarchy as Order." See my critique of this position in Chapter 2.

658 Şevket Pamuk, "The Ottoman Empire in Comparative Perspective," *Review* 11, no. 2 (1988).

demand for agricultural goods and raw materials. Ottoman agriculture, particularly in Western Anatolia, responded very strongly to this pull.[659]

In addition to increasing European demand, the growth of the domestic markets throughout the nineteenth century contributed to commercialization. The growing population of Anatolian towns—the estimated total population of Anatolia rose from 9-10 million in the early nineteenth century to 16-17 by the beginning of the twentieth century[660]—boosted agricultural demand. The demand for growing urban centers only heightened the bureaucratic elites' sensibilities regarding the supply of foodstuffs to the cities.

Even faster growing than the demand for agricultural goods was the domestic demand for commodities produced in Europe. The relative decline in production costs in Europe rendered their commodities more affordable for Ottoman consumers.[661] After the first quarter of the nineteenth century, Ottoman bazaars were filled with goods imported from Europe, particularly Britain, France, and the Habsburg Empire. Quataert describes the situation as follows: "[B]efore 1830, there was scarcely to be found in the bazaars a piece of European manufacture," whereas "in 1836, beleaguered Ottoman merchants in Trabzon had opened hundreds of shops filled with western manufactures."[662] The domination of the Ottoman domestic market by European manufacturers hurt the Ottoman manufacturers. The nascent industries mainly consisted of low-value textile production in Western Anatolia and had a hard time competing with cheap and higher-quality European products.

How exactly this new economic structure shaped the interests of the merchants is even more important than the effects of the competition with European markets on Ottoman manufacturing. Particularly after 1830, the Ottoman merchants who were driven out of the domestic markets repositioned themselves as suppliers of raw materials to European producers. In addition to the export of agricultural goods to Central and Western Europe through the Balkan trade routes, the Muslim merchants in the coastal towns of West Anatolia and the

---

659 Kasaba, "Incorporation of the Ottoman Empire, 1750-1820," 212-15.

660 Pamuk, *Osmanlı-Türkiye Iktisadi Tarihi, 1500-1914*, 216.

661 For a detailed review of economic consumption in the Ottoman Empire, see Donald Quataert, *Consumption Studies and the History of the Ottoman Empire* (State University of New York Press).

662 Quataert, *Manufacturing in the Ottoman Empire and Turkey, 1500-1950*, 94.

Black Sea region served as intermediaries to the European firms looking to purchase cheap raw materials.[663]

Unlike the mercantile classes in Bohemia, Moravia, and even parts of Hungary which demanded the state to step in and protect them from market externalities, Ottoman merchants were *not* in favor of a more hierarchical market structure maintained by a stronger state. The merchants' negative attitude toward greater state involvement in the economy was directly shaped by the provisionist economic policy of the state. As noted, the bureaucratic elite supported mercantile activities only when they remained within the boundaries drawn by the state, i.e., supply of foodstuffs and commodities to the cities. The export of such commodities was strictly controlled by the central administration in conjunction with the urban guilds.

By the end of the eighteenth century, the provisionist economic policy of the state had assumed a predatory character. Crumbling under the dearth of liquidity, the bureaucratic elite increased the pressure on the merchants and imposed further fiscal and administrative responsibilities on the merchants to extract additional resources from them. Areas of manufacturing and trade that had the greatest proto-industrial potential suffered under predatory policies. Those who produced or traded cloth, thread, iron, timber, pitch, hemp, etc. were particularly burdened.[664] Wealthier merchants (in addition to the owners of commercial estates) were required to equip troops and send them to the front on their own account. By the end of the eighteenth century, "compulsory loans" had become a common practice. For the first time in its history, the Ottoman state began confiscating the private properties of wealthy individuals. Under these conditions, "the obstacles to capital accumulation and investment reached a peak."[665]

With the proclamation of the *Tanzimat* Decree in 1839 and the *Islahat* Decree in 1856, which guaranteed private property rights and promised to support manufacturing and trade, the central administration was trying to assuage the well-justified concerns of merchants and capital holders. However, the provisionist policies did not incentivize the capital holders to respond positively to the central bureaucracy's attempt to enlist their support. Even while they vouched

663 For a critical review of the evidence regarding a comprador bourgeoisie in this period, see Reşat Kasaba, "Was There a Comprador Bourgeoisie in Mid-Nineteenth Century Western Anatolia?," *Review* xi, no. 2 (1988).

664 Genç and Quataert, "Ottoman Industry in the Eighteenth Century: General Framework, Characteristics and Main Trends."

665 Ibid., 66.

for guaranteeing private property rights and supporting trade, the bureaucratic elite continued to implement economic policies that directly undermined mercantile activities.

Consider the extension of rights and privileges provided to foreign merchants in the nineteenth century. The capitulations existed since the sixteenth century; they typically granted individual Christian communities (*millets*) autonomy in governing their affairs, including commercial activities. Capitulations were part of the Ottoman foreign policy to use trade privileges for diplomatic purposes [666] and temporary measures to increase customs revenue. However, at the end of the eighteenth century, the central administration began to grant more extensive benefits to foreign merchants that went beyond those available to local merchants. The low customs duties that most European merchants were subject to practically eliminated the chances for domestic manufacturers to compete with their European counterparts.[667]

The policy of providing selective benefits to European merchants culminated in the infamous Baltalimanı Commerce Treaty of 1838, which fully opened Ottoman agricultural markets to foreign merchants. In return for Britain and France's continuing political and economic support, the bureaucratic elite granted a wide range of selective benefits to the merchants of these countries. The most important clause of the treaty involved domestic customs duties. Before 1838 all merchants, Muslim and non-Muslim alike, were subject to 8 percent customs fees and taxes whenever they moved a commodity from one town to another. With the Baltalimanı Treaty, non-Muslim merchants were declared exempt from domestic customs duties, while Muslim merchants were kept outside the exemption.[668]

Once again, note the contrast between Ottoman and Habsburg trade policies. Particularly after 1740, all Habsburg rulers including the conservative government of Francis I protected domestic manufacturers from foreign competition through tariffs, subsidies, and other mercantilist instruments. In contrast, Ottoman economic policies were guided by fiscal concerns and the political rationale of the bureaucratic elite, undermining the already limited competitive capacity of Ottoman merchants and manufacturers. Given the persistence of the provisionist policies aimed at subjecting all mercantile activity to the political

---

666 The first capitulations were granted to France in the sixteenth century to forge a Franco-Ottoman alliance against the Habsburgs.

667 Pamuk, *Osmanlı-Türkiye Iktisadi Tarihi, 1500-1914*, 165-6.

668 Ibid., 206.

interests of the elite, it is hardly surprising that capital holders did not respond positively to the bureaucratic elites' efforts to forge an alliance but instead sided with the export-oriented landlords.

The common interests of the merchants and export-oriented landlords were based on more than their shared aversion to a centralized state apparatus. The two groups were also connected by strong financial ties. As previously noted, urban capital holders, particularly the non-Muslim groups like Greek, Armenian, and Levantine communities in Istanbul, traditionally faced barriers in capital accumulation. Since they could not directly invest in profitable businesses such as exports (and contraband trade), they turned their merchant capital into finance capital. Throughout the eighteenth century, non-Muslim capital holders supplied large loans, particularly to the owners of *çiftlik*s and *malikane*s. Consequently, they developed a vested interest in decentralized fiscal structure and export-oriented agriculture.

In most cases, the legal ownership of both types of properties was divided into many, in some cases dozens of, subcontracts. However, in rare circumstances, the capital invested in acquiring *çiftlik*s originated from the *çiftlik* owner. The actual owners of these estates were heavily indebted to a relatively small number of private financiers. As Kasaba shows, "starting from the *çiftliks*' inception, the development of the *çiftlik* agriculture was determined by the pure monetary interests of the financiers who in turn imposed a framework that shaped the *çiftlik* owners' attitude toward farming and toward their estates."[669]

Jewish, Greek, and Armenian entrepreneurs were integrated into the operation of tax farming and commercial agriculture as bankers, brokers, and accountants. Financiers were also heavily engaged in speculative activities surrounding tax farming contracts. In the absence of a well-developed banking and credit system, usury became the most profitable sector of the existing tax farming. Private finance firms derived substantial profits by arbitrating between different kinds of money circulating in Anatolia.[670]

A well-documented phenomenon in Ottoman financial history is the rise of the *Galata Bankerleri* (Bankers of Galata).[671] The predominantly Jewish and

669 Kasaba, "Incorporation of the Ottoman Empire, 1750-1820," 829.

670 Kasaba reports, for instance, that "it was not uncommon for a firm to transfer the contract that they had just received on the spot to another firm for a profit of hundred percent or more." Kasaba, "Was There a Comprador Bourgeoisie in Mid-Nineteenth Century Western Anatolia?," 219.

671 Haydar Kazgan, *Osmanlı'da Avrupa Finans Kapitali* (Ankara: Roma Yayınları, 2005).

Armenian capital holders, geographically concentrated in the *Galata* district of Istanbul, formed a well-connected financial network.[672] Having accumulated considerable wealth both by collecting commissions in long-distance trade and by investing in or otherwise indirectly benefiting from life-term tax farming contracts, these financiers were heavily engaged in the domestic borrowing of the Ottoman state. After 1760, the Bankers of Galata provided sizeable loans to the Porte. In addition to lending their capital, these bankers brokered short-term loans from European banks to the Ottoman treasury.[673]

5. Conclusion

By the mid-nineteenth century, the structure of the intra-elite conflict in the Ottoman Empire was marked by a clash between the merchants and export-oriented landlords, who favored a more rapid financial and commercial integration into the European economy, and the central bureaucratic elite, who feared that further integration would endanger their political survival. The reform movement, which started with Selim III and Mahmud II and culminated in the 1839 and 1856 edicts, turned out to be nothing more than "the class project of the bureaucracy attempting to preserve and defend themselves against the perceived class project of the rising bourgeoisie."[674] By offering several side payments to the merchants and other capital holders, the central bureaucracy tried, and ultimately failed, to short-circuit the alliance of merchants and export-oriented landlords.

The commercial activities of Ottoman merchants in the first half of the nineteenth century—exporting raw materials and agricultural commodities and importing finished products—did not fit well with the centralized fiscal state apparatus. Even more importantly, the provisionist and anti-merchant policies of the central bureaucracy rendered a rapprochement between the state elites and the capital holders too costly for the latter.

In terms of the explanatory framework of this book, the outcome of the institutional transformation of the Ottoman state from 1600 to 1881 was the combined product of the demand- and supply-side dynamics of intra-elite conflict.

---

672 Galata historically belonged to the Genoese merchants who enjoyed a privileged status since the conquest of Constantinople in 1453. Crowley, *1453: The Holy War for Constantinople and the Clash of Islam and the West.*

673 Pamuk, *Osmanlı-Türkiye Iktisadi Tarihi, 1500-1914*, 174-77.

674 Çağlar Keyder, "Bureaucracy and Bourgeoisie: Reform and Revolution in the Age of Imperialism," *Review* 11, no. 2 (1988): 159.

While supply-side concerns, i.e., the desire of the bureaucracy to undermine the power of the landowners resulted in the centralizing efforts, demand-side dynamics, i.e., the strong preference of the merchants for a decentralized fiscal state apparatus, resulted in the failure of centralization.

The exclusion of the capital from the ruling alliance had crucial economic and fiscal consequences for the Ottoman Empire and the Turkish state that would succeed it. First, the failed centralization stunted economic growth throughout the empire and facilitated the peripheralization of the Ottoman economy. Second, the persistent inability of the state to extract resources from the merchants and export-oriented landlords paved the way for excessive external borrowing, spiraling debt, and, ultimately, insolvency.

The relative importance of Ottoman manufacturing and trade declined throughout the nineteenth century. In 1830, the Ottoman economy accounted for 3 percent of the global trade; by 1910, this share had dropped to under 1 percent.[675] Even though certain sectors of the economy expanded in size, their relative share in European trade continued to decline.[676] The only sector that showed signs of dynamism was textiles, including raw cotton, dyestuffs, yarn, and cloth production. Yet even textiles remained low-value manufacturing, based chiefly on handicraft and putting-out systems. Lacking the capital to upgrade technologies and streamline production, textile manufacturers could not compete with European textile producers. In the late seventeenth century, textile manufacturers in the Balkan provinces, particularly Salonica, controlled a relatively promising market share in Italy, France, and Central Europe. By the middle of the nineteenth century, however, almost all Ottoman cotton and wool cloth producers had lost their market shares.[677]

Only a few privately owned factories opened in the nineteenth century. They were concentrated in certain regions: Balkan provinces, port cities of Anatolia (Istanbul, Izmir, and Trabzon in particular), and a few larger urban centers in southeastern Anatolia. Production in these sites was almost exclusively geared toward domestic markets. The first mechanized cloth factory in the empire was opened in 1908 (more than 150 years after the establishment of mechanized weaving in Britain) in the Balkan province of Niuasta. Another modernized textile workshop was opened in Salonica in 1909. The other notable examples of privately owned enterprises were the Ottoman Cloth and Material Factory in

675 Quataert, *Manufacturing in the Ottoman Empire and Turkey, 1500-1950*, 16.
676 Ibid.
677 Ibid., 89-90.

Istanbul and the cotton and wool weaving mills that opened in the Izmir region just before the First World War.

Unlike the Habsburg state, which actively promoted industrialization through incentives and subsidies, the Ottoman state adopted a market policy toward commerce and manufacturing in the late nineteenth century. State involvement remained limited to the few state-owned textile manufacturing workshops in Istanbul that were established to meet the demands of the palace and the military exclusively. These state-funded factories were "subsidized establishments with guaranteed markets."[678]

Unable to tap into the resources generated by the merchants and export-oriented landlords, the bureaucratic elite was in an even deeper fiscal abyss. The unfavorable trade balance, along with the longest streak of inflation in Ottoman history (between 1780 and 1850, prices increased 12 to 15 times throughout the empire[679]), depleted the liquidity to cover the expenses of the state and the central army. In the 1840s, the government began to borrow from European creditors through their financial connections in Istanbul.

The onset of large-scale external borrowing came during the Crimean War in 1854.[680] To pay for the war, the Ottoman government began to sell long-term bonds in European financial markets. Ottoman bonds were in high demand in Europe; they yielded about 11-20 percent annual return, very high compared to 3.5-4.5 percent interest rates in Britain and even lower rates in France.[681] From 1854 to 1873, external funds became the "most important means of dealing with the recurring budgetary difficulties" as the government borrowed large amounts with high-interest rates in London, Paris, Vienna, Frankfurt, and other major capital markets in Europe.[682]

---

678 Ibid., 3.

679 Pamuk, *Osmanlı-Türkiye Iktisadi Tarihi, 1500-1914*, 26; Şevket Pamuk, "The Ottoman Empire and The "Great Depression" Of 1873-1896," *Journal of Economic History* 44 (1984).

680 Kazgan, *Osmanlı'da Avrupa Finans Kapitali*, Ch 20.

681 Emine Kıray, *Osmanlı'da Ekonomik Yapı Ve Dış Borçlar* (Istanbul: İletişim Yayınları, 1995), 25.

682 Pamuk, "The Evolution of Fiscal Institutions in the Ottoman Empire, 1500-1914," 24. From 1854 to 1862, England was the most important lender to the Ottoman state; about 90 percent of all bonds sold in Europe were sold in London. By 1869, France grabbed leadership with 66 percent. Germany, even though they joined the party rather late, would become the second biggest lender by the end of the century. Kıray, *Osmanlı'da Ekonomik Yapı Ve Dış Borçlar*.

As Pamuk documents, most of the funds were spent on the daily expenditures of the government and on building new palaces and a new navy.[683] Only a trivial fraction of the revenue generated by the long-term bonds was invested in infrastructure, industry, or any other means that would increase the capacity of the state to pay back. By the end of the 1860s, the Ottoman government reached a point where it had to issue new bonds to maintain debt payments.[684] As the government's capacity to repay its debts declined, European creditors, became less and less willing to invest in Ottoman bonds. The global depression and financial crisis of 1873 led to a complete halt of lending by the European creditors.[685] By 1875, the government had accumulated a debt of 200 million sterling with 11 million annual interest payments. In comparison, the total annual domestic revenue was 18 million sterling.[686]

Since cycling debt through new bonds was no longer an option, the government declared a moratorium on its outstanding debt in 1875-1876. After a long negotiation with the individual creditors and their governments, in 1881, the Ottoman administration agreed to establish the Ottoman Public Debt Administration (OPDA).[687] Acting as a multinational collection agency, the OPDA was authorized to control parts of the Ottoman finances and ensure the payment of the outstanding debts. The establishment of the OPDA in 1881 marked the fiscal collapse of the Ottoman state.

---

683 Pamuk, *Osmanlı-Türkiye Iktisadi Tarihi, 1500-1914*, 231. Also see, C. G. A. Clay, *Gold for the Sultan: Western Bankers and Ottoman Finance 1856-1881: A Contribution to Ottoman and to International Financial History*, International Library of Historical Studies (London; New York New York, NY: I.B. Tauris; In the U.S.A. and Canada distributed by St. Martin's Press, 2000).

684 Pamuk, "The Evolution of Fiscal Institutions in the Ottoman Empire, 1500-1914," 29.

685 Pamuk, "The Ottoman Empire and The "Great Depression" Of 1873-1896."

686 Pamuk, *Osmanlı-Türkiye Iktisadi Tarihi, 1500-1914*, 281.

687 Edhem Eldem, "Ottoman Financial Integration with Europe: Foreign Loans, the Ottoman Bank and the Ottoman Public Debt," *European Review* 13, no. 3 (2005): 431.

Chapter 7 Conclusion

1. Revisiting the Arguments

This book offered a causal explanation of the macro-structural changes in the Habsburg and Ottoman Empires from the seventeenth to the ninenteenth century. Both states experienced a fiscal crisis in the 1600s, which set off two separate chains of temporally ordered and causally connected events—"reactive sequences"[688]—transforming their fiscal institutions.

The puzzling aspect of the transformation was that the ultimate institutional outcomes in the two cases were the exact opposites of the initial institutional configurations. The Habsburg Empire started from a very disadvantageous position: its administrative structure was highly fragmented, its infrastructural reach was short, and its capacity to collect taxes was severely limited. Nonetheless, by the mid-nineteenth century, the Habsburg state attained a much higher infrastructural and fiscal capacity by centralizing tax collection. The state then used its infrastructural power to steer economic development by reforming agricultural relations, removing barriers to trade and manufacturing as well as providing incentives toward industrialization. Ottoman state, on the other hand, though it initially possessed a centralized administrative and fiscal apparatus supported by a strong military and treasury, ended up with much lower fiscal capacity. The declining infrastructural and fiscal capacity of the state not only failed to promote economic growth in the nineteenth century but also slowed and stifled development. I called the puzzling divergence in the developmental trajectories—the centralization of the Habsburg state and the decentralization of the Ottoman state—a *reversal of fortunes.*

I asserted that distributional conflict among elites is the key to solving this puzzle. I proposed an explanatory framework that connects the structure of the intra-elite conflict to institutional change by way of political coalitions. The causal chain I constructed had three main components:

(1) Antecedent conditions and independent variable (*the mode of imperial organization* and the *structure of intra-elite conflict*): I showed that the Habsburg Empire from 1300 to 1700 was *horizontally* organized; the central administration was dependent on local intermediaries for critical governmental

688 Mahoney, "Path Dependence in Historical Sociology."

functions, most notably tax collection. As a corollary, the Habsburg elite was severely divided between central and rural elites. In contrast, in the Ottoman Empire, where the central administration was linked to the provinces through relatively unmediated mechanisms, the elite ruled as a unified actor from 1300 to 1700. I also made two ancillary arguments:

(a) The mode of imperial organization (horizontal vs. vertical) is a legacy of the period of imperial expansion. Habsburg expansion in Central and Eastern Europe in the fourteenth and fifteenth centuries left strong landed nobilities intact, whereas Ottoman expansion in Anatolia and Eastern Europe in the same period was more successful in eliminating and co-opting native elites.

(b) The structure of the intra-elite conflict in both cases was directly shaped by the fiscal crisis, which not only altered the balance of power among different elite fractions but also shaped their preferences and thereby creating space for institutional change. The rise of export-oriented grain production paved the way for the enserfment of peasantry in Habsburg lands, which increased the power of landed nobility and intensified intra-elite conflict. External economic changes led to the expansion of mercantile activities in the Ottoman Empire, which aggravated the tensions between the bureaucratic elite and merchants.

(2) Intervening variable (*Capital Incorporation*): The post-crisis elite realignment mediates between the independent and dependent variables. In the Habsburg case, the ruling elite was increasingly threatened by the rising power of the landowners in the provinces and after the seventeenth-century crisis, the central elites allied with the capital owners to balance the power of the landowners. In the Ottoman case, elites were operating under a different set of structural constraints and incentives embedded in a different structure of intra-elite conflict. Threatened not by the landed nobility in the provinces but by the capital holders, the Ottoman elites divulged more power and authority to the elites in the countryside. The expansion of tax farming and the decentralization of resource extraction, in general, undermined the fiscal and infrastructural capacity of the state.

(3) Dependent Variable (*Fiscal Centralization*): In the Habsburg case, the central elites allied themselves with the capital. In their effort to redistribute resources to their allies as side payments, the central elites ended up centralizing fiscal structures. In the Ottoman case, the elites excluded the capital from the political coalition and allied themselves with tax farmers, which, in the long run, resulted in decentralization.

The fundamental finding of my research is the following: high levels of elite conflict in the Habsburg Empire produced the political incentives for the formation of stronger, more centralized fiscal institutions and a developmental state policy. Where such political incentives were lacking, as in the Ottoman Empire, a similar process of institutional change produced the opposite set of political and economic outcomes.

2. Contribution to the Literature

2.1 Demand- and Supply-Side in Institutional Change

I argued that there are two primary ways to explain the institutional outcomes as products of elite conflict. The first approach—demand-side theories—starts from the institutional preferences of social actors, most notably merchants. Merchants have two alternative preferences: protection (the state is involved in the economy and alleviates market imperfections) or independence (minimal state involvement). The choice between the two preferences is primarily contingent on objective constraints, e.g., the type of trade that the merchants are engaged in. The social actors demand institutional changes in accordance with their objectively driven interests. The actual outcomes, i.e., whether the merchants' demands from the rulers are realized, are then contingent on the relative strength of bargaining parties. If merchants are strong enough to steer state policy, then they realize their institutional preferences.[689] The second approach—supply-side theories—starts from the preferences of the rulers (kings, monarchs, bureaucratic elite, etc.). The preferences of the ruler, who by definition is the supplier of institutions, are shaped again by external objective factors such as the economic structure, international context, and the form of government.[690]

I argued in Chapter 2 that isolating demand-side dynamics from the supply-side generates incomplete explanations. Instead of focusing on either the demands of social actors or the interests of revenue-maximizing rulers, my explanation theorizes about and empirically substantiates the preferences of all major actors involved in the conflict: the ruling elite in the imperial center, the urban capital holders, and the rural elites. In addition to examining how objective factors (such as the exogenous changes in the international economy) alter

---

689 Spruyt, *The Sovereign State and Its Competitors: An Analysis of Systems Change.*

690 Theda Skocpol, *States and Social Revolutions: A Comparative Analysis of France, Russia, and China* (Cambridge; New York: Cambridge University Press, 1979); Tilly, *Coercion, Capital, and European States, AD 990-1992*; Levi, *Of Rule and Revenue.*

the preferences of the actors, my explanation also endogenizes interest formation by explaining how exactly the strategic interactions among these actors shaped their interests. Thus, my explanation of the differential outcomes of state reformation in the Habsburg and Ottoman cases stitches together the demand- and supply-sides of elite conflict.

2.2 The Question of "East vs. West"

Ottoman-Habsburg comparison is significant due to the unique location of the two states along the "great divide" between the East and the West—the historical developmental gradient in Europe. The Ottoman Empire was located between the East and the West: the origins of the state were Near Eastern, but its political, economic, and geo-strategic orientation was predominantly European. The state elite was Islamic, but the empire was multi-religious and multi-ethnic. In terms of its institutions and social structure, the Ottoman state was the main heir to Byzantium as much as it was a continuation of the Turkic states in Anatolia. The Ottoman Empire, in short, was the West of the East.

By the same token, the Habsburg Empire was the East of the West. As the official heir to the Holy Roman Empire, the ruling elite of the Habsburg state was Catholic. Yet, like their Ottoman counterparts, they reigned over a multi-ethnic and multi-religious empire, which contained Muslim and Protestant populations. Even more importantly, in terms of its economic and political development until the latter half of the eighteenth century, the Habsburg state consistently lagged its western neighbors.

My research showed that in terms of their future political and economic prospects, the differences between these two states were not particularly evident before 1660. I argued that the path of the Ottomans and Habsburgs diverged decisively only after the seventeenth century. I accounted for the divergence in paths as a product of the strategic interactions among rational, revenue-maximizing actors. Elites in these two cases acted differently in the face of a shared problem, not because of their ideas or cultural predispositions but because they were responding to different structural constraints as self-interested actors seeking to perpetuate their position vis-à-vis their rivals.

In that respect, my research not only contributes to the institutionalist analyses by explaining the origins of the fiscal institutions in the Ottoman and Habsburg cases but also adds to our understanding of why and how the developmental trajectory of the East was differentiated from that of the West. While the Habsburg rule in Central and Eastern Europe and the Ottoman rule in Southeast Europe and the Balkans did not singlehandedly cause the differentiation of the East from the West, it was a key aspect of the long-term social change.

The East-West gradient, which was both mirrored in and facilitated by the Ottoman-Habsburg divide, continues to shape the developmental prospects of the successor states. After more than a century of independence and the imposition of communist rule on most of these states, they still bear the marks of the empires they were once a part of.

While the evidence that imperial legacies continue to shape contemporary economic and political outcomes is strong, our understanding of *how* exactly such legacies are transferred and reproduced over time is relatively limited. A starting point into the mechanisms of imperial legacies would be to reconceptualize the moment of transition from empire to nation-state as one of continuity rather than rupture. By explaining when, how, and why the paths of the Habsburg and Ottomans diverged and how the divergence was reproduced over time, my research extends the temporal and spatial boundaries of the scholarship on European state formation as well as the comparative research on empires and their legacies.

Bibliography

Abu-el-Haj, Rifaat Ali. *Formation of the Modern State: The Ottoman Empire, Sixteenth to Eighteenth Centuries*. Albany: State University of New York Press, 1996.

Acemoglu, Daron, and James A. Robinson. "Economic Backwardness in Political Perspective." The American Political Science Review 100, no. 1 (2006): 115–31.

Acemoglu, Daron, Simon Johnson, and James A. Robinson. "The Colonial Origins of Comparative Development: An Empirical Investigation " *The American Economic Review* 91, no. 5 (2001): 1369-401

Acemoglu, Daron, Smith Johnson, and James A. Robinson. "Reversal of Fortune: Geography and Institutions in the Making of the Modern World Income Distribution." In *NBER Working Paper no. 8460*. Cambridge, MA: National Bureau of Economic Research, 2001.

Adanır, Fikret, and Suraiya Faroqhi. "The Ottomans and the Balkans." In *Ottoman Empire and Its Heritage*, 445. Leiden; Boston: Brill, 2002.

Agoston, Gabor. "Habsburgs and Ottomans: Defense, Military Change and Shifts in Power." *The Turkish Studies Association Bulletin* 22, no. 1 (1998): 126-41.

Agoston, Gabor, Gaza David, and Pal Fodor. "The Costs of the Ottoman Fortress-System in Hungary in the Sixteenth and Seventeenth Centuries." In *Ottomans, Hungarians and Habsburgs in Central Europe. The Military Confines in the Era of Ottoman Conquest*. Leiden; Boston: Brill, 2000.

Aksan, Virginia. "Review Article: Ottoman Military Matters." *Journal of Economic Literature* 6, no. 1 (2002): 52-62.

Aksan, Virginia. *Ottoman Wars 1700-1870: An Empire Besieged*, Modern Wars in Perspective. Harlow, England: Longman/Pearson, 2007.

Aksan, Virginia, and Eric Zürcher. "Ottoman Military Recruitment Strategies in the Late Eighteenth Century." In *Arming the State: Military Conscription in the Middle East and Central Asia, 1775-1925*, 21-39. New York: I.B. Tauris, 1999.

Anderson, Perry. *Lineages of the Absolutist State*. London: New Left Books, 1974.

Arneth, A. von. *Maria Theresa Und Joseph II. Ihre Correspondenz*. Vienna, 1868.

Aston, T. H. *Crisis in Europe, 1560-1660, Essays from Past and Present*. London: Routledge & Kegan Paul, 1975.

Bak, János M., and Béla K. Király. *From Hunyadi to Rákóczi: War and Society in Late Medieval and Early Modern Hungary*. Boulder; New York: Brooklyn College Press, 1982.

Barkan, Ömer Lütfi. "The Price Revolution in the Sixteenth Century." *International Journal of Middle East* (1975).

Barkan, Ömer Lütfi, and M. A. Cook. "Research on the Ottoman Fiscal Surveys." In *Economic History of the Middle East*, 163-71. London: Oxford University Press, 1970.

Barker, Thomas Mack. *Army, Aristocracy, Monarchy: Essays on War, Society, and Government in Austria, 1618-1780*, East European Monographs. Boulder; New York: Social Science Monographs; Distributed by Columbia University Press, 1982.

———. *Double Eagle and Crescent; Vienna's Second Turkish Siege and Its Historical Setting*. Albany: State University of New York Press, 1967.

Barkey, Karen. *Bandits and Bureaucrats: The Ottoman Route to State Centralization*, Wilder House Series in Politics, History, and Culture. Ithaca, NY: Cornell University Press, 1994.

———. *Empire of Difference: The Ottomans in Comparative Perspective*. New York: Cambridge University Press, 2008.

———. "Negotiated Paths to Nationhood: A Comparison of Hungary and Romania in the Early Twentieth Century." *East European Politics and Societies* 14, no. 3 (2000): 497.

———. "Rebellious Alliances: The State and Peasant Unrest in Early Seventeenth-Century France and the Ottoman Empire." *American Sociological Review* 56, no. 6 (1991): 699-715.

Barkey, Karen, Hasan Kayali, Joseph W. Escherik, and Eric Van Young. "Changing Modalities of Empire: A Comparative Study of Ottoman and Habsburg Decline." In *Empire to Nation: Historical Perspectives on the Making of the Modern World*. Washington, DC: Rowman & Littlefield Publishers, 2006.

Barkey, Karen, and Mark Von Hagen. *After Empire: Multiethnic Societies and Nation-Building: The Soviet Union and the Russian, Ottoman, and Habsburg Empires*. Boulder, CO: Westview Press, 1997.

Barkey, Karen, and Rudi Batzell. "Comparisons across Empires: The Critical Social Structures of Ottomans, Russians and Habsburgs." In *Empires in Contention: Sociology, History and Cultural Difference*, edited by P. F. Bang and C. A. Bayly: In press, 2008.

Bates, Robert H., *Markets and States in Tropical Africa: The Political Basis of Agricultural Policies*, 2005th ed. Berkeley: University of California Press, 2005.

Bean, Richard. "War and the Birth of the Nation State." *Journal of Economic History* 33 (1973): 203-21.

Beller, Steven. *A Concise History of Austria*. Cambridge, UK; New York: Cambridge University Press, 2006.

———. *Francis Joseph*. London; New York: Longman, 1996.

Benedikt, Heinrich. *Die Wirtschaftliche Entwicklung in Der Franz-Joseph-Zeit*. Wien: Verlag Herold, 1958.

Bennett, Andrew, and Colin Elman. "Qualitative Research: Recent Developments in Case Study Methods." *Annual Review of Political Science* 9 (2006): 459-60.

Berend, Ivan, and Gyorgy Ranki. *European Periphery and Industrialization: 1780-1914*. Cambridge, MA: Cambridge University Press, 1982.

Berend, Ivan., and Gyorgy Ranki. *East Central Europe in the 19th and 20th Centuries*. Budapest: Akademiai Kiado, 1977.

Berend, Ivan. *History Derailed: Central and Eastern Europe in the Long Nineteenth Century*. Berkeley: University of California Press, 2003.

Berend, Ivan, and Gyorgy Ranki. *Underdevelopment in Europe in the Context of East-West Relations in the 19th Century*, Studia Historica Academiae Scientiarum Hungaricae. Budapest: Akadémiai Kiadó, 1980.

Berenger, Jean. *A History of the Habsburg Empire*. London; New York: Longman, 1994.

Berg, Peter Arend Jan van den. *The Politics of European Codification: A History of the Unification of Law in France, Prussia, the Austrian Monarchy and the Netherlands*. Groningen: Europa Law Pub., 2007.

Berktay, Halil. "The Search for Peasant in Western and Turkish History." *Journal of Peasant Studies* 183-4 (1992): 109-84.

Best, Geoffrey Francis Andrew. *War and Society in Revolutionary Europe, 1770-1870*, War and European Society. Montreal: McGill-Queen's University Press, 1998.

Birdal, Mehmet Sinan. *The Holy Roman Empire and The Ottomans: From Global Imperial Power to Absolutist States*. London, New York: I.B.Tauris, 2011.

Black, Jeremy. *European Warfare: 1453-1815*. New York: St. Martin's Press, 1999.

Blum, Jerome. *Noble Landowners and Agriculture in Austria 1815-1848: A Study in the Origins of the Peasant Emancipation of 1848*. Baltimore: Johns Hopkins University Press, 1948.

———. "The Rise of Second Serfdom in Eastern Europe." *American Historical Review* 62 (1957): 807-36.

———. "Transportation and Industry in Austria." *Journal of Modern History* 15 (1943).

Bonney, Richard. *The Rise of the Fiscal State in Europe, C. 1200-1815*. Oxford; New York: Oxford University Press, 1999.

Braudel, F. P., and F. Spooner. "Prices in Europe from 1450 to 1750." In *The Cambridge Economic History of Europe, Vol IV.*, Cambridge: Cambridge University Press, 1967, 374-486.

Braudel, Fernand. *The Mediterranean and the Mediterranean World in the Age of Philip II*. New York: Harper & Row, 1972.

Brenner, Robert. "Agrarian Class Structure and Economic Development in Pre-Industrial Europe." *Past and Present* (1976): 30-75.

———. "Origins of Capitalist Development: A Critique of Neo-Smithian Marxism." *New Left Review* 104 (1977): 25-93.

Brewer, John. *The Sinews of Power: War, Money, and the English State, 1688-1783*. London; Boston: Unwin Hyman, 1989.

Brown, Carl. *Imperial Legacy: The Ottoman Imprint on the Balkans and the Middle East*. New York: Columbia University Press, 1996.

Brunner, Otto. *Land and Lordship: Structures of Governance in Medieval Austria*. Philadelphia: University of Philadelphia Press, 1992.

Bulut, Mehmet. "The Role of the Ottomans and Dutch in the Commercial Integration between the Levant and the Atlantic in the Seventeenth Century." *Journal of Economic and Social History of the Orient* 45, no. 9 (2002): 197-230.

Bunce, Valerie. "The National Idea: Imperial Legacies and Post-Communist Pathways in Eastern Europe." *East European Politics and Societies* 9, no. 3 (2005): 406-42.

Calhoun, Craig J., Frederick Cooper, Kevin W. Moore, and Social Science Research Council (U.S.). *Lessons of Empire: Imperial Histories and American Power*. New York: New Press: Distributed by W.W. Norton, 2006.

Carl, Hempel. "The Function of General Laws in History." In *Readings in the Philosophy of Science*, edited by M. Martin and L.C. McIntyre. Cambridge, MA: MIT Press, 1997.

Chirot, D. "The Rise of the West." *American Sociological Review* 50 (1985): 181-95.

Chirot, Daniel. *The Origins of Backwardness in Eastern Europe: Economics and Politics from the Middle Ages until the Early Twentieth Century*. Berkeley: University of California Press, 1989.

Chirot, Daniel, and Thomas D. Hall. "World-System Theory." *Annual Review of Sociology* 8 (1982): 81-106.

Çizakça, Murat. *A Comparative Evolution of Business Partnerships: The Islamic World and Europe, with Specific Reference to the Ottoman Archives*. Leiden: Brill, 1996.

———. "Price History and the Bursa Silk Industry: A Study in Ottoman Industrial Decline, 1550-1650." *The Journal of Economic History* 40, no. 3 (1980).

Clay, C. G. A. *Gold for the Sultan: Western Bankers and Ottoman Finance 1856-1881: A Contribution to Ottoman and to International Financial History*, International Library of Historical Studies. London; New York, NY: I.B. Tauris; In the U.S.A. and Canada distributed by St. Martin's Press, 2000.

Collier, David, and James Mahoney. "Insights and Pitfalls: Selection Bias in Qualitative Research." *World Politics* 49 (1996): 56-91.

Cooley, Alexander. *Logics of Hierarchy: The Organization of Empires, States and Military Occupations*. Ithaca: Cornell University Press, 2005.

Crankshaw, Edward. *Maria Theresa*. New York: Viking Press, 1970.

Crowley, Roger. *1453: The Holy War for Constantinople and the Clash of Islam and the West*. 1st ed. New York: Hyperion, 2005.

Curta, Florin. *East Central & Eastern Europe in the Early Middle Ages*. Ann Arbor: University of Michigan Press, 2005.

Darling, Linda. "Ottoman Fiscal Administration: Decline and Adaptation." *Journal of European Economic History* 26 (1977): 157-83.

———. *Revenue-Raising and Legitimacy: Tax Collection and Finance Administration in the Ottoman Empire, 1560-1660*, The Ottoman Empire and Its Heritage. Leiden; New York: E.J. Brill, 1996.

Denemark, Robert, and Kenneth Thomas. "The Brenner-Wallerstein Debate." *International Studies Quarterly* 32 (1988): 47-65.

Desch, Mike. "War and Strong States, Peace and Weak States?" *International Organization* 50 (1996): 237-68.

Dickson, P. G. M. *Finance and Government under Maria Theresa, 1740-1780*. 2 vols. Vol. 1. Oxford: Claredon Press, 1987.

———. *Finance and Government under Maria Theresia, 1749-1780*. 2 vols. Vol. 2. Oxford: Claredon Press, 1987.

———. "Monarchy and Bureaucracy in Late Eighteenth Century Austria." *The English Historical Review* 110 (1995): 323-67.

Dimitrova-Grajzl, Valentina P. "The Great Divide Revisited: Ottoman and Habsburg Legacies on Transition." *Kvlos* 60, no. 4 (2007): 539-58.

Doukas, and Harry J. Magoulias. *Decline and Fall of Byzantium to the Ottoman Turks*. Detroit: Wayne State University Press, 1975.

Downing, Brian M. *The Military Revolution and Political Change: Origins of Democracy and Autocracy in Early Modern Europe*. Princeton, NJ: Princeton University Press, 1992.

Edith, Konrad. "Absolutismus Der Habsburger Im 16. Und Beginnenden 17. Jahrhundert." Salzburg: Paris-Lodron Universitaet Salzburg, 1987.

Eisenstadt, S.N. The Political Systems of Empires. London [New York]: Free Press of Glencoe, 1963.

Eldem, Edhem. "Ottoman Financial Integration with Europe: Foreign Loans, the Ottoman Bank and the Ottoman Public Debt." *European Review* 13, no. 3 (2005): 431-45.

Elster, Jon. *Political Psychology*. Cambridge; New York: Cambridge University Press, 1993.

Erbe, Michael. *Die Habsburger (1493-1918): Eine Dynastie Im Reich und in Europa*. Stuttgart, Berlin, Köln, Kohlhammer: Urban-Taschenbuecher, 2000.

Ertman, Thomas. *Birth of the Leviathan: Building States and Regimes in Medieval and Early Modern Europe*. Cambridge: Cambridge University Press, 1997.

Evans, R. J. W. *Austria, Hungary and the Habsburgs: Essays on Central Europe, C. 1683-1867*. New York: Oxford University Press, 2006.

Evans, R. J. W., and T. V. Thomas. *Crown, Church and Estates: Central European Politics in the Sixteenth and Seventeenth Centuries*, London: Palgrave Macmillan, 1991.

Faroqhi, Suraiya. *Towns and Townsmen of Ottoman Anatolia: Trade, Crafts, and Food Production in an Urban Setting, 1520-1650*, Cambridge Studies in Islamic Civilization. Cambridge, Cambridgeshire; New York: Cambridge University Press, 1984.

Faroqhi, Suraiya, and Gilles Veinstein. *Merchants in the Ottoman Empire*, Collection Turcica. Paris [etc.]: Peeters, 2008.

Fichtner, Paula. "Dynastic Marriage in Sixteenth-Century Habsburg Diplomacy and Statecraft: An Interdisciplinary Approach." *The American Historical Review* 81, no. 2 (1976): 243-265

Fichtner, Paula. *Ferdinand I of Austria: The Politics of Dynasticism in the Age of Reformation*. New York, 1982.

———. *The Habsburg Monarchy, 1490-1848: Attributes of Empire*, European History in Perspective. Houndmills, Basingstoke, Hampshire; New York: Palgrave/Macmillan, 2003.

Findley, Carter V. *Bureaucratic Reform in the Ottoman Empire: The Sublime Porte, 1789-1922*, Princeton Studies on the near East. Princeton, NJ: Princeton University Press, 1980.

Finkel, Caroline. *The Administration of Warfare: The Ottoman Military Campaigns in Hungary, 1593-1606*, Beihefte Zur Wiener Zeitschrift Für Die Kunde Des Morgenlandes. Wien, 1988.

Fischel, Alfred. *Christian Julius Von Schierendorff: Ein Vorlaufer Des Liberalen Zentralismus Im Zeitalter Josefs I Und Karls VI*, 1906.

Fodor, Pal. *In Quest of the Golden Apple: Imperial Ideology, Politics, and Military Administration in the Ottoman Empire*, Analecta Isisiana. Istanbul: Isis Press, 2000.

Fodor, Pal, and Gaza David. *Ottomans, Hungarians, and Habsburgs in Central Europe: The Military Confines in the Era of Ottoman Conquest*, Ottoman Empire and Its Heritage. Leiden; Boston: Brill, 2000.

Freudenberger, Herman. "An Industrial Momentum in the Habsburg Monarchy." *Journal of European Economic History* 12 (1983).

———. *The Industrialization of a Central European City: Brno and the Fine Woolen Industry in the Eighteenth Century*. Edington, Willts: Pasold, 1977.

———. *The Waldstein Woolen Mill: Noble Enterpreneurship in Eighteenth-Century Bohemia*. Massachusetts: Cambridge University Press, 1963.

Geddes, Barbara. *Paradigms and Sand Castles: Theory Building and Research Design in Comparative Politics*, Analytical Perspectives on Politics. Ann Arbor: University of Michigan Press, 2003.

Genç, Mehmet. "15. Ve 16. Yüzyıllarda Osmanlı Ekonomisinde İç ve Dış Ticaret." In *Osmanlı İmparatorluğunda Devlet ve Ekonomi*, edited by Mehmet Genç. İstanbul: Ötüken, 2003.

———. "Osmanlı Ekonomisi ve Savaş." *Yapıt* IV-V (1984): 86-93.

———. "Osmanlı Iktisadi Dünya Görüşünün İlkeleri." In *Osmanlı İmparatorluğunda Devlet Ve Ekonomi*, edited by Mehmet Genç. İstanbul: Ötüken, 2003.

———. "Osmanlı Iktisadi Dünya Görüşünün Klasik Prensipleri Ve Temel Değerleri." In *Osmanlı İmparatorluğunda Devlet ve Ekonomi*, edited by Mehmet Genç. İstanbul: Ötüken, 2003.

———. "Osmanlı İmparatorluğu'nda Devlet ve Ekonomi." In *Osmanlı İmparatorluğu'nda Devlet Ve Ekonomi*, edited by Mehmet Genc. İstanbul: Otuken, 2003.

———. "Osmanlı Maliyesinde Malikane Sistemi." In *Osmanlı'da Devlet Ve Ekonomi*, edited by Mehmet Genc. İstanbul: Ötüken, 2003.

———. "Ottoman Economy and War in the Eighteenth Century." *Yapıt, Toplumsal Araştırmalar Dergisi* 49-50 (1984): 86-93.

———. "The Principle of Ottoman's Economical World View." *Sosyoloji Dergisi* III, no. 1 (1988): 175-85.

Genç, Mehmet, and Donald Quataert. "Ottoman Industry in the Eighteenth Century: General Framework, Characteristics and Main Trends." In *Manufacturing in the Ottoman Empire and Turkey (1500-1950)*. New York: State University of New York Press, 1994.

George, Alexander L., and Andrew Bennett. *Case Studies and Theory Development in the Social Sciences*, Basic Studies in International Security. Cambridge, MA: MIT Press, 2005.

Gerber, Haim. "Jewish Tax-Farmers in the Ottoman Empire." *Journal of Turkish Studies* 10 (1986): 143-61.

Gerschenkron, Alexander. *Economic Backwardness in Historical Perspective, a Book of Essays*. New York: F. Praeger, 1965.

———. *An Economic Spurt That Failed: Four Lectures in Austrian History*. Princeton, NJ: Princeton University Press, 1977.

Goldstone, Jack A. "East and West in the Seventeenth Century: Political Crisis in Stuart England, Ottoman Turkey, and Ming China." *Comparative Studies in Society and History* 30 (1988): 103-42.

———. *Revolution and Rebellion in the Early Modern World*. Berkeley: University of California Press, 1991.

Good, David F. "Austria-Hungary." In *Patterns of European Industrialization: The Nineteenth Century*, edited by Richard Sylla and Gianni Toniolo. London; New York: Routledge, 1991.

———. *The Economic Rise of the Hapsburg Empire, 1750-1914*. Berkeley: University of California Press, 1984.

———. *Economic Transformations in East-Central Europe: Legacies from the Past and Prospects for the Future*: Routledge, 1994.

———. "Issues in the Study of Habsburg Economic Development." *East Central Europe* 6, no. 1 (1979): 47-62.

Goodwin, Jason. *Lords of the Horizons: A History of the Ottoman Empire*. London: Chatto & Windus, 1998.

Gorski, Philip S. *The Disciplinary Revolution: Calvinism and the Rise of the State in Early Modern Europe*. Chicago; London: University of Chicago Press, 2003.

Gould, S. J., Albert Somit, and Steven Peterson. "Punctuated Equilibrium in Fact and Theory." In *The Dynamics of Evolution: the Punctuated Equilibrium Debate in the Natural and Social Sciences*, Ithaca, NY: Cornell University Press, 1992.

Gross, Nachum. T., and Carlo M. Cipolla. "The Habsburg Monarchy." In *The Emergence of Industrial Societies, Part One*, 228-79: Fontana, 1973.

Gross, Nachum T., and John Komlos. "Austria-Hungary in World Economy." In *Economic Development in the Habsburg Monarchy in the Nineteenth Century*. New York: Columbia University Press, 1983.

Guilmartin, Jr John F. "Ideology and Conflict: The Wars of the Ottoman Empire, 1453-1606." *Journal of Interdisciplinary History* 18 (1988): 721-48.

Gunst, Peter. *Agrarian Development and Social Change in Eastern Europe, 14th-19th Centuries*. Varorium, 1996.

———. *Einige Probleme Der Wirtschaftlichen Und Sozialen Entwicklun Osteuropas*. Koln: Forschungsinst. fuer Sozial-u. Wirtschaftsgesch., 1977.

Gunst, Peter, Irene P. Winner, and Thomas G. Winner. "Some Characteristics of East European Economic and Social Development: Data and Reflections." In *The Peasant and the City in Eastern Europe: Interpenetrating Structures*. Schenkman, 1984.

Güran, Tevfik. "The State Role in the Grain Supply of Istanbul: The Grain Administration, 1793-1839." *International Journal of Turkish Studies* (1984): 27-41.

Hauszmann, Janos. *Ungarn*. Regensburg: Friedrich Pustet, 2004.

Hechter, Michael. *The Microfoundations of Macrosociology*. Philadelphia: Temple University Press, 1983.

Hechter, Michael, and Brustein William. "Regional Modes of Production and Patterns of State Formation in Western Europe." *American Journal of Sociology* 85, no. 5 (1980): 1061-94.

Hedström, Peter, and Richard Swedberg. *Social Mechanisms: An Analytical Approach to Social Theory*, Studies in Rationality and Social Change. Cambridge, UK; New York: Cambridge University Press, 1998.

Heindl, Waltraud. "Bureaucracy, Officials and the State in the Austrian Monarchy: Stages of Change since the Eighteenth Century." *Austrian History Yearbook* 37 (2006): 35-57.

———. "Burokratie Und Verwaltung Im Österreichischen Neoabsolutismus." *Oesterreichische Osthefte* 22, no. 3 (1980): 231-65.

———. *Gehorsame Rebellen: Burokratie Und Beamte in Österreich 1780 Bis 1848*, Studien Zu Politik Und Verwaltung. Wien: Bohlau Verlag 1991.

Heper, Metin. "The State and Public Bureaucracy." *Comparative Studies in Society and History* 27 (1985): 86-110.

Hintze, Otto. *The Historical Essays of Otto Hintze*. New York: Oxford University Press, 1975.

Hirschman, Albert O. *Exit, Voice, and Loyalty; Responses to Decline in Firms, Organizations, and States*. Cambridge, MA: Harvard University Press, 1970.

Hobsbawm, Eric. "The General Crisis of the European Economy in the 17th Century." *Past and Present* 5 (1954): 33-54.

Howard, Douglas A. *The Ottoman Tımar System and Its Transformation, 1563-1656*: Unpublished PhD Dissertation, Indiana University, 1987.

Hui, Victoria Tin-bor. *War and State Formation in Ancient China and Early Modern Europe*. New York, NY: Cambridge University Press, 2005.

İnalcık, Halil. "1431 Tarihli Tımar Defterine Göre Fatih Devrinden Önce Tımar Sistemi." In *Osmanlı İmparatorluğu: Toplum Ve Ekonomi*, edited by Halil Inalcik. İstanbul: Eren, 1996.

———. "Capital Formation in the Ottoman Empire." *Journal of Economic History* 29, no. 1 (1969): 97-140.

———. "Centralization and Decentralization in Ottoman Administration." In *Studies in Eighteenth Century Islamic History*, edited by Thomas Naff and Roger Owen, 27-52. Carbondale, 1977.

———. "Centralization and Decentralization in the Ottoman Empire, 1600-1700." *Archivum Ottomanicum* 6 (1980): 283-338.

———. "Decision Making in the Ottoman State." In *Decision Making and Change in the Ottoman Empire*, edited by Halil İnalcık and Ceaser E. Farah, 9-19. The Thomas Jefferson University Press, 1993.

———. "Impact of the Annales School on Ottoman Studies and New Findings." *Review* 3-4 (1978).

———. "Köy, Köylü ve İmparatorluk." In *Osmanlı İmparatorluğu: Toplum Ve Ekonomi*, edited by Halil Inalcik. İstanbul: Eren, 1996.

———. "Land Problems in Turkish History." *The Muslim World* 45 (1955).

———. "Military and Fiscal Transformation in the Ottoman Empire, 1600-1700." *Archivum Ottomanicum* VI (1980): 283-337.

———. *The Ottoman Empire; the Classical Age, 1300-1600*, History of Civilisation. London: Weidenfeld & Nicolson, 1973.

———. "Ottoman Methods of Conquest." *Studia Islamica* 2 (1954).

———. "The Rise of the Ottoman Empire." In *A History of the Ottoman Empire to 1730*, edited by M. Cook, 10-54. Cambridge, London, New York, Melbourne: Cambridge University Press, 1976.

———. "Sened-i Ittifak ve Gülhane Hatt-ı Hümayunu." *Belleten* 28 (1964): 605-90.

İnalcık, Halil, and Donald Quataert. *An Economic and Social History of the Ottoman Empire, 1300-1914*. New York, NY: Cambridge University Press, 1994.

İnalcık, Halil, and Rustow. "The Nature of Traditional Society." In *Political Modernization in Japan and Turkey*. New Brunswick, NJ: Princeton University Press, 1964.

Ingrao, Charles W. *The Habsburg Monarchy, 1618-1815*, New Approaches to European History. Cambridge, UK; New York: Cambridge University Press, 2000.

İslamoğlu-İnan, Huri. *Constituting Modernity: Private Property in the East and West*, Islamic Mediterranean. London; New York: I.B. Tauris; Distributed by Palgrave Macmillan in the U.S., 2004.

———. *The Ottoman Empire and the World-Economy*, Etudes Sur Le Capitalisme Moderne. Cambridge; New York; Paris: Cambridge University Press; Editions de la Maison des sciences de l'homme, 1987.

———. *State and Peasant in the Ottoman Empire: Agrarian Power Relations and Regional Economic Development in Ottoman Anatolia During the Sixteenth Century*, The Ottoman Empire and Its Heritage. Leiden; New York: E.J. Brill, 1994.

———. *State and Peasant in the Ottoman Empire: Agrarian Power Relations and Regional Economic Development in Ottoman Anatolia During the Sixteenth Century*. Leiden; New York: E.J. Brill, 1994.

İslamoğlu-İnan, Huri, and Çağlar Keyder. "Agenda for Ottoman History." In *The Ottoman Empire and the World Economy*. CUP, 1987.

Jacoby, Tim. *Social Power and the Turkish State*. London; Portland, OR: Frank Cass, 2004.

Janos, Andrew. *East Central Europe in the Modern World: The Politics of the Borderlands from Pre- to Postcommunism*. Stanford, CA: Stanford University Press, 2000.

———. "The Politics of Backwardness in Continental Europe, 1780-1945." *World Politics* 41 (1989).

Jászi, Oszkár. *The Dissolution of the Habsburg Monarchy*. Chicago: University of Chicago Press, 1961.

Jedlicka, Ludwig F. *Maria Theresia in Ihren Briefen Und Staatsscriften*. Wien: Bergland Verlag, 1955.

Kafadar, Cemal. *Between Two Worlds*. 221. Berkeley: University of California Press, 1995.

Kaminski, Andrzej. "Neo-Serfdom in Poland Lithuania." *Slavic Review* XXXIV (1975): 253-68.

Kann, Robert A. *The Habsburg Empire; a Study in Integration and Disintegration*. New York: Octagon Books, 1973.

Kann, Robert A., and Zdenek David. *The Peoples of Eastern Habsburg Lands, 1526-1918*. Seattle, 1984.

Kaplan, Steven Laurence. *Provisioning Paris: Merchants and Millers in the Grain and Flour Trade During the Eighteenth Century*. Ithaca, New York: Cornell University Press, 1984.

Karniel, Josef. *Die Toleranzpolitik Kaiser Josephs II*. Gerlingen, 1986.

Karpat, Kemal. "The Transformation of the Ottoman Empire, 1789-1908." *International Journal of Middle East Studies* 3, no. 2 (1972).

Kasaba, Reşat. *Cities in the World-System*, Studies in the Political Economy of the World-System. New York: Greenwood Press, 1991.

———. "Incorporation of the Ottoman Empire, 1750-1820." *Review* X, no. 5/6 (1987).

———. *The Ottoman Empire and the World-Economy: The Nineteenth Century*, Suny Series in Middle Eastern Studies. Albany: State University of New York Press, 1988.

———. "Was There a Comprador Bourgeoisie in Mid-Nineteenth Century Western Anatolia?" *Review* xi, no. 2 (1988): 215-31.

Katus, Laszlo, and E. Pamlenyi. "Economic Growth in Hungary During the Age of Dualism 1867-1913: A Quantitative Analysis." In *Social and Economic Researches on the History of East-Central Europe*. Budapest: Akademiai Kiado, 1970.

Kautsky, John H. *The Politics of Aristocratic Empires*. Chapel Hill: University of North Carolina Press, 1982.

Kazgan, Haydar. *Osmanlı'da Avrupa Finans Kapitali*. Ankara: Roma Yayınları, 2005.

Kemp, Tom. *Industrialization in Nineteenth Century Europe*. London: Longman Group, 1971.

Kennedy, Paul. *The Rise and the Fall of Great Powers: Economic Change and Military Conflict from 1500-2000*. New York: Vintage, 1987.

Keyder, Çağlar. "Bureaucracy and Bourgeoisie: Reform and Revolution in the Age of Imperialism." *Review* 11, no. 2 (1988).

———. "Small Peasant Ownership in Turkey: Historical Formation and Present Structure." *Review* VII, no. 1 (1983).

———. *State and Class in Turkey: A Study in Capitalist Development*. London: Verso, 1987.

King, Gary, Robert O. Keohane, and Sidney Verba. *Designing Social Inquiry: Scientific Inference in Qualitative Research*. Princeton, NJ: Princeton University Press, 1994.

Kinross, Patrick Balfour. *The Ottoman Centuries: The Rise and Fall of the Turkish Empire*. New York: Morrow, 1977.

Kiraly, Bela K. "Neo-Serfdom in Hungary." *Slavic Review* 34, no. 2 (1975): 269-78.

Kıray, Emine. *Osmanlı'da Ekonomik Yapı Ve Dış Borçlar*. İstanbul: İletişim Yayınları, 1995.

Klima, Arnost. "Agrarian Class Structure and Economic Development in Pre-Industrial Bohemia." *Past & Present* 85 (1979): 49-67.

———. "The Beginning of the Machine-Building Industry in the Czech Lands in the First Half of the 19th Century." *Journal of European Economic History* (1975): 49-78.

———. "Industrial Development in Bohemia, 1648-1781." *Past and Present* (1957): 87-99.

———. "Mercantilism in the Habsburg Monarchy-s with Special Reference to the Bohemian Lands." *Historica* 11 (1965).

———. "The Role of Rural Domestic Industry in Bohemia in the 18th Century." *Economic History Review* 27 (1974): 48-56.

Klima, Arnost, and John Komlos. "Industrial Growth and Entrepreneurship in the Early Stages of Industrialization in the Czech Lands." In *Economic Development in the Habsburg Monarch in the Nineteenth Century*, 81-101. New York: Columbia University Press, 1983.

Klingenstein, Grete, and Charles W. Ingrao. "Between Mercantilism and Physiocracy: Stages, Modes and Functions of Economic Theory in the Habsburg Monarchy, 1748-63." In *State and Society in Early Modern Austria*. Indiana: Purdue University Press, 1994.

Knight, Jack. *Institutions and Social Conflict*. Cambridge: Cambridge University Press, 1992.

Komlos, John. *Economic Development in the Habsburg Monarchy and in the Successor States: Essays*, East European Monographs. Boulder; New York: East European Monographs; Distributed by Columbia University Press, 1990.

———. *The Habsburg Monarchy as a Customs Union: Economic Development in Austria-Hungary in the Nineteenth Century*. Princeton, NJ: Princeton University Press, 1983.

———. "Institutional Change under Pressure: Enlightened Government Policy in the Eighteenth-Century Habsburg Monarchy." *Journal of European Economic History* 15 (1986).

Komlos, Jon, and Markus Heintel. "The Threat of a Malthusian Crisis in the Habsburg Monarchy." *Journal of Interdisciplinary History* 30, no. 1 (1999): 91-98.

Komlosy, Andrea. "State, Regions, and Borders: Single Market Formation and Labor Migration in the Habsburg Monarchy, 1750-1918." *Review* XXVII (2004): 135-177.

Köprülü, Mehmet Fuat. *The Origins of the Ottoman Empire*, Suny Series in the Social and Economic History of the Middle East. Albany, NY: State University of New York Press, 1991.

Kramar, Konrad, and Petra Stuiber. *Habsburgs Leere Kassen*. Wien: Verlag Carl Ueberreuter, 2001.

Krieger, Karl Friedrich. *Die Habsburger Im Mittelalter: Von Rudolf I. Bis Friedrich III*, Kohlhammer Urban-Taschenbucher. Stuttgart: W. Kohlhammer, 1994.

Kuran, Timur. "Islamic Commercial Crisis: The Institutional Root of Economic Underdevelopment in the Middle East." *Journal of Economic History* 63, no. 3 (2003): 414-46.

Lachmann, Richard. *Capitalists in Spite of Themselves: Elite Conflict and Economic Transitions in Early Modern Europe*. New York: Oxford University Press, 2000.

Lampe, John R. *Yugoslavia as History: Twice There Was a Country*. 2nd ed. Cambridge: Cambridge University Press, 2000.

Lampe, John R., and Marvin R. Jackson. *Balkan Economic History, 1550-1950: From Imperial Borderlands to Developing Nations*, The Joint Committee on Eastern Europe Publication Series. Bloomington: Indiana University Press, 1982.

Lane, F. C. "The Mediterranean Spice Trade." *The American Historical Review* (1940).

Levi, Margaret. *Of Rule and Revenue*, California Series on Social Choice and Political Economy. Berkeley: University of California Press, 1988.

Liebek, Helen. "Free Trade and Protectionism under Maria Theresa and Joseph II." *Canadian Journal of History* 14 (1979).

Little, Daniel. *Microfoundations, Method and Causation: On the Philosophy of the Social Sciences*, Science and Technology Studies. New Brunswick, NJ: Transaction Publishers, 1998.

Lowry, Heath W. *The Nature of the Early Ottoman State*, Suny Series in the Social and Economic History of the Middle East. Albany: State University of New York Press, 2003.

Lustick, Ian. "History, Historiography, and Political Science: Multiple Historical Records and the Problem of Selection Bias." *American Political Science Review* (1996): 605-18.

Lybyer, Albert Howe. *The Influence of the Rise of the Ottoman Turks Upon the Routes of Oriental Trade*. Washington, 1916.

Macartney, C. A. *The Habsburg and Hohenzollern Dynasties in the Seventeenth and Eighteenth Centuries*, The Documentary History of Western Civilization. New York: Harper & Row, 1970.

MacHardy, Karin J. "The Rise of Absolutism and Noble Rebellion in Early Modern Habsburg Austria, 1570 to 1620." *Comparative Studies in Society and History* 34, no. 3 (1992): 407-38.

Mahoney, James. "Long-Run Development and the Legacy of Colonialism in Spanish America." *American Journal of Sociology* 109, no. 1 (2003): 50-106.

———. "Path Dependence in Historical Sociology." *Theory and Society* 29, no. 4 (2000): 507-48.

Mahoney, James, and Dietrich Rueschemeyer. *Comparative Historical Analysis in the Social Sciences*, Cambridge Studies in Comparative Politics. Cambridge, UK; New York: Cambridge University Press, 2003.

Makkai, Laszlo. "Neo-Serfdom: Its Origin and Nature in East Central Europe." *Slavic Review* XXXIV (1975): 225-38.

Mandaville, Jon E. "Usurious Piety: The Cash Waqf Controversy in the Ottoman Empire." *International Journal of Middle East Studies* 10 (1979): 289-308.

Mann, Michael. "The Autonomous Power of the State: Its Origins, Mechanisms and Results." *Arch. Europ. Sociol.* XXV (1984): 185-213.

———. *The Sources of Social Power*. Cambridge, Cambridgeshire; New York: Cambridge University Press, 1986.

Mardin, Şerif. *The Genesis of Young Ottoman Thought a Study in the Modernization of Turkish Political Ideas*. 1st Syracuse University Press ed. Syracuse, NY: Syracuse University Press, 2000.

Maria, Theresa, and Alfred Arneth. *Briefe Der Kaiserin Maria Theresia an Ihre Kinder Und Freunde*. 4 vols. Osnabrück: Biblio Verlag, 1978.

Maria, Theresa, Antoinette Marie, and Alfred Arneth. *Maria Theresia und Marie Antoinette: Ihr Briefwechsel Während Der Jahre 1770-1780*. Osnabrück: Biblio Verlag, 1978.

Matis, Herbert. "Technik Und Industriealisierung Im Österreichischen Vormarz." *Technikgeschichte* 36 (1969): 12-37.

Mautz, J. E. "Transmission of Directives from Center to Periphery in the Ottoman State until the Seventeenth Century." In *Decision Making and Change in the Ottoman Empire*, edited by F. Farah Ceaser. Kirksville, Missouri: The Thomas Jefferson University Press, 1993.

McGowan, Bruce. *Economic Life in Ottoman Europe: Taxation, Trade, and the Struggle for Land, 1600-1800*. Cambridge; New York: Cambridge University Press, 1981.

Mears, John A. "Thirty Years War, the 'General Crisis' and the Origins of the Standing Professional Army in the Habsburg Monarchy." *Central European History* 21 (1988): 122-41.

Meeker, Michael E. *A Nation of Empire: The Ottoman Legacy of Turkish Modernity*. Berkeley: University of California Press, 2002.

Milward, Alan S., and S. B. Saul. *The Economic Development of Continental Europe, 1780-1870*. London: Allen&Unwin, 1973.

Mraz, G. *Maria Theresia Als Koenigin Von Ungarn*. Eisenstadt, 1984.

Myska, Milan, Sheilagh C. Ogilvie, and Cerman Markus. "Proto-Industrialization in Bohemia, Moravia and Silesia." In *European Proto-Industrialization*, 188-208. Cambridge: Cambridge University Press, 1996.

Naima. "Tarih-i Naima." Istanbul: Danışman Yayınevi, 1968.

North, Douglass. *The Rise of the Western World*. Cambridge: Cambridge University Press, 1973.

Norwich, John Julius. *Byzantium: The Decline and Fall*. New York: Knopf, 1996.

Okey, Robin. *The Habsburg Monarchy: From Enlightenment to Eclipse*. New York: St. Martin's Press, 2001.

Özkaya, Yücel. *Osmanlı İmparatorluğunda Ayanlık*. Ankara: AUDTCF Yayınları, 1977.

Özveren, Eyüp. "Black Sea & the Grain Provisioning of Istanbul: Imperial Legacies in Retrospect." (2002).

Pach, Pal Zsigmond. "Diminishing Share of East-Central Europe in the 17th Century International Trade." *Acta Historica* 16 (1970): 296-306.

———. "The Shifting of International Trade Routes in the 15th-17th Centuries." *Acta Historica* 14 (1968): 287-321.

Padover, Saul K. *The Revolutionary Emperor: Joseph II of Austria*. London: Eyre&Spottiswoode, 1967.

Pamuk, Şevket. "The Evolution of Fiscal Institutions in the Ottoman Empire, 1500-1914." Paper Presented at the Thirteenth International Economic History Congress, Buenos Aires, 2002.

———. "Fiyat Devrimi'nin Osmanlı İmparatorluğundaki Yansımalarına Yeniden Bakış." In *Osmanlı Ekonomisi Ve Kurumları*, edited by Şevket Pamuk. İstanbul: Türkiye İş Bankası Kültür Yayınları, 2007.

———. "Institutional Change and the Longevity of the Ottoman Empire, 1500-1800." *Journal of Interdisciplinary History* 35 (2004): 225-47.

———. "A Monetary History of the Ottoman Empire." In *Cambridge Studies in Islamic Civilization*, 276. New York: Cambridge University Press, 2000.

———. *Osmanlı Ekonomisi ve Kurumları*. İstanbul: Türkiye İş Bankası, 2007.

———. "Osmanlı Ekonomisinde Devlet Müdahaleciliğine Yeniden Bakış." In *Osmanlı Ekonomisi Ve Kurumları*. İstanbul: Türkiye İş Bankası Kültür Yayınları, 2007.

———. *Osmanlı-Türkiye Iktisadi Tarihi, 1500-1914*. Istanbul: İletişim, 2005.

———. "The Ottoman Empire and The "Great Depression" Of 1873-1896." *Journal of Economic History* 44 (1984): 107-18.

———. "The Ottoman Empire in Comparative Perspective." *Review* 11, no. 2 (1988).

———. "The Price Revolution in the Ottoman Empire Reconsidered." *International Journal of Middle East Studies* 33 (2001): 69-89.

———. "Prices in the Ottoman Empire, 1469-1914." *International Journal of Middle East Studies* 36 (2004): 451-68.

Pamuk, Şevket, and Huri İslamoğlu-İnan. "Commodity Production for World-Markets and Relations of Production in Ottoman Agriculture, 1840-1913." In *Ottoman Empire and the World Economy*, 1987.

Parker, Geoffrey. *Europe in Crisis, 1598-1648*, Blackwell Classic Histories of Europe. Oxford, UK; Malden, MA: Blackwell Publishers, 2001.

———. *The Military Revolution: Military Innovation and the Rise of the West, 1500-1800*. Cambridge; New York: Cambridge University Press, 1996.

Parker, Geoffrey, and Smith Parker. *The General Crisis of the Seventeenth Century*. London: Routledge & Kegan Paul, 1978.

Pierson, Paul. "Big, Slow-Moving and…Invisible: Macrosocial Processes in the Study of Comparative Politics." In *Comparative Historical Analysis in the Social Sciences*. Cambridge: Cambridge University Press, 2003.

———. "Increasing Returns, Path Dependence, and the Study of Politics." *American Political Science Review* 94 (2000): 251-267.

Quataert, Donald. *Consumption Studies and the History of the Ottoman Empire*. State University of New York Press, 1999.

———. *Manufacturing in the Ottoman Empire and Turkey, 1500-1950*, Suny Series in the Social and Economic History of the Middle East. Schoharie, NY: State University of New York Press, 1994.

Ranki, Gyorgy and Ivan Berend. "On the Economic Development of Austrio-Hungarian Monarchy." In *Underdevelopment and Economic Growth: Studies in Hungarian Social and Economic History*, 97-110. Budapest: Akademiai Kiado, 1979.

Ranki, Gyorgy, and John Komlos. "On the Economic Development of Austro-Hungarian Monarchy." In *Economic Development in the Habsburg Monarchy*, 47-65. New York: Columbia University Press, 1983.

Roberts, Clayton. *The Logic of Historical Explanation*. University Park, PA: Pennsylvania State University Press, 1996.

Rosenberg, Hans. *Bureaucracy, Aristocracy, and Autocracy: The Prussian Experience, 1660-1815*. Boston: Beacon Press, 1966.

Rudolph, Richard L. "The Pattern of Austrian Industrial Growth from the Eighteenth to the Early Twentieth Century." *Austrian History Yearbook* XI (1975): 3-25.

Rudolph, Richard L. *Banking and Industrialization in Austria-Hungary*. Cambridge: Cambridge University Press, 1976.

Rudolph, Richard L., and David F. Good. *Nationalism and Empire: The Habsburg Empire and the Soviet Union*. New York, NY: St. Martin's Press in association with the Center for Austrian Studies, University of Minnesota, 1992.

Rudolph, Richard L., and John Komlos. "Economic Revolution in Austria? The Meaning of 1848 in Austrian Economic History." In *Economic Development in the Habsburg Monarchy*, 165-83. New York: Columbia University Press, 1983.

———. "Social Structure and the Beginning of Austrian Economic Growth." In *Economic Development in the Habsburg Monarchy and the in the Successor States*, 133-49. New York: Columbia University Press.

Salzman, Ariel. "An Ancien Regime Revisited: "Privatization" And Political Economy in the Eighteenth-Century Ottoman Empire." *Politics and Society* 21 (1993): 393-423.

Salzmann, Ariel. *Tocqueville in the Ottoman Empire: Rival Paths to the Modern State*, Ottoman Empire and Its Heritage. Leiden; Boston: Brill, 2004.

Schwartz, Herman. "Dependency or Institutions? Economic Geography, Causal Mechanisms, and Logic in the Understanding of Development." *Studies in Comparative International Development* 42, no. 1 (2007): 115–35.

Shafer, D. Michael. *Winners and Losers: How Sectors Shape the Developmental Prospects of States*, Cornell Studies in Political Economy. Ithaca: Cornell University Press, 1994.

Shaw, Ezel. "Tanzimat in the Ottoman Empire Age of Reform in Europe." Paper presented at the Tanzimat'ın 150. Yıldönümü Uluslararası Sempozyumu, İstanbul 1989.

Shaw, Stanford. "The Aims and Achievements of Ottoman Rule in the Balkans." *Slavic Review* 21, no. 4 (1962): 597-616.

Shaw, Stanford J. *Between Old and New; the Ottoman Empire under Sultan Selim III, 1789-1807*, Harvard Middle Eastern Studies. Cambridge, MA: Harvard University Press, 1971.

———. "The Origins of Ottoman Military Reform: The Nizam-i Cedid Army of Sultan Selim III" *The Journal of Modern History* 37, no. 3 (1965): 291-306.

Shaw, Stanford, and Ezel Shaw. *History of the Ottoman Empire*. Vol. III. Cambridge: Cambridge University Press, 1977.

Sked, Alan. *The Decline and Fall of the Habsburg Empire, 1815-1918*. Harlow, England; New York: Longman, 2001.

Skocpol, Theda. *States and Social Revolutions: A Comparative Analysis of France, Russia, and China*. Cambridge; New York: Cambridge University Press, 1979.

———. "Wallerstein's World Capitalist System: A Theoretical and Historical Critique." *The American Journal of Sociology* 82, no. 5 (1977): 1075-90.

Slater, Dan, and Erica Simmons. "Informative regress: Critical antecedents in comparative politics." *Comparative Political Studies* 43, no. 7 (2010): 886-917.

Somel, Selçuk Akşin. *Historical Dictionary of the Ottoman Empire*, Ancient Civilizations and Historical Eras. Lanham, MD: Scarecrow Press, 2003.

Spruyt, Hendrik. "Institutional Selection in International Relations: State Anarchy as Order." *International Organization* 48 (1994): 527-57.

———. *The Sovereign State and Its Competitors: An Analysis of Systems Change*, Princeton Studies in International History and Politics. Princeton, NJ: Princeton University Press, 1994.

———. "War, Trade and State Formation." In *The Oxford Handbook of Comparative Politics*, edited by Carles Boix and Susan Stokes. Oxford: Oxford University Press, 2007.

Steensgaard, Niels. "Asian Trade and World Market: Orders of Magnitude in the 'Long Seventeenth Century." In *Actes Du Colloque Franco-Polonais D'histoire*. Nice: Laboratoire d'Histoire Quantitative: Univesite de Nice, 1981.

———. "The Seventeenth-Century Crisis and the Unity of Eurasian History." *Modern Asian Studies* 21 (1990): 683-697.

Stoelzl, Christoph. *Die Aera Bach in Boehmen: Sozialgeschichte Studien Zum Neoabsolutismus, 1849-59*. Munich, 1971.

Stokes, Gale. "Social Origins of East European Politics." In *The Origins of Backwardness in Eastern Europe: Economics and Politics from the Middle Ages until the Early Twentieth Century*. California: University of California Press, 1991.

Stollberg-Rilinger, Barbara. *Das Heilige Romische Reich Deutscher Nation Vom Ende Des Mittelalters Bis 1806*. Munich: Beck, 2006.

Sturmberger, Hans. *Aufstand in Böhmen; Der Beginn Des Dreissigjährigen Krieges*. München: R. Oldenbourg, 1959.

Subrahmanyam, Sanjay. "A Tale of Three Empires: Mughals, Ottomans and Habsburgs in Comparative Contexts." *Common Knowledge* 12, no. 1 (2006): 66-92.

Sunar, Ilkay, and Huri Islamoğlu-Inan. "State and Economy in the Ottoman Empire." In *The Ottoman Empire and the World Economy*: Cambridge University Press, 1987.

Szabo, Franz A. *Kaunitz and Enlightened Absolutism, 1753-1780*. Cambridge: Cambridge University Press, 1994.

Taylor, A. J. P. *The Habsburg Monarchy, 1809-1918; a History of the Austrian Empire and Austria-Hungary*. London: H. Hamilton, 1948.

Theresia, Maria. "Political Testament." In *The Habsburg and Hohenzollern Dynasties in the Seventeenth and Eighteenth Centuries*, edited by C. A. Macartney, London: Macmillan, 1970, 94-132.

Tilly, Charles. *Coercion, Capital, and European States, AD 990-1992*, Studies in Social Discontinuity. Cambridge, MA: Blackwell, 1992.

Tilly, Charles, Gabriel Ardant, and Politics Social Science Research Council. Committee on Comparative. *The Formation of National States in Western Europe*, Studies in Political Development. Princeton, NJ: Princeton University Press, 1975.

Toifl, Leopold, and Hildegard Leitgeb. *Ostösterreich Im Bocskay-Aufstand, 1605*, Militärhistorische Schriftenreihe. Wien: Bundesverlag, 1990.

Trevor, Roper. "The General Crisis of the Seventeenth Century." In *Crisis in Europe, 1560-1660. Essays from Past and Present*. London: Routledge & Kegan Paul, 1975.

Turchin, Peter. *War and Peace and War: The Life Cycles of Imperial Nations*. New York; London: Pearson Education, 2005.

Unterreiner, Katrin. *Emperor Franz Joseph, 1830-1916: Myth and Truth*. 1st ed. Wien: C. Brandstätter, 2006.

von Graevenitz, Christel Maria. *Die Landfriedenspolitik Rudolfs Von Habsburg (1273-1291) Am Niederrhein Und Im Westfalen*. Koln, Weimar, Wien: Boehlau Verlag, 2003.

Waldner, David. "From Intra-Type Variations to the Origins of Types: Recovering the Macroanalytics of Statebuilding." University of Virginia: Unpublished manuscript, 2004.

———. *State Building and Late Development*. Ithaca, NY: Cornell University Press, 1999.

Wallerstein, Immanuel. *The Modern World-System I: Capitalist Agriculture and the Origins of the European World-Economy in the Sixteenth Century*. New York: Academic Press, 1974/2011.

———. *The Modern World-System II: Mercantilism and the Consolidation of the European World-Economy, 1600-1750*. New York: Academic Press, 1980.

Wallerstein, Immanuel, Hale Decdeli, Reşat Kasaba, and Huri İslamoğlu-İnan. "The Incorporation of the Ottoman Empire into the World-Economy." In *The Ottoman Empire and the World Economy*. CUP, 1987.

Walt, Stephen M. *The Origins of Alliances*, Cornell Studies in Security Affairs. Ithaca: Cornell University Press, 1987.

Walter, Friedrich. *Die Geschichte Der Oestterichischen Zentralverwaltung Unter Maria Theresia*. Vienna, 1938.

Wandruszka, Adam. *The House of Habsburg; Six Hundred Years of a European Dynasty*. London: Sidgwick and Jackson, 1964.

———. *Leopold II*. Wien: Verlag Herold, 1963.

———. *Maria Theresia: D. Grosse Kaiserin*. Göttingen; Zürich; Frankfurt [Main]: Muster-Schmidt, 1980.

Wangermann, Ernst. *The Austrian Achievement, 1700-1800*. New York: Harcourt Brace Jovanovich, 1973.

Watzenig, Werner. "Die Finanz- Und Wirtschaftspolitik in Den Erblaendern Und Im Reich Unter Maximilian I in Den Jahren 1493 Bis 1507." Karl-Franzens Universitaet, 1983.

Webber, Carolyn, and Aaron Wildawsky. *A History of Taxation and Expenditure in the Western World*. New York: Simon & Schulster, 1986.

Weber, Max. *Economy and Society: An Outline of Interpretive Sociology*. Berkeley: University of California Press, 1978.

———. *The Theory of Social and Economic Organization*. New York: Free Press, 1997.

Weiker, Walter F. "The Ottoman Bureaucracy: Modernization and Reform." *Administrative Science Quarterly* 13, no. 3 (1968): 451-70.

Wheatcroft, Andrew. *The Habsburgs: Embodying the Empire*. London: Folio Sociert, 2004.

Wilson, Peter, and Jeremy Black. "Warfare in the Old Regime, 1648-1789." In *European Warfare, 1453-1815*, 69-96. New York: St. Martin's Press, 1999.

Wittek, Paul. *The Rise of the Ottoman Empire*, Royal Asiatic Society Monographs. London: The Royal Asiatic Society of Great Britain and Ireland, and sold by its agents Luzac and co., Ltd., 1958.

Wright, W. E. *Serf, Seigneur and Sovereign. Agrarian Reform in Eighteenth Century Bohemia*. Minneapolis: University of Minnesota 1996.

Wright, William E. "Neo-Serfdom in Bohemia." *Slavic Review* XXXIV (1975).

Index

www.ingramcontent.com/pod-product-compliance
Ingram Content Group UK Ltd.
Pitfield, Milton Keynes, MK11 3LW, UK
UKHW011005120926
8556IPUK00027B/65

9 783631 896181